*Hinterland Warriors and Military Dress*

# Dress, Body, Culture

Series Editor **Joanne B. Eicher,** *Regents' Professor, University of Minnesota*

Advisory Board:

**Ruth Barnes,** *Ashmolean Museum, University of Oxford*
**Helen Callaway,** *CCCRW, University of Oxford*
**James Hall,** *University of Illinois at Chicago*
**Beatrice Medicine,** *California State University, Northridge*
**Ted Polhemus,** *Curator, "Street Style" Exhibition, Victoria & Albert Museum*
**Griselda Pollock,** *University of Leeds*
**Valerie Steele,** *The Museum at the Fashion Institute of Technology*
**Lou Taylor,** *University of Brighton*
**John Wright,** *University of Minnesota*

Books in this provocative series seek to articulate the connections between culture and dress which is defined here in its broadest possible sense as any modification or supplement to the body. Interdisciplinary in approach, the series highlights the dialogue between identity and dress, cosmetics, coiffure, and body alternations as manifested in practices as varied as plastic surgery, tattooing, and ritual scarification. The series aims, in particular, to analyze the meaning of dress in relation to popular culture and gender issues and will include works grounded in anthropology, sociology, history, art history, literature, and folklore.

ISSN: 1360-466X

*Previously published titles in the Series*

**Helen Bradley Foster,** *"New Raiments of Self": African American Clothing in the Antebellum South*
**Claudine Griggs,** *S/he: Changing Sex and Changing Clothes*
**Michaele Thurgood Haynes,** *Dressing Up Debutantes: Pageantry and Glitz in Texas*
**Anne Brydon and Sandra Niesson,** *Consuming Fashion: Adorning the Transnational Body*
**Dani Cavallaro and Alexandra Warwick,** *Fashioning the Frame: Boundaries, Dress and the Body*
**Judith Perani and Norma H. Wolff,** *Cloth, Dress and Art Patronage in Africa*
**Linda B. Arthur,** *Religion, Dress and the Body*
**Paul Jobling,** *Fashion Spreads: Word and Image in Fashion Photography*
**Fadwa El-Guindi,** *Veil: Modesty, Privacy and Resistance*

DRESS, BODY, CULTURE

# Hinterland Warriors and Military Dress
## European Empires and Exotic Uniforms

*Thomas S. Abler*

Oxford • New York

First published in 1999 by
**Berg**
Editorial offices:
150 Cowley Road, Oxford, OX4 1JJ, UK
70 Washington Square South, New York, NY 10012, USA

© Thomas S. Abler 1999

All rights reserved.
No part of this publication may be reproduced in any form
or by any means without the written permission of Berg.

Berg is an imprint of Oxford International Publishers Ltd.

**Library of Congress Cataloging-in-Publication Data**
A catalogue record for this book is available from the Library of Congress.

**British Library Cataloguing-in-Publication Data**
A catalogue record for this book is available from the British Library.

ISBN    1 85973 201 1 (Cloth)

Typeset by JS Typesetters, Wellingborough, Northants.
Printed and bound in the UK by WBC Book Manufacturers, Bridgend

UC
485
.E85
A25
1999

# Contents

| | | |
|---|---|---|
| Preface | | vii |
| *1* | Introduction: Empires and Hinterland Warriors | 1 |
| *2* | The Military Uniform: General Principles of Its Evolution | 11 |
| *3* | Hussars: Horsemen of the Eastern Frontier | 23 |
| *4* | Other Horsemen from the East: Uhlans and Cossacks | 47 |
| *5* | 'Ladies from Hell' | 67 |
| *6* | North African Mameluks and Zouaves | 99 |
| *7* | Khaki – 'Not a Bad Colour for Work' | 111 |
| *8* | North America: Feathers and Leather | 131 |
| *9* | The Frontier Experience and the Military Uniform | 149 |
| Glossary | | 159 |
| Notes | | 165 |
| Bibliography | | 173 |
| Index | | 189 |

# Preface

This is a book that owes its birth to Berg Publishers. I had not the faintest of intentions of picking up this topic academically before a brochure came across my desk announcing Berg's series under the editorship of Professor Joanne Eicher concerned with 'dress, body, culture'. Having long had an interest in the history of military uniforms, albeit an interest I was sometimes reluctant to admit to fellow anthropologists, I was spurred to send off an outline and copy of my *curriculum vitae*, and to my surprise Berg's managing director, Kathryn Earle, responded that Professor Eicher and Berg were interested. Thus I never would have been involved in the task of producing this work had Professor Eicher and Berg not launched their series. I also owe a considerable debt to Professor Eicher and Ms Earle for their patience as the production of drafts of this study failed to meet deadlines which I had been convinced were reasonable and which I had been certain that I could meet. I must also thank Berg's external reader, Dr Malcolm Young, who undertook the refereeing process with far greater enthusiasm than is usual and whose extensive commentary has led to a much improved final draft.

Many individuals and institutions aided in the acquisition of the illustrations used here. These include Peter Harrington, Curator, the Anne S. K. Brown Military Collection, John Hay Library, Brown University; Sue Fletcher, the Royal Collection, Windsor Castle; Christina La Torre, the National Army Museum, Chelsea; Kathleen D. Stocking, New York State Historical Association, Cooperstown; Kim Walters, the Southwest Museum, Los Angeles; France Duhamel, the National Gallery of Canada; Leslie Redman, the Canadian War Museum, Ottawa; and staff at the Toronto Reference Library, the British Library, the New York Public Library and the Dana Porter Library, University of Waterloo. Photographs of items in my own modest collection were made by my colleague, Dr Maria Liston.

Computing support was provided by the Dean of Arts, University of Waterloo, and Keith McGowan of the Arts Computing Office fixed two computer crashes that would have delayed the production of this work even longer. Faye Schultz, secretary for anthropology at the University of Waterloo, runs our lives with great efficiency, leaving the department faculty the time and energy to pursue scholarly goals.

*Preface*

My interest in military uniforms began as a hobbyist, and I must also thank the members of the various hobbyist groups that I have joined from time to time for sustaining my interest and enlightening me over the years. These include the Ontario Model Soldier Society, the British Model Soldier Society, the British Flat Figure Society and the Illinois Military Miniature Society.

Thirty-five years ago, when I was a graduate student at the University of Wisconsin-Milwaukee, Dr Nancy O. Lurie saw some of the notes on military dress that I had been making from holdings of the Milwaukee Public Library. I disregarded her advice that I pick up military uniforms as a topic for my master's thesis. Among other issues, information was not readily accessible on the topic. This study owes a large debt to the efforts of numerous students of military dress whose work has been published over the last three decades. I hope at least some readers will proceed from this effort to the items I list in the bibliography. If they do, a great deal of pleasure awaits them.

# 1

# Introduction: Empires and Hinterland Warriors

'Forward, the Light Brigade!
Charge for the guns!' he said:
Into the valley of Death
Rode the six hundred.

Alfred, Lord Tennyson
The Charge of the Light Brigade

## Prologue

The charge of the Light Brigade at Balaclava in the Crimea, immortalized in the poetry of Alfred, Lord Tennyson, ranks as one of the best-known episodes of glory (and disaster) in British military history. In addition to Tennyson's poem, the famous charge has been the subject of at least two feature-length films (one, from 1936, starred Errol Flynn and Olivia De Havilland; the other, produced in 1968, was directed by Tony Richardson and featured Trevor Howard, David Hemmings, John Gielgud and Vanessa Redgrave). The event also has been the focus of one of the rare historical studies that successfully bridge the gap between popular and scholarly history (Woodham-Smith 1953). Countless schoolboys in English-speaking countries have been stirred by Tennyson's description of the charge of the 600 at the Battle of Balaclava on 25 October 1854; those who continued to pursue military topics learned the judgement of French General Bosquet who watched the cool, parade-ground precision of the charge from the heights above the Valley of Death: 'C'est magnifique, mais ce n'est pas la guerre!' ['It is magnificent, but it isn't war!'] (Woodham-Smith 1953: 247).

This display of English courage and foolhardiness was for the most part carried out by Englishmen dressed up as either Hungarians or Poles. Of the Light Brigade, only the 4th and the 13th Light Dragoons did not wear such exotic dress. The 17th Lancers dressed as Poles, wearing strange, square-topped headgear, whereas the two regiments of hussars (the 8th and the 11th) and the commander of the Light Brigade, Lord Cardigan, were in Hungarian garb with gaudily braided jackets, curved sabres of oriental pattern, and tall fur caps. One might wonder why the English, who normally exhibit pity for anyone so unfortunate as to have been born 'foreign', should dress themselves in the exotic costume of wild horsemen from regions much nearer to the borders of their Russian foe than to London, Liverpool, or Manchester.

Earlier in the day at Balaclava, a single regiment of British Infantry beat back the advancing Russian masses, establishing a phrase to characterize British coolness under pressure – 'the thin red line'. This single battalion of infantry, the 93rd Regiment of Foot, two ranks deep, was the only obstacle in the path of the advancing Russians. It stood its ground and with two volleys drove off a charge of a large body of Russian cavalry. The first was not fired until the Russian cavalry came within range – 500 yards. This stopped the Russian charge. The second volley, 'as clear and compact as at an ordinary field-day', caused the Russians to wheel and flee (Calthorpe 1979: 73). The excitement of the moment caused some of the infantry to surge forward, but their brigade commander, Sir Colin Campbell, held them back, calling out, '93rd, 93rd, damn all that eagerness' (McElwee 1972: 21). The 93rd were described as 'the thin red line',[1] and the phrase was picked up with pride by the army as a whole, being used by military historians and commentators to characterize British courage in actions long before as well as after the encounter at Balaclava.

However, the infantry regiment forming the thin red line was not dressed like the vast majority of the Royal Army. The original thin red line was formed by Highland Scots, the 93rd (Highland) Regiment of Foot (later the Argyle and Sutherland Highlanders). They fought in the Crimea in their feather bonnets and kilts, and not in the more conventional (even more 'civilized') attire of shakos and trousers worn by the vast majority of British infantry who served in regiments of English, Irish, or lowland Scottish origins. The captured Russian Major-General Karganoff referred to the Highlanders as 'savages without trousers' (Calthorpe 1979: 42).

The Light Brigade and the thin red line at Balaclava represent the impact of hinterland warriors on the armies of the metropolis. By metropolis I mean the core of an empire, the population and institutions that control imperial expansion and profit from such colonial activity. The hinterlands constitute the frontiers of the empire, almost always ethnically distinct from the metropolis. From the first, states have expanded into their hinterlands, and many scholars point to expansive or 'aggregative' warfare as a key variable in the initial evolution of the state (Carneiro 1992; Cohen 1984). From the earliest expansion of states into their hinterlands, imperial commanders have found the militant, ethnically-distinct and (in the view of the metropolis) 'uncivilized' peoples on their borders a fertile ground from which to raise 'irregular' bodies of soldiers. Eventually some of these become incorporated into the imperial army, become 'regularized' as it were, but wearing a stylized (often almost to the point of caricature) version of their national dress. The Highland Scots battalion, which formed 'the thin red line', is an example of this process of recruitment of hinterland warriors.

The dress of these ethnic soldiers often comes to represent a particular style of fighting. Hungarians and Poles had long been employed in continental European armies as light cavalry, and their dress came to be associated with the skill and *élan* with which they carried out that role. Austria had long recruited light cavalry from the hinterlands of her eastern frontier. Hence the members of the Light Brigade, like other many other units of light cavalry in armies of the industrial world, dressed in a fashion derived from the clothing of the horsemen of eastern Europe.

## Empires and their Frontiers

As empires expand into new territories, their military forces encounter peoples of different cultural and military traditions from their own. Some of these are enemies of the expanding empire, but others come to serve the empire in its expansion as allies or auxiliaries to the imperial forces. Ferguson and Whitehead (1992: 21) point out: 'Ethnic soldiers and martial tribes have been an aspect of state expansionism from earliest times.' Farwell noted similarities between the imperial British in India and the imperial Romans in Germany with 'lightly armed militia and local auxiliaries (Frontier Scouts) . . . as a first line of defence' and regular imperial troops 'in camps well behind the frontiers but close enough to support them if necessary' (Farwell 1989b: 197–8). Keeley (1996: 74) also recognized that 'the history of European expansion' is marked by 'extensive use of natives as scouts or auxiliaries . . . necessary because civilized soldiers alone were inadequate for the task.'

In this volume I intend to consider the impact this employment of such troops has on the military culture of the imperial army, looking particularly at the issue of dress. The performance of hinterland warriors or ethnic soldiers on the battlefield has led to incorporation of items of their dress in the uniform of elements of the imperial army, whether recruited on the frontier or not, and has diffused to other armies of industrial states. This book considers the following: 1) the reasons the empire chooses to employ hinterland warriors, 2) the role such troops play in military actions on the frontier, 3) the incorporation of such troops into the metropolitan army, 4) some general principles concerning styles of military dress, and 5) the diffusion of the style of dress of such troops beyond the frontier where they were first employed.

Although it is not the aim of this book to present a detailed history of the employment of frontier peoples by imperial armies, it is worth noting the long history and wide geographical spread of the practice. As early as 2000 BC the Egyptian Empire was employing Nubians from its southern frontier in its armies (Wise 1981: 21). In 1288 BC, the Sherdens, one of the 'sea peoples' from the north, helped Rameses defeat the Hittites (Thompson 1985: 65). In its invasion of Greece in 480 BC, the army of the Persian Empire under Xerxes included numerous frontier units among its personnel. These included chariots from India and archers from Ethiopia (Warry 1995: 38–9). The keys to Hannibal's victory over Rome at Cannae in 216 BC were the Numidian light cavalry, which the Carthaginians recruited in what is now Algeria, and the heavy cavalry recruited in Spain and Gaul (Lawford 1976: 38–41). It has been observed that the Roman military itself recognized the need to recruit from the frontiers as early as the third century BC. As a result, it 'soon became an accepted fact and many strange garbs and weapons were to be found side by side with the legionaries in most major wars' (Webster 1985: 141). Hinterland warriors were also important in mediaeval Europe. The importance of archers in the armies of Plantagenet England was established with the recruitment by Edward I of archers from Wales. He is said to have employed nearly 11,000 Welsh archers when he defeated the Scots under William Wallace at Falkirk in 1298 (Thompson 1985: 79).

All of these examples come from a time before the appearance of military uniforms on the battlefields of the world, although the exotic dress of many of these ethnic auxiliaries was distinct from that of their imperial employers. In a strict sense, the military uniform is a late development in the history of war, for it was not until the late seventeenth century that units in uniform dress dominated the battlefield, and it was only in the following century that the state bureaucracy seriously began to regulate the style of military clothing. As the topic of military uniforms forms the primary focus of this study, rather than issues of imperial expansion or frontier warfare and tactics, early instances of the imperial use of frontier warriors are not considered in this volume.

## Advantages in Recruiting from the Hinterlands

There are obvious reasons for colonial powers to employ peoples on the frontiers of an empire to fight for them. A group co-opted to act as an ally is one less group that might act to resist. For example, a suspicious Hanoverian government in London took the opportunity to recruit Highland Scots and send them overseas as a way of removing potential supporters of the Stuarts from England's northern frontier. Any positive impact these strange, even wild, Gaelic-speaking clansmen might make on continental battlefields was considered as a bonus (see Prebble 1975).

Local fighting men, of course, possess local knowledge with respect to warfare. Feest (1980: 11) claimed that 'all colonial powers' found it necessary to use local fighting men because of their knowledge of local traditions. The uses of frontier troops as 'guides' for imperial armies long predates the founding of the corps which bore that name on the northwest frontier of British India. Locally recruited men not only know the terrain and territory but also understand the tactics of the empire's enemies on the frontier.

If war has been tradition on a frontier, then local warriors will have been socialized in a militaristic society, and need less training than city clerks or farm boys in the skills of waging war. Mason (1976: 314) notes that the British found 'it was easy to train Sikhs and Gurkhas for the business of war', and both Gurkhas and Sikhs were enlisted in the imperial army immediately following British wars with these peoples.

A tradition of hostility of course makes it easier for the empire to form an alliance with one group in a war against that group's enemy – for as the French proverb states, 'the enemy of my enemy is my friend' (Brussell 1970: 217). To cite an American example, in 1876 George Armstrong Custer had with him Crow Indian scouts as he carried out his campaign against the Sioux and Cheyenne, and which culminated in the Battle of the Little Big Horn – popularly known as 'Custer's last stand'. The Crow had never fought against the advancing Americans, instead choosing to ally themselves with the Americans against their own traditional enemies such as the Sioux and Cheyenne. That the Crow found killing American soldiers not a sufficient challenge to their talents, as is sometimes stated, may or may not be true. In any case, Bordewich (1996: 26–9) has pointed to the irony that when modern hobbyists 're-enact' the battle on the site of Custer's defeat, the part of the Sioux and Cheyenne is taken by Crow Indians from their reservation which adjoins the battlefield.

Frontier peoples frequently have a style of fighting that also complements that of the more normal or conventional components of the imperial army – 'such a soldier's skills are with some specialized weapon [or tactics] alien to the military system which employs him' (Thompson 1985: 10). Most often these involve those skills associated with 'light' troops – scouting and skirmishing. This employment of hinterland warriors fits with the stereotype of such people held by the military establishment of the imperial army that has recruited them.

In addition, to the empire, the political cost of sustaining casualties among frontier auxiliaries is not as great as it would be if large numbers of young men from the heart of the metropolitan area were dying in the imperial wars of expansion. Hence there are numerous political and tactical reasons to employ local populations as auxiliaries in the expansion of an empire.

## Negative Factors in Employing Hinterland Warriors

There are, of course, negative factors in the employment of frontier peoples as soldiers in the army of the empire. To do so involves supplying arms to a potential enemy. The possibility of mutiny exists. The first and most famous of the regiments of Highland Scots in the employ of the British, the Black Watch, mutinied in the first decade of its existence when it believed it was to be sent to the West Indies. This set a pattern for mutiny among units of Highland Scots in the British Army (see Prebble 1975). A turning point in the military history of British India occurred with the Mutiny of 1857, but Indian regiments in the British service mutinied both before and after that violent and bloody year.

Another negative factor concerning the employment of ethnic soldiers relates to stereotypes of frontier peoples possessed by the enemies of the empire, and even in the empire itself. On the one hand there are positive stereotypes (the 'noble savage') but there are also negative ones (the 'merciless savage'). Enemies of the empire, and even political opponents at home, will use the latter stereotype to condemn the imperial use of frontier peoples in warfare, particularly if this use is in warfare against 'civilized' populations rather than other 'savage' peoples. For example, the rebellious portion of the American colonies fabricated a good deal of propaganda about the British use of Indian allies during the American Revolution. A particularly nasty piece of such false propaganda, attributed to Benjamin Franklin, was published in the Boston Chronicle of 12 March 1782. This claimed to be the text of a letter accompanying bundles of scalps being sent to Frederick Haldimand, Governor of Canada. The sources of the scalps are identified as 43 from soldiers, 359 from farmers, 88 from women, 193 from boys, 211 from girls, 122 from a variety of ages and genders and 29 from infants ripped from their mothers' wombs. In 1845, the American historian William L. Stone expressed regret that the tale was still being represented as truth (see Mathews 1963: 72, 177).

Even though Indians had not yet done almost no fighting (although they had been employed in very limited roles by *both* sides) in the attempt to suppress the American rebellion before 4 July 1776, when the American

Declaration of Independence was signed, that document claimed 'he [King George III] ... has endeavored to bring on the inhabitants of our frontiers the merciless Indian Savages, whose known rule of warfare is an undistinguished destruction of all ages, sexes and conditions' (Bailey 1968: 111). Opponents of the government at home in London were quick to repeat these fabrications. Lord Chatham (William Pitt) in 1777 damned the government by asking who 'dared to authorize and associate to our arms the tomahawk and scalping knife of the savage? To call into civilized alliance the wild and inhuman savage of the woods; to delegate to the merciless Indian the defense of disputed rights; and to wage the horrors of his barbarous war against our brethren?' (Bailey 1968: 114).

So powerful was the taboo against using 'native' troops against 'Europeans' that the British did not use its seasoned veterans from the Northwest Frontier of India in the Anglo-Boer War of 1899–1902. Speculating on 'what if' in history is usually unproductive, but it is tempting to wonder if the Boers might have found Guides, Gurkhas and Sikhs more formidable opponents than the British regulars they held a bay for so long. More recently, persons who objected to the participation of the 7th Duke of Edinburgh's Own Gurkha Rifles in the Falklands campaign had placed a sign on the Queen Elizabeth II (which had carried the Gurkhas, among others, to and from the Falklands) when the liner had re-entered civilian service and docked in New York to pick up trans-Atlantic passengers. It read (spelling as in the original): 'BEWARE! IN THIS SHIP ARE HIDING 500 YOUNG ARGENTINIAN HEAD DECAPITATED BY ITS FOMERS PASSENGERS THE GURKHAS MERCENARIES' (Farwell 1984: 172). The Argentinean propaganda campaign against the use of the Gurkhas may have become counterproductive. It has been reported that Argentine troops 'fled in panic back into the arms of the Scots Guards' rather than face the Gurkhas. The commander of the Gurkha battalion, Lieutenant Colonel David Morgan, commented on the refusal of Argentineans to resist the advances of the Gurkhas. 'When all is said and done, if we can win by reputation, who wants to kill people?' (quoted in Farwell 1989a: 82).

## Use of Local Dress by Imperial Forces

One might also note that the conditions of warfare on the frontier sometimes favour the adoption of local dress by imperial troops. Imperial armies were often ill-equipped to deal with climatic conditions far different from those at home, so intense heat and intense cold led to modification to uniforms designed for the more moderate battlefields of Europe. The ample problems of supplying troops on the frontier often led to the adoption of locally supplied clothing. Even the United States in the 1870s had difficulty clothing its small army on its western frontier, despite huge stocks of clothing left over from the Civil War and the benefits of rail transport to carry uniforms and equipment over much of the journey to the west (see Chappell 1972; McChristian 1995).

Issues of status and prestige may also influence the adoption of local dress by frontier elements of the metropolitan army. The military culture of imperial armies often values the combat officer over the parade-ground soldier, and acquisition of items of exotic clothing provide evidence of participation of the metropolitan soldier in distant campaigns. Conversely, there was the widely held nineteenth-century notion that fighting in colonial wars was not as worthy an occupation as fighting a European foe, so it was a task avoided by some aristocratic officers with the means and social connections to enjoy advancement up the ladder of promotion while remaining at home. For the upwardly mobile middle-class officer, the frontiers of the empire provided an opportunity, perhaps the only opportunity, to advance. By donning the exotic dress of the frontier, an officer could signal that he was a veteran of this theatre of operations. Possession of such memorabilia indicated a moral if not social superiority to the aristocratic officers who served in units seldom seeing foreign action.

## Exotic Dress and Military Uniform

There is a process through which exotic dress worn by frontier peoples becomes incorporated in the symbolic set of what is considered an appropriate or proper military uniform. I would characterize this as a series of four stages. As in any evolutionary process, there are numerous cases that do not clearly fall into one stage or another but rather fall into the border area somewhere between. The stages in the evolution of uniforms dealt with in this study are:

Native dress → modified native → stylized native → stylized military

'Native dress' is the normal fighting garb of the frontier fighting man and is adopted as the dress of 'irregular' units first raised to aid imperial expansion. This is then modified to give the unit a 'military' character, entering the 'modified native' stage. Such modification may initially be the standardization of arms and equipment. However, usually colour becomes uniform in the unit rather than being a matter of individual taste. Officers, whether from the imperial power or from the local population, carry weapons and exhibit badges of rank of the imperial army. The dress is continually modified over time to conform to military ideals of 'smartness' and to reflect changing military fashion, becoming 'stylized native'. Elements in the original 'native dress' may be elaborated to a degree that their origins are obscure. Finally the dress becomes simply a military style, no longer associated with the region in which it originated.

## Prospectus

In the next chapter the origins of the military uniform will be discussed along with social and psychological forces that, coupled with the practical constraints, have dictated its development and form. Included in that discussion is an indication of the sorts of evidence available about the dress of the soldier. As will be seen, the survival of actual uniforms is rare and both contemporary illustrations and later reconstructions of what was worn have impaired value.

The next three chapters look at specific examples of the pre-nineteenth-century recruitment of hinterland warriors. Chapter 3 considers the classic case of the Hungarian horsemen whose dress came to be found in armies around the world before the outbreak of World War I and which, indeed, continues to be worn in those enclaves where some approximation of the old 'full-dress' uniform is found. Chapter 4 looks two other groups of eastern horsemen, the Polish lancer or uhlan and the Russian Cossack. The former, as will be seen, was much more influential on the dress of the world's cavalry. Chapter 5 takes up the case of the Highland Scots and the presence of Scots dress in regiments recruited from the descendants of Scottish emigrants in many countries about the world. As will be seen, however, Scots military dress has come to be worn by many soldiers without roots in the north of Britain.

The recruitment of local troops as part of the French colonial adventure in North Africa had a global impact as outlined in Chapter 6. In particular, because of historical circumstances, which will be discussed, it had a strong impact on the armies recruited during the American Civil War. North African dress was also worn by troops recruited in Canada, the West Indies and Brazil; it had its impact on the dress of the Indian Army and was adopted by part of the army of the Ottoman Turks because of French influence. This was an era, lasting until the Franco–Prussian War, when military fashion around the globe imitated French originals. Chapter 7 shows how British colonial experiences in India, coupled with the changes taking place in military technology, led to the widespread adoption of khaki uniforms. The earliest example of its use was for a unit recruited from among the hill tribes on the

North-West Frontier with clothing dyed in a local bazaar. The next chapter will look at two issues. The first is that some hinterland warriors, notably Native North Americans, had relatively little influence on the dress of metropolitan armies beyond that of the officers who actually commanded them. The second is to look at diffusion going the other way – examples of the dress of soldiers and officers of the metropolitan army have an impact on the dress of the hinterland warrior. The book concludes with a discussion of the factors that encouraged and inhibited the adoption of the dress of hinterland warriors in the context of the racist and Eurocentric attitudes that dominated the mind set of those who founded and controlled the empires.

# 2

# The Military Uniform: General Principles of Its Evolution

> Soldier, Soldier won't you marry me
> With your musket, pipe and drum?
> Yes, oh yes, I would marry you
> But I have no clothes to put on
>
> Anonymous

## The 'Military Revolution' and the Origins of the Military Uniform

In this chapter several aspects of the literature on the history of military uniforms will be considered. It not the intention to present a general history of the military uniform (a formidable task – see the encyclopaedic treatment of Knötel, Knötel and Seig 1937), but rather to present principles that have been put forward as having an impact on the evolution of the military uniform, and to consider some of the limitations of the data and literature relevant to or describing military uniforms of the past. As the military uniform is a relatively recent European invention, I deal primarily with the military uniforms of European armies (and of those states that derive the organization and structure of their military forces from European models). There are aspects of uniform in the dress of military personnel found in other cultures at various times and places in world history, but by far the greatest number of individuals who went to battle and performed military tasks in uniforms have been members of modern European armies or forces modelled after European military establishments.

Uniform dress for infantry, artillery and cavalry units in European armies began with the 'military revolution' in northern Europe at the end of the sixteenth century and the beginning of the seventeenth (on the 'military revolution' see Roberts 1967; Parker 1988). This 'revolution' included the use of disciplined units of musketeers whose firepower could destroy enemy formations. It was the dominance on the battlefield of these hand-held firearms that led to the 'military revolution'.

Gunpowder had been making an increasing impact on European battlefields since its introduction early in the fourteenth century, but in the late sixteenth and early seventeenth centuries, when it became all-important, firearms were still crude and awkward. The matchlock, relying on a lighted match to ignite the charge of gunpowder, was the musketeer's weapon until the mid-seventeenth century it when was replaced by the flintlock, which used the spark of flint against steel to ignite the charge. The muzzle-loading, single-shot weapons in use from the sixteenth century until the late nineteenth century were slow to load. They frequently misfired. The Brown Bess musket, 'the most famous weapon that was ever placed in the hands of the British soldier' (Rogers 1960: 90), served the British Army from before 1720 to the 1830s and was more reliable than most. Despite this high reputation, a test conducted in 1834 showed the Brown Bess misfired more than 15 per cent of the time (Rogers 1960: 171 – misfiring could be increased with improper loading procedures in the heat of battle). The phrase, 'flash in the pan', which we still use in relation to ineffective behaviour derives from the failure of the powder in the pan of a flintlock musket to ignite the charge within the barrel. These military firearms were also smoothbores, lacking the accuracy of rifles. The spin put on the bullet by a rifled barrel ensures the bullet follows a straight course, unlike the erratic path of a bullet from a smoothbore weapon. The military musket of the eighteenth century was only accurate at a range up to 50 yards (Trubowitz 1985: 92), and in 1814 Colonel Hanger of the British Army observed that 'a soldier must be very unfortunate indeed who shall be wounded by a common musket at 150 yards, provided his antagonist aims at him; and as to firing at a man at 200 yards with a common musket, you may as well fire at the moon and have the same hope of hitting your object' (quoted in Rogers 1960: 95).

Military thinkers, notably Counts Maurice and William Louis of Nassau (Parker 1988: 18–19) and Gustavus Adolphus of Sweden (Roberts 1967), realized that the inadequacies of gunpowder weapons then available could be negated by the coordination of troops in battle. That is, while an individual firing his weapon had little likelihood of hitting a target, the combined fire of a large number of individuals could have a devastating impact on opposing troops. Cooperation between the musketeers and pikemen would allow the musketeers to inflict damage on attacking cavalry and then be protected by the pikes of their comrades from the shock action of the enemy horsemen. The only way to defeat a steady body of musketeers and pikeman was to use more effective volleys from better-disciplined bodies of musketeers accompanied by pikemen or to slaughter them from a distance with field artillery, an arm not well developed at the start of the 'military revolution'. Thus, with the 'military revolution', training and drill became crucial in the execution of war.

Firearms had replaced the dominant missile weapon of the past, the English (or Welsh) longbow, which had required a lifetime of training and a body modified (or deformed) to deal with the stresses of using the weapon (Bradbury 1985). Unlike the longbow, comparatively little training was required to use an early firearm effectively. The movements required to load and point it (aim is not an appropriate word to use for the exercise) were simple. However, a major task to be learned was the discipline to wait for the enemy to come into range and then to fire as a unit to devastate the attacking force. One then had to coordinate with other soldiers so that the frequency of the volleys could be maintained and the musketeers could be protected by pikemen from cavalry attacks.

This led to the establishment of permanent units, some of which exhibit a continuity with current regiments in European armies. Reflecting the mercenary past of European warfare, these troops were raised by individuals and offered for sale (lease might be a better term) to the government wishing to employ them. Providing clothing for these organizations was the responsibility of the commanders who raised them, and the provision of uniform dress was economical and also created recognition for the battalion, squadron or regiment. Joseph (1986: 134–5) refers to this as the 'patrimonial era' which extended to the mid-eighteenth century and beyond. It eventually became apparent that in order to prevent battlefield error (the danger of 'friendly fire') it was advantageous for some uniformity of dress to be extended beyond individual battalions to the army or national level. As state control increased over what had been originally a capitalist enterprise, central bureaucracies began to regulate dress and provide uniforms.

## Evolution of Military Dress

James Laver, from the Victoria and Albert Museum, has recognized several principles in the evolution of military dress. He saw three competing principles governing fashion through history, and argued that these have had an impact on the style of military dress as well as that of the civilian population. He named these three principles the hierarchical principle, the seduction principle and the utility principle (Laver 1945: 64–5). In times of peace the seduction principle and the hierarchical principle dominate, while the utility principle comes into play during long periods of war. He generalized about the role of the seduction principle in military uniform: 'A smart uniform enhances a man's masculinity . . . It gives him a head-dress which exaggerates his height; it puts a stripe on his trousers to exaggerate his apparent length of leg; it gives him epaulettes to exaggerate the width of his shoulders' (Laver 1969: 72–3).

Laver (1969: 72) succinctly summed up the way a 'smart' uniform can influence relations between the sexes: 'when off duty it is the Guardsman who gets the girls'. The impact of military uniforms on females was not confined to European society. John B. Glubb (Glubb Pasha) noted the impact the uniform of the desert patrol of the Arab Legion of Jordan, at the time of its formation in the 1930s.

> The uniform was cut in the same manner as their ordinary dress, long robes reaching almost to the ground and long white sleeves, but the outer garment was khaki in colour. With a red sash, a red revolver lanyard, a belt and bandolier full of ammunition, and a silver dagger in the belt, the effect was impressive. Soon the tribesmen were complaining that the prettiest girls would accept none but our soldiers for their lovers. (Glubb 1948: 103)

Joseph (1986: 107) has also called attention to the 'erotic' aspects of uniforms, pointing out that they 'enhanced the sexual attractiveness of their wearers, both to heterosexual and homosexual observers' and that 'sexual connotations of uniforms stem . . . from the function of violence as an aphrodisiac for some'. Uniforms dictated by the seduction principle tend to inhibit the actual performance of the soldier on the battlefield, however, and lengthy wars will lead the utility principle to modify the dress worn in the field. The hierarchical principle, which leads to highly visible symbols of distinctions of rank within the hierarchical structure of the military, also falls victim to the utility principle in time of war as officers find it practical, and less dangerous, to dress like their men.

Even in times of combat, however, when the exotic dress of hinterland warriors had been adopted by imperial forces, the seduction principle can be victorious (although it should also be noted that for much of the eighteenth and nineteenth centuries, the seduction principle was more than able to hold its own against the utility principle). It will be shown how the flamboyant dress of hinterland warriors became incorporated and even caricatured in the dress of metropolitan armies when they could have easily copied the tactics of their frontier allies and worn a much more utilitarian costume, avoiding the use and even absurd elaboration of the dress of their models from the hinterland. On the other hand, it will also be seen that a major victory of the utility principle, the adoption of a khaki uniform, also is derived from the dress of hinterland warriors.

The operation of the seduction principle, according to Laver, not only enhances the soldier's relationship with the opposite sex, but also inspires his pride in his unit, creating an *ésprit de corps*. Joseph notes the continuing process by which élites (and élite units within élites) differentiate their dress from others, only to have others copy that dress (Joseph 1986: 77). Only the airborne infantry (paratroopers in US parlance) wore the high topped, laced 'jump boots' in the US Army until late in World War II. These served as a proud symbol of this élite fighting corps. Bill Mauldin (1945: 138), the cartoonist champion of the ordinary 'GI Joe', noted that the 'jump boots' of the airborne infantryman were the most comfortable footwear available and wore a pair given to him by members of the 509th Parachute Battalion. However, this distinctive symbol was eventually widely adopted by others, many not even combat troops. It thus became deflated in value as a symbol of élite status (Todd 1954: Plate 28).

Laver concluded that his utility principle in time of war forces uniforms toward loose fit for easier movement and toward camouflage colouration. He saw these as 'modifications . . . likely to be first seen in the dress of Light Infantry and auxiliary troops generally, and in those engaged in "Colonial" warfare' (Laver 1948: 25).

Laver (1969: 63) also outlined six functions for military dress. These include increasing individual pride, having a negative impact on enemy morale, battlefield recognition, increasing unit *ésprit de corps*, making rank clear, and protection without interference in movements. Several of these relate to the dress of auxiliaries in imperial armies. Providing distinctive ethnic dress for auxiliaries can intimidate enemies and increase unit pride and morale. A negative factor in auxiliaries' wearing of ethnic dress is the possibility of being mistaken for the enemy who are similarly dressed and thus of drawing friendly fire. This is usually not an issue once the troops are incorporated into the imperial or metropolitan army and fighting on remote battlefields. However, if these items of ethnic dress diffuse to other imperial armies, this can cause problems of recognition on battlefields far removed from the frontier on which the uniform originated. The presence of Zouaves on both sides during the American Civil War led to instances of mistaken identity in the early stages of that conflict, and the fact that both French lancers and German uhlans dressed as Poles led to deaths from friendly fire in the Franco-Prussian War.

## Diffusion of Military Dress

Laver reached several conclusions directly related to issues discussed in this book. Indeed, it is fair to say that my own thoughts on military uniforms and their evolution were shaped some forty years ago by a reading of Laver's splendid little summary of the history of British uniforms. Among the conclusions he presented is the fact that 'military fashions are extremely imitative', for, as he noted: 'The dress of any successful troops will be copied, especially in unessentials, and any victorious nation tends to impose some detail of its uniform on the armies of the world' (Laver 1948: 25). Thus the nation reputed to be the best army in the world will find lesser powers imitating its uniforms. The idea, it seems, is that dress does make the soldier, and for much of the nineteenth century, the military reputation of France meant the world dressed in French uniforms. The Franco–Prussian War, however, led armies of the world to abandon their French shakos and kepis and to jam pickelhaube helmets on the heads of their soldiers (Laver 1948: 20–1). Colonel Frederick P. Todd (1954: Plate 23) has noted that the full dress of George Armstrong Custer's Seventh US Cavalry imitated Prussian military fashion.

The fact that hinterland warriors employed by imperial armies retained modified versions of their own dress has had its impact on the uniforms of the world's soldiers. Hinterland warriors were often employed in roles that differentiated them, at least initially, from troops in the regular army. According to Laver, with respect to mounted troops, imperial armies tend to lack light cavalry, who can act as scouts, the 'eyes of the army'. Light cavalry, because of their role, consequently enjoyed less prestige in imperial armies than heavy cavalry, which acted as shock troops in battle. With their local knowledge, hinterland warriors were often employed as light cavalry. This usage also suited military stereotypes about the strengths and weaknesses of hinterland warriors – bush skills were admired but ethnic soldiers were felt to lack the discipline to serve as part of the line in battle. Laver (1948: 12–13) has pointed out that the seventeenth century recruitment of light cavalry from the edges of European empires led to innovations in military dress of light cavalry. As Hungarians and Poles were recruited for this role, and because, as has just been pointed out, there is a feeling that dress makes the soldier, armies around the world dressed their light cavalry as Hungarian hussars or Polish lancers. Laver noted that the dress of these mounted warriors was copied, 'at first slavishly and then with increasing fantastication' (Laver 1948: 26), and hussar styles were adopted by many units playing a light cavalry role even though they were not officially designated as 'hussars' (as British Light Dragoons and French Chasseurs à Cheval). Even the first full dress uniform of the North West Mounted Police in Canada featured hussar braiding across the chest.

With respect to diffusion of military uniforms, it is notable that in imperial armies in recent times there has existed a differentiation between the regular army based at home and the forces serving overseas. There was a strong tendency among European colonial powers to dress their colonial troops like the colonial troops of other European powers. Britain, for example, dressed West Indians in North African costume (see Chapter 6), and Britain, Germany, France, Italy and Belgium all used the fez of Turkey and North Africa as headdress for sub-Saharan African troops. Khaki, of Indian origin, became the colour of choice for all colonial troops raised in sub-Saharan Africa (see Chapter 7). Although originally adopted from the dress of a particular locally recruited population, the military minds of Europe concluded such innovations signalled a style of dress to be worn by colonial troops generally. A tendency to see all 'natives' as similar, if not alike, led to the assumption they could and should be similarly dressed.

## The Study of Military Uniforms

Of necessity, because of the broad scope of this study, I have not engaged in primary research but instead I have had to rely more heavily than I would have liked on secondary sources, the detailed research others have published on the dress of particular armies, particular wars and even particular units and battles. These publications constitute a surprisingly large body of literature, although many of the publications on the history of the military uniform are aimed at a wide variety of persons with an amateur or peripheral interest in history. These include collectors of militaria, makers of military models (toy soldiers), historical re-enactment groups, costume designers for dramatic productions and the like. Most 'serious' students of military history do not attach great importance to such studies, although they may be willing to decorate their monographs with illustrations of military dress of varying degrees of accuracy. Those who do consume the literature on the history of military uniform approach it with varying degrees of sophistication, and the scholarship exhibited in the literature varies from the rigorous to sloppy and fluid indeed!

Part of the problem in the study of military uniform is the quantity and quality of primary sources for such study. Official 'dress regulations' appear relatively late in the history of military uniforms and were issued irregularly. In the British and Indian Army dress regulations, items are often described simply being of 'regimental pattern'. In any case, one Indian Army Cavalry officer commented 'Cavalry look upon *Dress Regulations* as a fair basis for disagreement, and seldom conform' (Harris 1979: 4). Troops on campaign or those stationed on the frontier would be less likely to conform to formal dress regulations than would troops in the capital of the empire.

A surprisingly small number of examples of military dress survive and are preserved in museum collections. Full dress is, by the very nature of its use, more likely to survive than items worn in combat or on campaign, and full dress is more likely to survive than items such as stable dress or drill clothing. Moreover, the dress of an officer is more likely to survive than that of a member of the other ranks, and some items of military dress are more likely to be preserved than others. Coats are more likely to be preserved than breeches. Coats, though, frequently lose their buttons or epaulets to collectors of those specific items of militaria, and these may be replaced by other, possibly incorrect, items. The 'little clothes' of the eighteenth-century British soldier, items such as the waistcoat worn under the coat (but exposed to view because the lapels of the coat were turned back), are very seldom preserved in museum collections. Even those items of military dress that do survive are often poorly documented. That family tradition suggests that Great-Great-Great Uncle Fred wore something on the field of Waterloo does not prove that the regimental coat was ever dampened by the rains of Belgium. W. Y. Carman (1957: xv) has pointed out that 'restoration and adaptation for theatrical purposes often creates false clues' as do surviving 'trial patterns . . . never adopted'. The Canadian War Museum published an entire monograph simply to demonstrate that a particular group of items of dress in its collection were not of military origin at all (Pothier and Grant 1975). Even an item that has survived intact with reasonable documentation may vary considerably from its appearance when actually worn. Dyes used in military uniforms were often unstable, and conditions of storage and display may have considerably changed the appearance of the item over time. It has been observed, for instance, that when the British blockade deprived Napoleonic France of its supply of indigo, the inferior dyes used for the regulation dark blue uniforms 'tended to end up any shade between a seasick green and royal purple after a little exposure to sun and rain' (Elting 1988: 440). It was not just blue that was unstable. Elting (1988: 440–1) cautions: 'Some shades of green required multiple dyeing – first with blue, then with yellow. Over the years the yellow might vanish, leaving a blue coat that now puzzles amateur uniformologists.' In a similar vein, an American officer after the Civil War complained of a lack of consistency in the colour of uniforms available for his men, which in theory were light blue trousers and a dark blue coat: 'In a lot of a hundred pairs of pants there are often found all shades from a deep to a pale muddy blue, while the uniform coats and blouses range from gray-green to black' (quoted in McChristian 1995: 8). For many years in the British army, the so-called 'rifle green' used in some uniforms posed a problem because of the instability of the dye, and uniforms officially 'rifle green' in hue were actually black. A contemporary referred to this colour as 'invisible green' and among the Guides on the northwest frontier of India, the sepoys of the 1st Punjab Rifles (officially clad in rifle green) were known as 'siah posh' (black coated) (Lumsden and Elsmie 1899: 85).

Carman has argued that the 'rich field' of contemporary illustrations is possibly more rewarding than scarce and often undocumented surviving specimens of military dress to show what actually was worn. He writes: 'a contemporary picture may not be accurate in detail, but at least it will have "the feel of the period", showing the fullness of the skirts, the style of the cuff or some other aspect' (Carman 1957: xv). However, contemporary illustrations also have their problems. It is often uncertain that the artist ever saw the troops depicted and sometimes full dress worn in London or Paris is falsely depicted as being worn on campaign. In the case of eyewitness drawings and paintings, the unit being shown may be in doubt and a naive artistic style may reduce the value of the drawing. The earliest illustrations that we have of Scots soldiers wearing the belted plaid (not the 'little kilt' which was invented later – see Trevor-Roper 1983) were produced in London and Germany by untrained artists with little skill in depicting either the nature of the garment or the intricacies of the tartan. Of some importance to our subject here is the fact that metropolitan artists often depicted stereotypes of 'savage' peoples rather than the realities the imperial troops were encountering in the hinterland.

It is often impossible to tell if a contemporary picture is in error or correctly reflects reality. Elting (1988: 717) has noted contemporary pictures of Napoleon's dragoons with purple lapels, collars and cuffs. This was never an authorized colour. However, he suggests there are two possible reasons why the pictures may reflect reality. It is possible that individual commanders ignored regulations for reasons of convenience or economy. It is also possible that the dyes meant to provide the officially correct pink or crimson were so poor or unstable that the purple hue resulted.

The illustrations of British military artist Richard Simkin are the pictorial equivalent of Rudyard Kipling's verse in providing for us an image of the Victorian 'Tommy Atkins'. Simkin produced a number of watercolours of British military personnel that served as the basis for lithographs documenting the contemporary dress of the British Army for *The Army & Navy Gazette* in the 1890s. These can be examined critically to uncover errors. In some cases a photograph survives which depicts the very model that Simkin used, and attests to his accuracy. In other cases errors have crept in. It has been noted Simkin provided medals for the Lieutenant Colonel of The Princess of Wales's Own (Yorkshire Regiment). 'Simkin's Commanding Officer is in a sense a cheat! Not one of the four regular and militia battalion COs had any active service and therefore none had any medals' (Simkin's officer has three – Walton 1986: 61). In another case, that of the Northamptonshire Regiment, Simkin erred in placing the wrong style of headdress on his subjects.

> All ranks are in Review Order and perhaps on their way to a grand parade in Aldershot where the 1st Bn were stationed for a while from late 1890. The only problem is that neither 1st nor 2nd Bn at this time wore the blue home service helmet; the 2nd Bn in the Straits Settlements would have been wearing the foreign pattern white helmet of the day, while the 1st had received the trial universal white helmet . . . in the early summer of 1889. (Walton 1986: 78)

The process of moving from original watercolours to lithographic reproduction compounded the errors. Walton (1986:108) notes that Simkin's correct use of black for the uniforms of a Bugler and Rifleman of the King's Royal Rifle Corps was changed by the colourist of *The Army & Navy Gazette* who 'put everyone in rifle green throughout – which was certainly wrong!'

Photographs also pose problems. Many undocumented photographs survive, providing a puzzle for the researcher. Perhaps photographs do not lie, but liars can take or pose for photographs. The great photographer of the Crimean War, Roger Fenton, 'enjoyed dressing up in a Zouave uniform he borrowed from General Bosquet's Division, had himself photographed in it by [his assistant] Sparling, and for a lark published it with the title "Zouave, 2nd Division"' (Gernsheim and Gernsheim 1954: 20–1). The curator of the West Point Museum, Michael J. McAfee, cautions collectors of American Civil War images to be wary of 'photos of strangely dressed individuals [which] appear in auction catalogues or on tables at militaria shows with the label "ZOUAVE" . . . generally at a price that will empty your wallet' (McAfee 1993: 6). Philip Katcher (1992: 20) warns such collectors that 'European military photographs are showing up on the American market . . . sold as soldiers of the North or South during the American Civil War.'

In addition to his paintings of the contemporary Victorian soldier, Richard Simkin also produced illustrations of historic British military dress that are still being reprinted (see Carman 1982, 1985). If one must be cautious in accepting the work of a contemporary to the subject being depicted, one must also be cautious about accepting the work of someone who attempts to reconstruct the military dress of the past. It is true that a modern artist, using all the sources available, may well provide a very accurate reconstruction of the dress of a soldier of the past. By examining contemporary illustrations, surviving clothing and equipment in museum and other collections, as well as written orders and other historical documents relating to the events, the modern artist may be able to provide a complete and satisfactory depiction of the dress of a participant in a past campaign. The modern reconstruction may even be much closer to the truth than a contemporary illustration. However, such reconstructions should be approached with caution; they should be viewed in the same way that one judges the writing of history – what are the sources used by the artist in his reconstruction and is it reasonable based on those sources? Whole uniforms from American and Loyalist regiments in the American Revolution have been reconstructed in illustrations based on newspaper notices in which the colours of coats of deserters (and only the colours of their coats) are described (see Lefferts 1926).

## Conclusion

In this chapter I have presented those principles that others have seen as determinants in the evolution of the military uniform. Most important, I suggest, is the tendency to copy the dress of those troops who successfully pursue a particular role. Since distinctively dressed hinterland warriors were so employed, their dress came to be imitated by troops expected to perform similar roles in other armies. Laver's seduction principle is also of great importance. Innovations established on the frontier become modified through the seduction principle to achieve a 'more military' or a 'smart' appearance. As some of the elements of the dress of the hinterland warriors became stylized and associated with military success generally, they spread even beyond troops performing tasks similar to those of the original hinterland warriors.

# 3

# Hussars: Horsemen of the Eastern Frontier

Un hussard qui n'est pas mort à trente ans n'est qu'en Jean Foutre
(A hussar who isn't dead at thirty is a blackguard)

Antoine-Charles Louis Comte de Lasalle

## Types and Tasks of Cavalry

The first frontier people to have an influence on military uniforms were the horsemen of eastern Europe. In the late seventeenth and the early eighteenth century, prior to the incorporation of these eastern warriors into imperial armies, two basic types of cavalry or mounted soldiers were found in the armies of European states. The first type was battle cavalry, usually designated 'horse' or 'cuirassiers'. The latter were often (but not invariably) equipped with body armour, a cuirass that protected the wearer's chest and abdomen and, if a full cuirass, also his back. The Life Guards and the Blues and Royals (formerly the Royal Horse Guards) who perform ceremonial duties in London wear cuirasses similar in pattern to those worn in combat three centuries ago. With the sword as their primary arm (they also carried pistols in holsters on their saddles and sometimes carbines), the main task of this heavy cavalry was to charge bodies of enemy infantry or cavalry on the battlefield and, by the weight and shock of the charge, drive the enemy from their position.

The second type of mounted soldier in these armies was termed dragoons. Dragoons were originally intended to be mounted infantry, dismounting to fight using the carbines they carried (the name derives from the name for their muskets – *dragone*). Samuel Johnson perhaps correctly defined dragoon as 'a kind of soldier that serves indifferently either on foot or horseback' (Johnson 1755). However, almost from the first, dragoons in battle played exactly the same role as Cuirassiers and Horse. Mollo (1973: 53) notes that the dress of these heavy cavalrymen, cuirassiers, horse and dragoons, 'was basically the same as the infantry' although this is a bit of an untruth. The cuirass was no longer worn by foot troops in the late seventeenth century. Also unique to cavalry were the heavy gauntlet gloves to protect hands gripping reins and sword. The real mark of the heavy cavalryman, however, was his boots. These, like his horse, were large and sturdy, to provide protection for his legs as he charged at the foe, stirrup to stirrup with his fellow troopers.

One aspect of the 'military revolution' of the seventeenth century was an increase in the mobility of armies through improvement in systems of logistics, allowing large armies to operate over long distances in the field. This created a demand for light cavalry, mounted troops who could locate enemy armies and screen one's own army from the eyes of enemy scouts. Typically the training and inclination of the cavalry recruited within the metropolis (the core of the empire) did not lead to development of the sorts of skills necessary to carry out these light cavalry duties. As late as the Peninsular War in Spain, British cavalry exhibited inadequate preparation for the light cavalry role and a lack of enthusiasm among officers to pursue it. Pimlott (1977: 37) notes 'important geographical features were not guarded, vedettes were easily picked off by the French, mutual support between posts or patrols was almost non-existent, and intelligence gathering was poor', laying the blame on the attitudes of the officers. 'Officers craved the glory of shock action and naturally regarded such tasks as reconnaissance or outpost duty as boring and mundane, if not a little beneath their dignity' (Pimlott 1977: 36). This was long after the value of the light cavalry had been demonstrated in wars on the continent.

In the eastern hinterlands of imperial Europe, however, there had been found recruits whose horsemanship and experience suited them well for the light cavalry task. These same troops 'were largely responsible for the introduction of a wider variety of military clothing, some of it of a very elaborate and fanciful nature' (Mollo 1972: 53).

## The Incorporation of Hussars into Continental Armies

These light cavalry were initially recruited from Hungary, and they came to be called by a local designation, 'hussars'. Chandler (1976: 95) notes 'The Austrians had in fact employed Hungarian Magyar irregular horsemen since the fifteenth century, but only in 1688 did they formally raise their first regiments of Hungarian hussars on a semi-permanent basis.' A nineteenth-century observer gave an opinion why Hungary was able to provide light cavalry:

> The Hungarian … learns to be a horseman in his childhood, and, having nothing better to do in that half-savage land, he teaches his horse all sorts of tricks, and acquires a peculiar mastery of that kind of equitation. His land is thinly populated and the dwellings are consequently sparse, which means that when he is out riding he must keep a sense of direction, in order to be able to retrace his path. With his kind of upbringing, the Hungarian becomes a perfect light cavalryman with further training. (Le Comte de Mirabeau, quoted and translated in Duffy 1977: 96)

Another commentator has remarked on the relationship between the Hungarian warrior and his horse.

> From his earliest youth the future Hussar is familiar with horses, they are his friends and his playmates; he eats with them and sleeps with them; he knows the meaning of every sound they make, and every movement and attitude of their frames; he has an intuitive and unerring knowledge of their habits, their likings and dislikings. The Hussar loves his horse, and speaks to it as if it were an intelligent creature; he tells it of his griefs, his fears, his hopes, and the sagacious animal replies with affectionate whinnyings and nuzzlings in the bosom of his master. The Hussar, whatever his fatigues or privations, will never dream of rest or refreshment for himself until he has first provided for the wants of his four-footed friend. (Quoted in Stacke 1970: 2–3)

Hungarian light cavalry honed their frontier skills while combating the mounted armies of Asia and Islam, and they have been described at 'ultimately a synthesis of "occident-orient," combining lightness and speed, the precision of the sword and the firepower of one or two good carbines and horse pistols' (Berenger 1980: 37). Both men and horses were small in hussar regiments. In the Austrian army, a cuirassier's horse stood at 16 hands (5 feet 4 inches to the shoulder), a dragoon's mount was at least 15 hands, and the horse of a hussar was a diminutive 14 hands (Duffy 1977: 104). Recruits to the Prussian hussar regiments of Frederick the Great could only be 5 feet 6 inches or less in height (Mollo 1977: 134). An anonymous eighteenth-century source described the role of hussars:

> reconnaissance work, or for launching quick attacks in battle and throwing the enemy into confusion. They never attempt to make a stand, especially when they come under heavy fire. They disperse like lightning, but they can reassemble in an instant. (Translated from German in Duffy 1977: 97)

A less charitable observer, the French General de la Colonie, viewed hussars as 'properly speaking, little more than bandits on horseback' (quoted in Chandler 1976: 95–6).[1] Hussars in the service of monarchs outside Austria were also damned by contemporaries. A British officer described the Black Hussars of the Prussian cavalry:

> A nasty looking set of rascals . . . [who] at night or when they rest . . . run their heads into some straw or any stubble and the rest of their persons lies soaking in the rain . . . They drink more brandy than water and eat I believe more tobacco than bread. (Quoted in Duffy 1988: 270–1)

## The Dress of the Hussar

Late seventeenth-century Hungarian national dress provided the template from which the hussar uniform evolved. Mollo (1972: 56–7) describes 'the original hussars with their shaggy caps and cloaks, their high cheek bones and turned-down Mongol moustaches, mounted on small Tartar bred horses, and armed with curved scimitars'. The headdress was a floppy stocking cap with a band of fur at its base or, alternatively, a cylindrical felt cap known as a *haiduk*. The short jacket was fastened at the front by cords and wooden toggles. A sheepskin slung over the left shoulder provided protection in cold weather. Tight breeches were worn and a rope for picketing the hussar's pony was wrapped about his waist. Hanging from the sword belt was a sack or envelope 'which contained necessaries and plunder' (Mollo 1972: 57).

The peasant dress of these Hungarian horsemen was soon modified by military tailors. In the case of the cap, the fur band was increased in height, overwhelming the bag, which flopped to one side, evolving into the headdress known as the colback or busby (see Plate 1). The former, variously spelled, is the term used on the continent for this fur headdress; the latter is the English name, 'after the firm of London military hatters responsible for making it' (Heathcote 1976: 109). The bag is known in French as the 'flamme' and Lieut-General F. H. Tyrrell (1922: 137) reports seeing an English translation of Hugo's *Les Miserables* in which the original 'Colbacks aux Flammes' is rendered 'flaming Colbacks'! In the Austrian army of the Seven Years War, the fur cap had reached a height of 10.5 inches (Duffy 1977: 98).

A second early innovation in hussar dress was the evolution of the cylindrical felt cap into the mirliton and the shako. The former was a slightly conical cap, smaller at the top than at the base (Duffy [1974: 99] likens it to 'an inverted flower pot'). It might be coloured or black, but attached to one side was a long triangular 'fly', the base of the triangle equalling the height of the cap and attached vertically to its left side. This fly bore a regimental colour on one side and was black on the other; it was long enough to be wound several times about the cap, exposing either the black or the coloured side (see Plate 2). Alternatively, it could simply be allowed to hang, drooping over the left shoulder of the hussar. The free apex of the fly was usually ornamented with a tassel. The wearing of the mirliton by some regiments of hussars appears very early in the history of the arm; by the Seven Years War it was possibly even more common than the colback among troops dressed as hussars. In Prussia and France, in particular, it was favoured during the second half of the eighteenth century.

The shako replaced the mirliton by the first decade of the nineteenth century. Unlike the mirliton, its sides were straight or even flared outward.

The elegant moustache of the original Hungarian trooper was a required element of the hussar 'look'. When Marbot joined the French Hussars he found younger members of his unit using boot polish to enhance their incipient moustaches (Elting 1988: 240). Also copied was the Hungarian coiffeur featuring braided pigtails falling over each temple to reach the shoulder or even the chest. An officer in the Hussars de Béon (in the British service at the close of the eighteenth century) described the hair style: 'we arranged our hair with a parting in the middle and took a handful on each side to form to plaits called "Cadenettes" which hung down on each side of the breast when fighting and thus protected the cheeks from sabre cuts' (quoted in Lawson 1940–67, Volume 4: 132).

The cording and toggles that kept the jacket (or 'dolman') closed in the original dress grew to rows of braiding and buttons that covered the entire front of the jacket from neck to waist. The hussars who charged with the Light Brigade at Balaclava had 18 rows of braid on their jackets, each row with one functional button, which closed the jacket at the front, and with an additional button at the end of each row of braid (in the case of enlisted men), or four additional buttons – one at each end and two others at the midpoints between these end buttons and the front edges of the jacket (this latter style worn by officers, giving an officer a total of 90 buttons on the front of his jacket alone! – see Mollo and Mollo 1991: 78–84). An officer's jacket surviving from the period contravenes regulations and has 19 rows of braid, hence 95 buttons.

About the waist, the picketing rope of the first hussars developed into a sash composed of numerous cords threaded through a series of tubes, which has come to be known as a barrel sash. Tight breaches were worn, and over these were sometimes worn leggings, also cut to fit close to the leg, which extended to the upper thigh. Elaborate braiding often ornamented the front of the breeches, extending from the waist to well down each thigh. Both breeches and leggings were tucked into boots which extended to the mid calf, of the style which has come to be known as 'Hessian boots'. Often the boots were dyed a garish colour.

The original animal skin thrown over the left shoulder was replaced by a jacket, known as a 'pelisse', corded like the dolman and edged with fur. Like the dolman, the pelisse had three or five rows of buttons – a French hussar officer's uniform in the Napoleonic era had a total of 156 buttons of five types (Elting 1988: 440).

A final distinctive element in the appearance of the hussar was and is the sabretache, a leather pouch or envelope, with an elaborately decorated face, which hung from the belt beside the sabre (the sabre itself was curved, unlike the straight-bladed sword of the heavy cavalry). Carman (1977: 114) has noted 'early Hungarian hussars wore tight breeches which did not permit pockets and so their purse or pouch . . . was worn on waist-belt'.

## Hussars Beyond the Austrian Empire

The armies of the eighteenth century often went far beyond their borders to recruit men for service; hence Hungarians, dressed and equipped as hussars, found their way in the cavalry of nations beyond the Austrian empire. An examination of the origins of over 700 officers of hussars in France under the *Ancièn Régime* revealed that the largest portion came from Hungary – 25.9 per cent. However, 25 per cent came from Alsace, 18.4 per cent from Germany, and 11.6 per cent from Lorraine (Chaduc 1986: 64). Soon, metropolitan armies began to dress locally recruited horsemen as hussars and trained them to use the light cavalry tactics that had gained a reputation for the Hungarians. Although Prussian king, Frederick William, felt 'a German lad does not make such a good hussar as an Hungarian or a Pole' (Duffy 1974: 99), a later Prussian cavalry general concluded 'it was not necessary to be born in Hungary to become a good Hussar' (Mollo 1972: 56). Table 1 presents the dates in which units designated as hussars were formally incorporated in the regular armies of several European states.

Table 1. *Creation of hussars in selected states*

| | | | |
|---|---|---|---|
| Austria | 1688 | Sweden | 1758 |
| Bavaria | 1688 | Saxony | 1791 |
| France | 1692 | The Netherlands | 1795 |
| Prussia | 1721 | Great Britain | 1806 |
| Württemberg | 1735 | Argentina | 1806 |
| Russia | 1740 | Mexico | 1843 |

*Sources:* Knötel, Knötel and Seig 1937; Ahliny 1973; Balaguer and Girado 1973; Hefter 1958.

Flamboyant use of colour was an aspect of hussar dress in the Austrian army from the first, and other armies similarly allowed their units of hussars to dress in unique colour schemes. This ran counter to the prevailing trend in European military uniforms for, by the early years of the eighteenth century, the armies of Europe were standardizing the colours worn by their men, at least by arm or branch of service. Obviously, such standardization improved the chances of battlefield recognition. Britain clothed its infantry and cavalry in red: Austrians and French both wore white for the most part; Prussians wore dark blue; Russians wore dark green. Sometimes a particular branch or arm might be clothed differently – both British and French artillery were dressed in blue while Prussian Cuirassiers wore white. In most armies, however, the hussar arm exhibited a 'rainbow' palette of hues, with each regiment wearing a unique combination of colours. The elements of the hussar uniform created ample opportunity for variation. The dolman and pelisse might be different colours, and the breeches might be a third. The dolman usually had collar and/or cuffs of a different colour from the body of the garment. The braid on both the dolman and pelisse usually matched, but it might be white, yellow, red, green, or possibly something else, including a mixture of two colours (for officers it was usually silver or gold). The colour of the fur on both the pelisse and the colback was another area open to variation, as was the colour of the sash and its barrels. The cloth bag of the colback also might be of a colour unique to the regiment. Tables 2, 3 and 4 give details of the dress of hussars in three different European armies.

Other states also followed this pattern. Frederick the Great's five hussar regiments, formed in 1741, were initially known by the predominant colour of their uniforms. The 1st through 5th Hussars were known respectively as the Green Hussars, the Red Hussars, the Blue Hussars, the White Hussars and the Black Hussars. Austrian hussars illustrated their contempt for the Prussian imitations by shouting 'baa, baa' at the sight of the 4th Hussars in their white uniforms (Duffy 1974: 100). Sweden's first two hussar regiments were styled the 'Blue Hussars' and the 'Yellow Hussars', the colours of the royal coat of arms and the national flag. The 'Blue Hussars', the *Kungliga Husarregementet*, created in 1758, wore a blue dolman, pelisse and leggings. Although the 'Yellow Hussars' (known as Wrangel's after their colonel), raised in 1760, wore a black dolman laced white, they took their name from their yellow pelisses and the yellow bags on their colbacks (Ahliny 1972).

## The Sombre British Hussar

The British Army formed a notable exception to this rule of variegated colouring for Hussars. The British initially formed troops and later light horse

**Table 2.** *Uniforms of Austrian hussars, 1762*

| Regiment | Dolman | Collar/cuffs | Pelisse | Braid | Breeches |
| --- | --- | --- | --- | --- | --- |
| Nadasdy | Red | Red | Dark blue | Yellow | Dark blue |
| Baranyay | Green | Green | Green | Red | Light blue |
| Szeczeny | Dark blue | Red | Dark blue | Red | Dark blue |
| Palffy | Light blue | Pink | Light blue | Pink | Light blue |
| Dessöffy | Light blue | Red | Light blue | Red | Red |
| Spleny | Green | Red | Green | White/red | Red |
| Hadik | Dark blue | Red | Dark blue | Yellow | Red |
| Bethlen | Light blue | Pink | Light blue | Pink | Light blue |
| Esterhazy | Light blue | Yellow | Light blue | Yellow | Red |
| Kalnoky | Light blue | Light blue | Light blue | Yellow | Red |
| Kaiser | Dark blue | Yellow | Dark blue | Yellow | Dark blue |
| Palatinal | Light blue | Crimson | Light blue | White | Red |
| Carlstädter | Dark blue | Red | Dark blue | Yellow | Dark blue |
| Kukez | Red | Red | Red | White | Red |
| Esclavonier | Green | Green | Green | Yellow/white | Red |

*Source:* Knötel et al. 1937: 278

regiments (styled 'Light Dragoons') in the mid-eighteenth century, resisting the continental practice of dressing light horse as hussars. They were given a distinct helmet, similar in form to the British light infantry cap of the period, but until 1784 continued to wear red coats like the majority of units of the British army. In that year their red coats were replaced with a blue jacket, which closed all the way to the waist and a sleeveless 'shell' worn over the jacket, also blue, but cut away to reveal the jacket. The jacket had three rows of thirteen buttons, connected by white cord and looped at the ends, hence the jacket closely resembled the dolman in style. Headdress, though, was the Tarleton helmet, named after Lieutenant-Colonel Banastre Tarleton, the leader of the British Legion, a Loyalist corps during the American Revolution. It featured a bearskin crest that ran fore and aft over a peaked leather cap or 'skull'. Thus the first blue uniform of the British light dragoons began an evolution toward hussar styles, but was still considerably removed from it (Barthorp 1984: 58–9). The shell was abandoned in 1796, and the buttons were placed closer together on the shortened jacket. Both the 'mirliton' (widely

## Hussars

**Table 3.** *Russian line hussars, 1809*

| Regiment | Dolman | Collar/cuffs | Pelisse | Braid | Breeches |
|---|---|---|---|---|---|
| Soum | Grey | Red | Grey | White | Red |
| Pavlograd | Dark green | Turquoise | Turquoise | Yellow | Dark green |
| Elizabethgrad | Grey | Grey | Grey | Yellow | Dark green |
| Mariupol | Dark blue | Yellow | Dark blue | Yellow | Dark blue |
| Alexandria | Black | Red | Black | White | Black |
| Olviopol | Dark green | Red | Dark green | White | Red |
| Isum | Red | Dark blue | Dark blue | White | Dark blue |
| Akhtyrsk | Brown | Yellow | Brown | Yellow | Dark blue |
| White Russia | Dark blue | Red | Red | White | Dark blue |
| Grodno | Dark blue | Light blue | Dark blue | White | Dark blue |
| Loubny | Dark blue | Yellow | Dark blue | White | Dark blue |

*Source:* Haythornthwaite 1987: 15

worn by continental hussars) and the pelisse were unofficially adopted by officers (Barthorp 1984: 70–2) and their foppish appearance invited the caricatures created by Robert Dighton the younger (Haswell Miller and Dawnay 1966–70, Volume 1, Plates 279, 280, 282, 283).

**Table 4.** *French hussars, 1812*

| Regiment number | Dolman | Collar | Cuffs | Pelisse | Braid | Breeches |
|---|---|---|---|---|---|---|
| 1 | Light blue | Light blue | Red | Light blue | White | Light blue |
| 2 | Brown | Brown | Light blue | Brown | White | Light blue |
| 3 | Grey | Grey | Red | Grey | Red | Grey |
| 4 | Royal blue | Royal blue | Red | Red | Yellow | Royal blue |
| 5* | Light blue | Light blue | White | White | Yellow | Light blue |
| 6 | Red | Red | Red | Royal blue | Yellow | Royal blue |
| 7 | Green | Red | Red | Green | Yellow | Red |
| 8 | Green | Red | Red | Green | White | Red |
| 9 | Red | Light blue | Light blue | Light blue | Yellow | Light blue |
| 10 | Light blue | Red | Red | Light blue | White | Light blue |
| 11 | Royal blue | Red | Red | Royal blue | Yellow | Royal blue |

*Source:* Knötel et al. 1937: 173
* See Plate 3 for the classic hussar dress of an officer of this regiment.

Thus when three light dragoon regiments (the 7th, the 10th, and the 15th) were given the official title, '(Hussars)' (placed in parentheses after their continued designation as Light Dragoons) there was little to change in their uniforms. The pelisse became official and was issued to all ranks, and the fur 'busby' (the British designation of the colback) was also issued to all ranks. However, these British light dragoons (hussars) retained the sombre dark-blue uniforms for both dolman and pelisse, reflecting the decision made a decade earlier to dress all of Britain's light dragoons in blue. Regimental distinctions for these regiments, and other light dragoons who later became light dragoons (hussars), were confined to such things as the colour of collar and cuffs, the colour of the busby bag, the colour of the braid (white or yellow), the colours in the barrel sash, and the colour of the fur on the pelisse and busby. At the time of the Crimean War, even these distinctions were lacking for most British Hussars, so that only the regimental number on the valises of the other ranks allowed one to identify regimental affiliation (Mollo and Mollo 1991: 78).

## Hussars and Ethnicity

The first hussars in the service of European states were of diverse origin, reflecting the fluid manner in which armies in the eighteenth century recruited their personnel. The troopers of the Hussar Regiment Berchény and Hussar Regiment Royal-Nassau in the French army were representative. Count Ladislaw de Berchény of Hungary initially recruited the former for France in Wallachia, which then was under Turkish rule. Stationed in Alsace, they then also recruited locally. 'Gradually, while the officers remained Hungarian, the men became increasingly natives of Alsace, until, in 1760 Frenchmen, provided their usual tongue was German, were permitted to serve in Hussar regiments' (Mollo 1977: 186). At the opening of the Seven Years War, France was still under strength in hussars so, in 1756, it incorporated an entire regiment of hussars, which had previously been in the army of the Prince of Nassau, into its service as the Hussar Regiment Royal-Nassau. They were part of the French army, which went down to defeat at Minden on 1 August 1759 (Mollo 1977: 160). German remained the language of drill and command within hussar regiments of the French Army until the Revolution (Mollo 1972: 56).

A brief history of a Hanoverian regiment is also illustrative of eighteenth-century recruiting of hussars. An officer in the Dutch military, Captain Nicolaus von Luckner, raised a troop of hussars for the service of Hanover in 1757. Three years later it was of regimental strength, nearly 700 men and horses. In the Seven Years War they performed yeoman service and have earned high praise. 'They were present at almost every action involving light cavalry work, whether outpost duty, raids, or skirmishing, and distinguished themselves by a courage verging on recklessness' (Niemeyer and Ortenburg 1977: 70–1). Luckner initially recruited foreigners, including some Hungarians, for his hussars, but as the unit grew to regimental strength, almost all of its men and officers were Hanoverians. At the end of the war, however, Luckner's Hussars were disbanded, and those within its ranks who remained in the Hanoverian army exchanged their white dolmans and crimson pelisses for light dragoon uniforms of British pattern (Niemeyer and Ortenburg 1977: 66–7, 70–1).

Although Great Britain did not have any hussars among the cavalry of the regular British Army until 1805, it employed the service of foreign regiments of hussars long before that date. As war broke out with revolutionary France, the British government, 'in its panic, eagerly seized on adding to its army the French Émigrés who had escaped from the butcheries of the Revolution and were anxious to fight for the restoration of their King' (Lawson 1941–67, Volume 4: 122). Some units were raised specifically for Britain by émigré officers, but others had already served in the forces of Austria, the Dutch, or the Armée de Condé. The British employment of these hussars was of short duration, with most serving primarily in the campaign in Holland. After this, many were disbanded or shipped to the West Indies where they perished in large numbers, forcing units to merge and eventually disband. The York Hussars (originally Irwin's British Hussars) lasted longer than most, not being disbanded until 1802. As Table 5 illustrates, these hussars conformed to the 'rainbow' palette mentioned above with respect to hussars.

## Hussars in North America

The first hussars on the North American continent have an interesting connection to another variety of frontier soldier, the American ranger (to be discussed in Chapter 8). The most famous of the units of rangers who fought the French through the Seven Years War (or the French and Indian War as it is now known in the United States) were Rogers' Rangers, commanded by Major Robert Rogers. With the outbreak of the American Revolution in 1775, Rogers raised a battalion of rangers from Connecticut and New York loyalists to aid the Royal cause. Although Rogers and several of his officers were dismissed under cloud of alleged irregularities in handling regimental funds, the unit distinguished itself, under the title of the Queen's Rangers, particularly at the battles of Brandywine and Germantown in Pennsylvania in 1777. Sir

Table 5. *Émigré hussars in British service, c. 1795*

| Regiment | Dolman | Collar/cuff | Pelisse | Fur | Braid | Breeches |
|---|---|---|---|---|---|---|
| Béon | Light blue | Red | Light blue | Black | White | Light blue |
| Damas | Light blue | Black | Grey | Black | * | Light blue |
| Hompesch | Green | Red | Green | Black | White | Red |
| Warren's | Red | Red** | Light blue | Brown | White | Blue grey |
| Slam | Red | Black | Black | White | White*** | Red |
| 1st Rohan | Light blue | Red | White | Black | Yellow | Light blue |
| 2nd Rohan | White | Red | Red | Black | Yellow | Red |
| Choiseul's | Green | Red | Green | Grey | **** | White |
| York | Red | Green | Green | White | White | Red |

\* Black and white twisted braid.
\*\* Red collar, light blue cuffs.
\*\*\* White braid on dolman, red braid on pelisse.
\*\*\*\* Red and yellow twisted braid.
*Source:* Lawson 1940–67, Volume 4: 131–60.

William Howe, the British commander of the force occupying Philadelphia, appointed John Graves Simcoe, an officer in the Grenadier Company of the 40th Foot, as a major in the Provincials to command the Queen's Rangers, replacing Major James Wemys, the previous commander who had been wounded at Germantown.

It was Simcoe, as he brought this well-respected Loyalist unit back up to strength, who conceived of adding hussars to complement its infantry. Simcoe, writing of himself in the third person, described his decision to mount some of his command.

> Sir William Erskine, in directing what duties Major Simcoe should do, had told him to call upon him for dragoons whenever he wanted them; upon this, Major Simcoe took the liberty of observing, 'that the clothing and habiliments of the dragoons were so different from those of the Queen's Rangers (the one being in red, and with white belts, easily seen at a distance, and the other in green, and accoutred for concealment) that he thought it would be more useful to mount a dozen soldiers of the regiment'. (Simcoe 1962: 3)

It was friendly fire, however, that persuaded Simcoe to dress these mounted men as hussars. One of the Queen's Rangers wearing the captured helmet of a Continental Light Dragoon was killed by a Hessian Jäger (rifleman).

The disaster that happened to the mounted Ranger determined Major Simcoe to provide high caps, which might at once distinguish them from both the rebel army and their own; the mounted men were termed Huzzars, were armed with a sword, and such pistols as could be bought, or taken from the enemy. (Simcoe 1962: 11)

A biographer of Simcoe reports the number of 'Huzzars' grew to fifty and provides the text of a recruiting advertisement from *Rimington's Royal Gazette* published while the Queen's Rangers were stationed in New York (Read 1890: 14–15):

ALL ASPIRING HEROES

Have now an opportunity of distinguishing themselves

by joining

THE QUEEN'S RANGERS HUZZARS,

Commanded by

LIEUTENANT-COLONEL SIMCOE.

Any spirited young man will receive every encouragement, be immediately mounted on an elegant horse, and furnished with clothing, accoutrements, etc., to the amount of FORTY GUINEAS, by applying to Cornet Spencer, at his quarters, No. 1033 Water Street, or his rendezvous, Hewitt's Tavern, near the Coffee House, and the depot at Brandywine, on Golden Hill.

Whoever brings a Recruit shall instantly receive TWO GUINEAS.

VIVANT REX ET REGINA!

Simcoe's enthusiasm for his 'Huzzars' did not extend to putting them in full hussar dress. It was only their headdress that marked them as hussars. This was cylindrical, with a silver crescent on the front. Our evidence for this headdress is a watercolour by a member of the Queen's Rangers, Captain James Murray (see Plate 4). Secondary sources have disagreed whether it was constructed of felt or fur (Lawson 1940–67, Volume 3: 232; McBarron and Smith 1974; Katcher 1973a: Plate D2), though I favour the latter view. The bag that hung over the left side from the top, green with a white tassel at the end, gave the headdress the distinctive appearance of a colback or busby. The only other hussar element in the accoutrements of the Queen's Ranger Huzzar is the curved sabre of the light cavalryman.

Serving with the Queen's Rangers, while that corps was quartered in New York, was another body of light cavalry, Diemar's Huzzars (the Black

Huzzars), formed from Germans who had been taken prisoner at Saratoga but had escaped rebel hands. Little is known about this unit, but it is reported they wore 'black or dark gray huzzar jackets' (Katcher 1973b: 85).

The Queen's Rangers Huzzars fought in Virginia in the Yorktown campaign, which effectively ended the war. On the opposing side in this same campaign was another unit in spectacular hussar dress, the hussars of Lauzun's Legion, part of the French Expeditionary Force under Rochambeau. Like the Queen's Rangers, Lauzun's Legion had both an infantry and mounted component. The hussars of Lauzun's Legion wore a black mirliton with a red wing, a sky blue dolman with lemon yellow cuffs and yellow lace, braid, and buttons, and red breeches laced yellow. In the heat of Virginia they are reported to have abandoned use of the sky blue pelisse. Boots were black with a white tassel (Chartrand 1991: 33–4, 40–2, Plate D1).

The United States never adopted the designation of 'hussar' nor did it adopt significant portions of hussar dress for its regular army. Indeed, until the Civil War (1861–65) mounted troops were not a significant part of its army. For a brief period, during the 1812–15 conflict with Britain, United States Light Dragoons wore dolman-like dark blue jackets with three rows of silver buttons and black braid in full dress, but with this wore light dragoon helmets patterned after earlier British models rather than the colback, mirliton or shako of the true hussar (Katcher 1975: 123). For much of the nineteenth century, however, American gentlemen enjoyed playing soldier in part-time volunteer units; these units of weekend soldiers paid for their own uniforms, hence those with a wealthy membership often impressed the townsfolk, especially the ladies, with gaudy and elaborate uniforms. Their uniforms surrendered completely to Laver's seduction principle. It is doubtful than anything approaching a complete list of volunteer units could ever be compiled, but it is worth mentioning a few of them who called themselves Hussars or who wore the hussar dress.

One of the more flamboyant hussar units among the American Volunteer Militia was the Boston Hussars, raised in 1810 but disbanded just seven years later. They wore a green dolman with a crimson pelisse, both braided with yellow cord (gold for officers) and a black bell shako. Unlike their continental namesakes, however, the regiment did not present itself for parade on light, small horses. All horses in the unit had to be at least 15½ hands high (McBarron 1977). Other Volunteer Militia units adopted hussar dress, including the Chatham Hussars formed in Savannah, Georgia, in 1812, and who then combined with the Chatham Light Dragoons in 1816 to form the Georgia Hussars. Their dark blue dolmans with five rows of silver buttons and white braid continues as mess dress for this unit in the Georgia National Guard (McBarron, Todd and Elting 1977; Katcher 1989: 7–8). Both the

Governor's Horse Guards of New Hampshire and the 3rd Regiment (Hussars) of New York wore distinctive hussar dress (McBarron and Todd 1982a; Katcher 1989:17, 42, Plate B1).

The 3rd New Jersey Volunteer Cavalry, also designated the 1st US Hussars, actually saw combat, distinguishing itself in the final year of the American Civil War. It was raised in the early months of 1864 and was reviewed by President Abraham Lincoln as it passed through Washington on its way to the front. The veterans of the Army of the Potomac quickly dubbed them 'the butterflies' because of their elaborate uniforms. With ordinary US cavalry trousers of light blue, they wore a dark blue dolman braided yellow (gold for officers) with orange patches on the standup collar. Headgear was a yellow braided version of the ordinary kepi, but without the usual leather peak. They were supplied with a short, hooded light-blue cloak, which they wore over the left shoulder in the manner of a pelisse, but some officers equipped themselves with light blue pelisses edged in black fur. It was not just a unit of dandies, however, for on 13 September 1864, along with the 2nd Ohio Cavalry, they captured the 8th South Carolina Infantry including its colours and commander. This unit was 'apparently ... the only full-strength [US] regiment ... to carry the title of "Hussar" into battle' (Risley, Elting and Sturcke 1982).

Hussars also appeared in Canada. As cavalry regiments in the Canadian Militia were numbered consecutively, and not all were designated Hussars, the numbers of hussar units do not follow a consecutive sequence. Nine of the regiments in 1907 bore the title 'Hussars', the senior regiment being formed in London, Ontario, in 1892. Regulation headdress was the Universal Pattern White Helmet although it is clear that the busby was worn by some of these units (for example, the 8th Princess Louise's New Brunswick Hussars). The dark-blue tunic with its gold braid and a buff collar was identical for all except the 6th Hussars who had a white collar (Ross and Chartrand 1977: 32a, 33, 46–9).

### Hussars in Latin America

Hussars and Hussar-style dress have made numerous appearance in the military forces of Latin America. A definitive listing and description is probably impossible, given the chaotic conditions of revolution in the early decades of the nineteenth century.

When the British invaded the then Spanish colony of Argentina in 1806 (Spain was still an ally of Napoleon) among the forces opposing the invasion was a locally raised unit of hussars. Initially named Húsares del Rey (King's

Hussars), they were later known as Húsares de Pueyrredón and still later after Argentina began to assert independence from colonial Spain as Húsares de la Patria (Balaguer and Girado 1973). In 1814 in Argentina a squadron of Hussars in blue dolmans with red pelisses served as the Guard for the 'Supremo Director de las Provincias Unidas'. The next year this unit took the name 'Union Hussars' and were replaced as the Guard to the Supreme Director by a small corps of mounted guides ('Guias de Caballeria'), also in hussar dress (Balaguer and Fernández 1974a). Still another hussar regiment, 'Cazadores a Caballo', was created in 1817 (Balaguer and Fernández 1974b).

Hussar uniforms were popular in the armies fighting for the liberation of South America in the early decades of the nineteenth century under Simon Bolivar and José de San Martin. Some were recruited overseas from veterans of the Napoleonic wars. Bolivar's forces included a British Legion and an Irish Legion. In the former were the 1st and 2nd Venezuelan Hussars whereas the latter included a unit styled Hussar Guards. The 2nd Venezuelan Hussars wore a red dolman and overalls with light blue collar and cuffs. The hussars of the Peruvian Legion were quite British in appearance with a brown fur colback with a red bag, blue dolman laced yellow and a blue pelisse. As commander of an army of *gauchos* (Argentine cowboys), General Martin Miguel de Guemes wore a white hussar uniform braided gold (Hooker and Poulter 1991).

In 1840 Brazil had an elaborately dressed unit of National Guard Hussars, but because they wore the Polish headdress, the *czapka*, they will be discussed in the next chapter.

Mexico had formed a Presidential Bodyguard of Hussars in 1843, bearing the title Hussars of the Guard of the Supreme Powers (Hefter 1958: 45, 73–4; Hooker 1972). Later, when the Hapsburg Archduke Maximilian, with French support, attempted to establish himself as Emperor of Mexico in 1864, he brought with him a large contingent of French, Belgians and Austrians. The French were regular troops from the French metropolitan and colonial establishments but the Austro-Belgian troops were raised specifically for the service of the new Mexican Emperor. These included a large body of hussars, recruited in Hungary. They wore a tiny felt hat, its brim turned up all round, ornamented with an eagle feather on its left side, rather than a colback or shako, and a hip-length green tunic piped white with five rows of white cording rather than a dolman. No pelisse was worn, but the tunic was sometimes worn over the left shoulder in the fashion of a pelisse, revealing a dark blue blouse. A portion of these hussars were designated the Empress' Own Hussars of the Guard and when the French abandoned Maximilian in 1867, some 1000 continued to serve the Habsburgs in new red uniforms leading to a common designation, the Red Hussars (Hefter 1982).

The republican harassment of the French supporters of Maximilian led the latter to create a force of Contra-Guerrillas that in part wore hussar dress. This was a multi-ethnic unit, including French, Greeks, Spaniards, Mexicans, North Americans, South Americans, English, Italians, Dutch and Swiss in its ranks. What they seem to have had in common was a lack of character. A contemporary observer noted 'this pack of ferocious adventurers did not know the meaning of discipline' and a French officer asked for recruits for the corps admitting sending 'the worst types from my company'. The two squadrons of cavalry in the corps wore dolmans, red for the first and blue for the second, laced black in both cases. Headgear was a large sombrero or a large straw hat. Artillery (the corps had two mountain guns) and officers of infantry also wore the red dolman (Leliepvre, Hefter and Elting1982).

## The Java Hussars

With respect to ethnic origin, possibly the most unusual unit of hussars was raised by Britain in India. These were the Java Hussars who were formed in 1812 under the command of Captain L. H. O'Brien of the Madras Cavalry. They served for the brief period Britain occupied Java and when the colony was returned to the Dutch in 1816 the regiment was disbanded. A trooper is illustrated by the contemporary artist C. Hamilton Smith (Plate 5) wearing a blue dolman with yellow collar and cuffs and white braid. Most interesting, though, is the headgear: a red turban trimmed white (Carman 1961: 196). There is, of course, no evidence of a pelisse, certainly superfluous in the Indonesian archipelago.

Although the Java Hussars had both the title of 'hussar' and modified hussar dress, they were far from unusual in wearing the dolman in British India. In Hamilton Smith's illustration, both the Governor General's Body Guard and the Bengal Cavalry wear dolmans (Carman 1961: 3, 24–5).

## Evolution of the Hussar Uniform

There were relatively few modifications to the hussar style of dress before the French Revolution. However, the mirliton became a casualty of the Napoleonic wars, and disappeared from fashion in the first decade of the nineteenth century, replaced by the shako, which evolved from the mirliton or its ancestor, the cylindrical felt cap. The hussar shako was frequently coloured – for example, the British 10th (Prince of Wales's Own Royal) Light Dragoons (Hussars) wore red shakos at the Battle of Waterloo. Accompanying this disappearance of the mirliton from fashion was the abandonment of the braided cadenette hairstyle. Another earlier affectation abandoned in the first years of the nineteenth century was the long leggings or hose that had covered the legs from the boot to mid-thigh. At the same time, the dolman became shorter, exposing the sword belt that hung about the hips, and the colback (worn by some, but not all, units of hussars) became reduced in height and increased in diameter. Following these changes in the first decade of the nineteenth century, hussar uniforms did not alter greatly for nearly fifty years, and the hussars who charged with the Light Brigade at Balaclava in the Crimea in 1854 would not have looked out of place at Waterloo thirty-nine years earlier.

Before the outbreak of the Crimean War, however, military uniforms among some European powers made a decided shift, following developments in civilian fashion. The shift was away from the tailed coat, cut straight across the front at the waist, to a tunic or frock coat. Soldiers wearing these benefited from their looser cut, and the skirts of the tunic extended to the top of the thigh, whereas those of the frock coat, much fuller, extended to mid-thigh or even the knees. The hussars of Austria and Prussia led the way in the adoption of the tunic. The mass of cording across the front of the jacket was eliminated from the tunic, but was replaced by five or six rows of looped braid often referred to as 'brandenburgs' (Plate 6). The mass of cording on the pelisse suffered a similar fate. Britain's hussars adopted this style shortly after the Crimean War, but those of France retained the old heavily-laced dolman in full-dress into the twentieth century. In Britain the Royal Horse Artillery also retained the old style of jacket rather than adopting the new hussar tunic and, to this day, one mounted battery (the King's Troop) continues to wear it in full dress. After the Crimean War the pelisse disappeared for ever from the dress of British hussars (made official in the *Dress Regulations for the Army, 1857* – see Bowling 1972: 39–40), as it had among the hussars of Germany in 1853. In the German army the pelisse was restored to the dress of the Life-Guard Hussars in 1865, and subsequently to eight other hussar regiments, although the 13th Hussars never wore theirs, granted to them in 1913, because of the outbreak of World War I (Hagger, Fosten and Marrion 1974: 22–5).

Both Germany and Russia retained distinctive colours for their various regiments of hussars until 1914. The 21 German regiments of hussars wore tunics of Bright Red (Life-Guard, 3rd), Black (1st, 2nd, 17th), Brown (4th), Dark Red (5th), Dark Green (6th, 10th, 11th), Russian Blue (7th), Dark Blue (8th, 14th, 15th), Cornflower-blue (9th, 12th, 13th, 16th), Light Blue (18th, 19th) and Field Grey (20th) (Hagger, Fosten and Marrion 1974: 21). In France the multicoloured dress of hussar units disappeared in army reorganizations following the defeat of 1870, dressing all its hussars in a light blue dolman and madder red trousers (Stacke 1970: 28). In Britain, the hussar in full dress continued to wear his conservative dark blue tunic and overalls. Austria clothed its hussars in tunics of either light or dark blue, but this did not completely eliminate the peacock passions of designers of hussar dress. For Imperial (*kaiserlich und königlich* or kuk) the parade shako was of regimental colour, being dark blue, white, madder red, ash grey, or light blue. The combination of tunic colour, shako colour and colour (gold or silver) of the toggles and olivets (false buttons at the end of the brandenburgs) ornamenting the tunic was unique to each regiment (Lucas 1987: 11, 106–11; Knötel et al. 1937: 280). In addition to these units, the Austro-Hungarian Empire had as a separate army the Hungarian Honved, and all of the ten Honved cavalry regiments were hussars, although Regiment No. 10, recruited in Croatia-Slovenia, was dressed and equipped as lancers from its formation in 1874 until it was changed to hussars in 1882. Their dress resembled that of the Imperial Army in cut, but the tunic was invariably dark blue. The olivets were universally gold. Half of these regiments wore madder red shakos, and the other five wore unique colours (grey, white, light blue, dark blue, and grass green) and hence were readily identifiable (Lucus 1987: 117–20, 181–2).

## Influence of Hussar Dress on Other Arms

As has been mentioned above, light cavalry frequently dressed as hussars even if they did not include the word 'hussars' in their regimental title. Perhaps the most famous hussar-style uniform ever worn was that of the Chasseurs à Cheval of Napoleon's Imperial Guard. Certainly it could be argued that Théodore Géricault's famous equestrian portrait of Lieutenant Dieudonné in the full dress of the Guard Chasseurs with colback, dolman, pelisse and barrel sash is history's best-known painting of a soldier below the rank of general. Dieudonné was killed in the retreat from Moscow the same year (1812) that Géricault won a gold medal for the painting exhibited in the Salon in Paris (Young 1971: 30–1; Lachouque 1961: 524). With respect to Chasseurs à Cheval of the line in Imperial France there was considerable conflict between many regimental commanders, who tried to dress their men as hussars, and an economy-minded bureaucracy, which favoured a more sober and less expensive uniform.

Items of hussar dress were adopted by other arms, particularly those that, like the hussars, emphasized independent action and mobility. Possibly the most unusual of these was the *Régiment de dromadaire* formed by the French in Egypt in April, 1799 (Plate 7). As their name suggests, their mounts were camels, considerably larger than the traditional hussar pony. This short-lived unit went through several changes in dress in its three years of service. Troopers seem to have always worn a sky blue dolman with red cuffs and sky blue (red after October 1800) hussar breeches. The original service dress headgear was a turban, but from February 1800, a black bicorne with a large white feather plume was worn. In full dress a long coat with half sleeves and laced in hussar fashion was worn over this with a crimson barrel sash with white barrels. Trumpeters wore a scarlet dolman, breeches and pelisse (Haythornthwaite 1981: 117–8; Large 1965: Plate 7).

From their formation in 1800 the officers of British regiments of rifles have dressed as hussars, albeit in sombre rifle green with black braiding rather than a typical flamboyant hussar colour scheme. They wore a pelisse of rifle green and carried the curved hussar sabre while fighting Napoleon's armies in the Peninsula (Windrow and Embleton 1974: 150–1).

Both the original laced dolman and the later braided hussar tunic were adopted by other arms. Horse Artillery in both Napoleonic France and in Britain wore hussar-style dolmans. Officers in the Northwest Mounted Police who, according to legend, brought law and order (as well as peace with the native population) to the Canadian west wore red tunics with hussar braiding as part of their original full dress uniforms adopted in 1876 (Ross and May 1988: 33, 41, Plate A2).

In 1842 a print depicting an Officer of the Cape Mounted Rifles in South Africa illustrated a splendid hussar uniform in black or rifle green with black braiding and black fur edging the pelisse. He wears a shako with a large black plume of a hanging cluster of black feathers which is as large as the shako itself (Crescent Books 1973: 43). The unit recruited from persons of diverse origin. All the officers were British, but a portion (the exact numbers varied through time) was recruited from among the Cape Coloured population. It had been raised in 1817 as the Cape Corps, consisting of both infantry and cavalry, but in 1827 was reorganized into three companies known as the Cape Mounted Riflemen. An 1820 military tailor's pattern book describes the officer's jacket of the Cape Corps as 'Green Hazzar Jacket' (Anderson 1939). The Cape Mounted Riflemen had a band riding greys. The unit wore its rifle green uniforms until 1867 when the uniforms were changed to blue. It was disbanded in 1870 (Tylden 1938).

A century later, the apartheid regime in South Africa maintained a Presidential Guard whose dress reflected the Hussar tunic. On ceremonial duties this unit wore a blue shako laced gold and a grey-green tunic with orange-gold brandenburgs, four in number, three across the chest above the white waist belt and one below. Grey-green trousers with an orange-gold stripe were worn. I am uncertain how long this uniform continued in use, but it is reported to have been worn on ceremonial occasions in Pretoria in 1969 (Cassin-Scott and Fabb 1973: Plate 67).

Modified Hussar dress also was found among troops recruited in insular southern Asia. On the island of Borneo in the British protectorate of Sarawak in 1914 the Dyaks and Sikhs of the Sarawak Rangers wore a white tunic frogged with black brandenburgs (Nevins 1992:276).

On mainland south Asia, the laced dolman largely disappeared from cavalry in the Indian Army following the mutiny of 1857. It was replaced by two Indian knee-length garments, quite similar to each other in style, the *alkhalak* and the *kurta*. For a very brief period, in the mid-1860s, the Governor General's Bodyguard wore hussar tunics (Harris 1979: 5) and until 1914 and even later, British officers in many Indian cavalry regiments wore hussar tunics in full dress, which in some units worn on parade with their troops and in other cases as a dismounted full dress.[2] British officers of the Governor General's Bodyguard; the Governor's Bodyguard, Madras and the Governor's Bodyguard, Bengal all wore scarlet hussar tunics and were equipped with the sabretache (Wilson 1970: 21–3; Bowling 1971: 5–6).

For much of its history the Indian Army was in fact three armies, belonging to the Bengal, Madras and Bombay Presidencies, and the hussar tunic was worn by British Officers in the last two as well as by officers in the Central Indian Horse, the Hyderabad Contingent and the Erinpura Irregular Horse. These tunics disappeared from the four regiments of Madras Cavalry as the uniform of the other ranks and Native Officers became Indianized and the regiments were converted to lancers in the last two decades of the nineteenth century. Of the four Hyderabad regiments, the 1st (in 1903 the 20th Deccan Horse) continued to wear the hussar tunic in dismounted full dress but the other three Hyderabad cavalry regiments all lost the hussar tunic when they converted to Lancers in 1890. British Officers of the two regiments of Central Indian Horse in full dress wore a handsome drab hussar tunic, laced gold with maroon collar and cuffs (Nicholson 1970b: 9–10; Bowling 1971).

The Indian Army also utilized a hussar-like tunic, which had originated among French colonial troops in North Africa. The tunic closes with hooks and eyes and the braid passes loosely over the chest (and over the pouch belt) anchored at each end to toggles and lace loops. In 1863 both British and Indian Officers in the 9th to 19th regiments of Bengal cavalry were to wear this garment and in 1865 it was specified for Frontier Force cavalry, including cavalry of the Guides (Plate 8). As was the case with the more conventional hussar tunic, the conversion of regiments to lancers led to the abandonment of this style (Nicholson 1970b: 7–8; Bowling 1971; Harris 1979).

Mention should also be made of the cavalry of Imperial Japan in the first decades of the twentieth century. For full dress they wore blue hussar tunics laced white with three rows of silver buttons for the line and laced red with yellow metal buttons for the guard. The braid on officers' tunics was black. Red trousers had green stripes and collars and cuffs were also green (Knötel, Knötel et al. 1937: 387). Another source asserts that, in China in 1900, the Japanese cavalry wore a blue dolman laced red with blue collar and cuffs and blue trousers with a red stripe. The peaked forage cap was blue with a red band and red piping about the crown. Officers wore a similar dolman but with black frogging and a red collar and blue cuffs piped red (Bodin 1979: 32–3, 37–8).

In the days leading up to the conflict of 1914, hussar braiding on the tunic of generals and staff officers was popular in European armies. In the Imperial Army of Austro-Hungary those generals who had previously commanded a hussar regiment were privileged to wear 'Hungarian' dress rather than the more conservative 'German' uniform. The gala dress of these Generals was very colourful indeed, and included a colback of marten fur – the only use of the colback in the Austro-Hungarian Army at this time. Both tunic and breeches were scarlet with heavy gold lace. The pelisse was white lined with scarlet silk and edged with marten fur again with heavy gold cording. These same officers wore a service dress consisting of a pike grey tunic with the Hussar cording gold with black threads. The Hussar shako was worn and trousers were blue grey with two red stripes. The service dress pelisse was pike grey and edged with mink (Lucas 1987: 187–8).

This gala dress was worn by Austrian officers with earlier hussar connections, but Britain put all its general staff in scarlet tunics laced gold in hussar fashion. This full dress uniform for staff officers was worn with only minor changes for 43 years, finally being replaced by a less ornate tunic in 1897 (Holding 1894: 24–5, Plate VII; Nicholson 1970a).

## The Shako

Although armies far removed from the Hungarian homeland adopted the dolman and pelisse of the hussar, it is the headgear of this trooper that had the greatest impact on military dress worldwide. When body armour, including helmets, fell into disuse early in the seventeenth century, hats worn by military personnel became identical to those of their civilian counterparts. There was a concession to uniformity in the way the hat was laced and a cockade of national colours was worn thereon, but civilian and military hats, at least the hats worn by the vast majority of the military, followed parallel evolution through the eighteenth century.

The first exception to this was the development of the grenadier cap, a variety of headgear associated only with the military. Initially grenadiers were specialist troops who threw grenades into enemy fortifications and formations. They were selected from ordinary recruits on the basis of their greater height and upon demonstrated courage, hence the grenadier company of a battalion was an élite unit expected to spearhead offensive actions. These grenades were round bombs with short fuses that the grenadier had to light, using a slow match held in his left hand, before throwing the grenade with his right. Since both hands were occupied in throwing the grenade, the grenadier could not hold his musket and had to sling it across his back. The brim of the ordinary civil-military hat of the time made such an action inconvenient, so grenadiers replaced the hat with a cap resembling a stocking cap. Someone came upon the idea of stiffening this cap so that it stood upright upon the head. Eventually this grew so tall that the slinging of the musket probably again became awkward, but by that time this did not matter since grenades were no longer used in battle. However, the title grenadier had been retained for élite companies and regiments who marked their status by wearing grenadier caps. In the early eighteenth century these caps had cloth or metal fronts, but in the latter portion of the century they were made partially of fur. Entirely made of fur, these grenadier caps (or 'bearskins' as they are commonly called) are still worn on ceremonial by the five foot regiments of the Brigade of Guards in the British Army.[3]

The second distinctly military variety of headgear introduced into European armies in the eighteenth century was that worn by hussars,[4] and it is this item of headdress that changed the look of the soldier for nearly a century. I do not here refer to the colback or busby, which continues to be associated primarily with hussars and those troops dressed in hussar style.[5] Rather, I refer to the cylindrical cap worn as a warm-weather alternative to the colback and the mirliton that evolved from it. This headdress was adopted, early in Napoleonic times, by French Light Infantry.[6] By 1806 the shako, as the cylindrical headdress came to be known, was worn by the entire infantry (both Line and Light Infantry battalions), much of Napoleon's Guard, and by those Hussars and Chasseurs à Cheval who did not wear the colback. The shako, whose origins were on the Hungarian frontier, remained the standard military headdress for most of the nineteenth century.

The hat the shako replaced was the bicorne, which, with its ancestor, the tricorne, had been the standard military and civilian male head covering for more than a century. This headgear of the *ancient régime* had given way in civilian circles by 1800 to the top hat. The bicorne, which had been the hat of the monarchy, ironically continued to be worn by the armies of Revolutionary France and indeed by the Army of Imperial France through the era of its greatest victories. The bulk of the magnificent infantry and artillery troops who established Napoleon's genius on such fields as Jena and Austerlitz in silhouette were identical to the soldiers of Louis XVI some twenty years earlier. Thus the rejection of the bicorne for the rank and file (it continued to be worn in many armies by senior officers until full dress largely passed from the scene in 1914) could be anticipated given the fall from favour of the bicorne among civilians. However, with the introduction of the shako, the evolution of military headgear took a divergent path from the evolution of hats among the male civilian population. From this point in time, the hat as well as the arms served to distinguish the military man from the civilian.

## Conclusion

Given the nature of warfare in the era prior to the invention of barbed wire and the machine gun, a problem commonly faced by imperial armies was the recruitment of men skilled in the role of light cavalry. They were important in discovering the lay of the land, locating roads, bridges and obstacles that lay in the path of an advancing army. These men were needed to locate the enemy and report its movements; they were needed for intelligence through the interception of communications being sent by messenger from one enemy division to another; they were needed to form a screen to prevent their own army from being surprised by the enemy and they were needed to pursue the disintegrated forces of a broken and retreating enemy. They were necessary to destroy the confidence and morale of an enemy by harassing stragglers. At times of retreat or strategic withdrawal, light cavalry were also needed to protect the army against harassment by enemy cavalry.

In the eighteenth century several European powers found it easy to recruit men with these skills from the populations on their frontiers. Their success in pursuing these tasks led to the association of their style of dress with the role they played, so that even troops recruited within the metropolis were uniformed in copies of that dress when expected to play a light cavalry role. Soon a stylized version of the dress became associated not only with the light cavalry but with the military generally, so the dress of these frontier horsemen came to be worn even by an officer corps recruited from among the nobility of the empire.

# 4

# Other Horsemen from the East: Uhlans and Cossacks

> He saw the lances rise and fall for a moment, and a friend of his went down. The horses began to rear and bite and kick, and man after man went down among their feet and he saw them trying to ward off the lances with their hands. And then the horse he had taken was killed by a thrust of a lance and he was down himself and thought he was done for, and lay there under the hoofs and heard the clash of arms, the shouting of men, the neighing and moaning of the horses.
>
> David Howarth
> *A Near Run Thing: The Day of Waterloo*

## The Lance as a Military Weapon

The second uniform inspired by the dress of horsemen from Eastern Europe was that of lancers or uhlans. The former term is used by the British Army, the latter was a German usage. Lances have been carried by a variety of cavalry through the ages, and, indeed, the mounted lancer in the early mediaeval era was the epitome of the warrior, the armoured knight. Among the cavalry of Western Europe, lances went out of fashion with the advent of infantry armed with firearms and pikes. The latter, five metres or so in length, could be utilized by infantrymen to prevent cavalry (whose lances to be carried by men on horseback were of necessity much shorter than the pike handled by the foot soldier) from spearing them. The conservative military mind is such that when pikes themselves went out of fashion, being replaced by the bayonet on the end of the musket, no one suggested that lances of a length reasonable enough to handle on horseback could do damage to an infantry formation that was relying upon bayonets for defence. Of course, even armed with lances, cavalry was susceptible to being destroyed by musketry before reaching the infantry.

While the lance was abandoned in the face of pikes and musketry in western European warfare, it continued to be used in the east by peoples such as the

Poles, Tartars and Cossacks. Poland, possibly because of its confused, and confusing, political situation, falling under the jurisdiction of an number of foreign powers, became the source for recruiting men skilled with the use of the lance on horseback for the armies of Western Europe.

First employed by Saxony, Poles entered the French service as the *Voluntaires de Saxe* in 1743. Maurice de Saxe, born in 1696 as the illegitimate son of the Elector of Saxony and made a Marshal of France in 1747 just three years before his death, introduced uhlans (lancers) into the army of France. The *Voluntaires de Saxe* consisted of both dragoons and uhlans and both wore helmets of neo-classical style. Given the Marshal's 'particular penchant for actresses' it is suggested that this headgear had theatrical 'inspiration' (Mollo 1972: 57). This was an innovation that had considerable influence on the later appearance of dragoons and other heavy cavalry, and seems to have been worn by the uhlans of the *Voluntaires de Saxe* until they were disbanded after the death of Marshal Saxe. For uhlans in other armies, and later in France, as we will see, the prescribed headdress was a headdress of Polish origin.

## Uhlans of Austria and Prussia

The hallmark of the dress of the uhlan or lancer is the Polish headdress, the *czapka* (also spelled *tchapka*) or *konfederatka*. The *czapka*'s square top is its distinguishing feature, worn so that the angles of the square point to the front and back and to each side.[1] Originally made of soft cloth, often with a fur band about the bottom, it was soon given a rigid construction. The square upper portion of the headgear became, for many armies, a place to display a distinctive regimental colour. The *kurtka*, the characteristic lancer jacket, appeared at an early date among Polish uhlans in the Austrian service and, like the *czapka*, came to symbolize the uhlan. It had a blaze of regimental colour from neck to waist formed by turned-back lapels or a cloth 'plastron' buttoned over the chest that mimicked the appearance of lapels on the front of the jacket. The *kurtka* also featured piping in the regimental colour along the seams that curve from the shoulder to the waist on the back and along the rear seams of the sleeves. A third feature of lancer dress was the girdle, a broad decorative waistband with three or five stripes of two colours, usually of yellow or white (gold or silver) with one or two stripes of the distinctive regimental colour.

Prior to the division of Poland in 1795 between Prussia, Russia and Austria, the *konfederatka* was worn by a large portion of the Polish army. It was worn only by officers (not by other ranks) in the infantry and artillery, but in the cavalry, all ranks wore this headdress (von Pivka 1979: 185–6). The last Polish King, Stanislas Poniatowski, had an elegantly dressed bodyguard of lancers wearing the *konfederatka* with a black fur band and a gold-laced white top. They wore a sleeveless long coat of cobalt blue over a sleeved red waistcoat. The coat was heavily laced in gold and featured a red plastron, also heavily laced in gold. The uniform also featured gold epaulets and red boots (Cassin-Scott and Fabb 1973: Plate 54).

The *czapka* soon made an appearance in other European armies. From 1782 to 1790 Vienna was treated to the sight of the magnificent appearance of the Galician (or Polish) Noble Guard. They wore a white *czapka* trimmed with gold and each had a leopard skin thrown over his left shoulder in the fashion of hussars. Their lances carried a black and yellow pennon[2] (Martin 1963: 94, Plate 6).

The Austrian line cavalry saw the formal organization of a regiment of uhlans in 1792. Their original *czapka* was low, of yellow cloth with a fur band and no peak. Thus it resembled the *konfederatka* worn by Polish officers and troops of the time. The original coat was worn open, not closed to the waist like the *kurtka*. It was green with red facings. Both plume and lance pennon were yellow and black. A second regiment of uhlans was formed in 1798. By this time the *kurtka* had come into use and the *czapka* had lost its fur trim (see Plate 9). The lower portion of the headgear was of black leather with a peak. The *czapka* was increased in height and width three years later when a third regiment was formed. A fourth regiment was formed in 1813. The top or square portion of the *czapka* was yellow for the 1st, dark green for the 2nd, scarlet for the 3rd, and white for the 4th Uhlans (Haythornwaite 1986: 35–6).

Russia soon followed this fad for clothing cavalry armed with the lance in the Polish fashion. In 1803 two regiments of Light Horse, the Polish and Lithuanian regiments, were dressed in the Polish manner with the *czapka* and a *kurtka* fronted with a plastron and piped on the seams of the sleeves and back (Mollo 1979: 27). By 1812 there were six regiments of lancers, including a regiment of Life Guards, these Life Guards attired in a *czapka* with a blue top, with a *kurtka* with red collar, piping and plastron, and yellow epaulettes and buttons (Von Pivka 1979: 227).

Prussia adopted the lance for some of its cavalry, but initially their dress reflected ethnic origins outside Poland. The cavalry of Frederick the Great included the Bosniaks who were armed with the lance. They were originally recruited in the Ukraine by an Albanian jeweller, Stephan Serkis, and in 1745 they formed a squadron attached to the Prussian 5th Hussars. In 1770, the unit was granted an independent regimental status as ninth on the list of Prussian Hussars. They originally wore a white turban wrapped about a red skull cap and an ankle-length black coat with half sleeves over a red jacket. Sometime before 1780 the turbans were replaced by a fur cylindrical headdress with a cloth top (not a busby bag) of red cloth (Haythornthwaite 1991: 35–6). Among Frederick's troops there were uhlans in a unit of irregulars, the *Frei Korps von Kleist*, who wore a cloth cylindrical cap with a thin fur band. These Uhlans von Kleist were disbanded in 1763 (Marrion 1965).

When Prussia gained possession of part of Poland in 1795, the Bosniaks (9th Hussars) recruited its lancers from among the Polish nobility. They (the 9th Hussars) became known as *Towarczys*. An independent battalion of *Towarczys* was also formed. Following the defeats at Jena and Auerstädt the Prussian army was reorganized in 1808, with two lancer regiments, now designated uhlans. Their uniform, though, was not distinctive, being the Prussian double-breasted jacket and ordinary shako. A concession to the classic uhlan dress, however, was the lancer girdle worn about the waist of the other ranks. With the formation of the *Leib-Uhlanen* squadron in 1808, the Prussian cavalry finally embraced a unit dressed in *czapka*, *kurtka* and girdle. The *Leib-Uhlanen* wore a dark blue *czapka* and a dark blue *kurtka* with red collar, cuffs, lapels and piping (Von Pivka 1979: 208–9; Melegari 1968: 116–17). When the *Leib-Uhlanen* were renamed the *Garde-Uhlanen-Eskadron* in March 1810 they replaced the *kurtka* with the ordinary Prussian cavalry jacket (Nash 1972: 56–7).

As the Napoleonic wars moved into their final phase, Prussia recruited large numbers of men to its newly formed 'Landwehr'. Over one hundred squadrons strong, this force was armed with the lance. Given the conditions in which it was raised, one could well expect great variation in the uniforms provided to these cavalry. The shako was the official headgear, but a Rheinish regiment and either the 3rd or the 7th Silesian regiments (or both) wore the *czapka*. The uhlan girdle also was worn by some of these units, including a Westphalian squadron (Nash 1972: 63–7).

## Napoleon's Lancers

This early employment of lancers in Polish costume was significant in the armies of Austria, Russia and Prussia, but it was the incorporation of Polish lancers in the *Grande Armée* of Napoleon that established *czapka* and *kurtka* as featured items of dress among the world's cavalry. Carman (1957: 109) notes: 'The glories achieved by the Polish Lancers in the service of Napoleon reflected all around Europe, and most countries tried to capture some of their spirit by equipping or raising their own version of these showy horsemen.'

## Other Horsemen from the East

In December 1806 Napoleon entered Warsaw and was provided with a guard of honour composed of local aristocracy. He ordered the formation of four troops of *chevau-legers Polonais* in March 1807. Recruited from the élite, its men paid for their own uniforms and provided their own horses. Their *kurtka* was dark blue with crimson lapels and the cloth top of their *czapka* was also crimson. In this uniform on 30 November 1808, they established the legend of the Polish cavalryman at Somosierra in Spain, where they charged 2,500 metres uphill to sabre the gunners of four entrenched batteries, an action in which every officer was killed or wounded. The last battery was stormed by Lieutenant Niegolewski and his men. As Niegolewski lay wounded by one of the captured Spanish guns, Napoleon took off his own medal of the Legion of Honour and pinned it on the *kurtka* of the Polish lieutenant. Ironically, this legendary action occurred before the unit was armed with lances. The regiment did not become lancers until 1809, and the lances the first carried are said to have been captured from Austrian uhlans (Windrow and Embleton 1974: 40; Lachouque 1961: 135–6; Etling 1988: 193–4). However, from this point on, Poles and lances were an integral, flamboyant and highly visible part of Napoleon's *Garde*. The association of these Poles with the little Corsican continued to grow and was so strong that a squadron accompanied him to his first exile on the Island of Elba (Lachouque 1961: 438).

Napoleon's famed Imperial Guard eventually had three additional regiments of lancers dressed as Poles. On 17 December 1809 the Lancers of Berg, resplendent in white *kurtkas* faced with pink, a creation of the flamboyant Marshal of France, Joachim Murat as the Grand Duke of Berg, became part of the Imperial Guard. In September 1810, the former Hussars of the Guard of the Dutch army were incorporated in Napoleon's Guard as the 2nd Regiment of Lancers of the Guard. They were clothed from *czapka* to ankle in red, hence their designation, *Lanciers rouge* (Plate 10). A 3rd Regiment of Lancers of the Guard was recruited from Poles in July, 1812. This regiment did not survive the invasion and retreat from Russia (Lachouque 1961: 507).

Poles served with the French élite in the Imperial Guard, but Poland was also a recruiting depot for ordinary troops in Napoleon's army. In his search for men Napoleon created Polish Legions as had his Republican predecessors. These included the *Légion du Nord* and the Legion of the Vistula, the latter fighting in Spain from 1808 to 1812 (Etling 1988: 379). The Lancers of the Vistula Legion became an independent unit (*$1^e$ Lanciers de la Vistule*) in April, 1810, and 14 months later became the *$7^e$ Chevau-lèger lanciers* in the French line cavalry (Windrow and Embleton 1974:134). The first six regiments of *Chevau-lèger lanciers* of the French line were converted from Dragoon regiments and were not in Polish dress, wearing instead a modified dragoon helmet and green uniforms, the same colour they had worn in their former existence as dragoons. The 7th, 8th and 9th Regiments, however, wore full Polish dress with blue uniforms faced with yellow for the 7th, blue for the 8th and chamois for the 9th (Elting 1988: 242; Riehn 1959: 24).

## British Lancers

Britain also had an early regiment of lancers, although not part of the regular army, the 'Hulans britanniques' recruited from among French émigrés fleeing the new Republic (Plate 11). The regiment was raised in November 1793 by Marquis Louis de Bouillé, and in addition to its French personnel, it also had a large German contingent. The 'Hulan' wore a white *czapka*, closely resembling the original *czapka* of Polish and Austrian units, and a red sleeved cut-away coat, laced in the same pattern as the contemporary British Light Dragoon sleeveless shell, over a green waistcoat. Having served in varied locales, the regiment was shipped to Haiti in 1796 where it met the fate of many another European detachment when encountering the tropical diseases endemic there. By August of that year, its surviving members had been incorporated into the Légion Britannique de Saint-Domingue (Lawson 1940–67, Volume 4: 161–3; Chartrand 1996: 12–14) .

Lancers were not authorized for the British army until a quarter century after the formation of the Hulans Britanniques. However, the uhlan uniform influenced the dress of the British cavalry. In 1812 those British light dragoons who had not been converted into hussars (see above) were given a new uniform, including the *kurtka* and uhlan girdle of the continental lancers. The fact that this jacket was identical in cut and ornament to the *kurtka* has not received comment (see Carman 1957: 106). The headdress with this new uniform was a shako. Many observers commented unfavourably on the shako, lamenting the loss of the serviceable Tarleton helmet and noting the frequent instances in which the new shako led to its wearers' being mistaken as French and thus attracting friendly fire (Carman 1957: 106).

In 1816 Britain converted the 9th, 12th, 16th and 23rd Light Dragoons to Lancers. When the 23rd Light Dragoons (Lancers) were disbanded a year later in an economy move by the peacetime government, the 19th Light Dragoons became Lancers. As was the case when British Light Dragoons became Hussars, the old numbers were retained. In addition to carrying lances and discarding their carbines, the other changes in the appearance of these troops were the adoption of fully cut 'Cossack' trousers (more on this below) and the adoption of the *czapka*, with its cloth top the regimental facing colour. Since the British Light Dragoon jacket was already cut in lancer fashion, their was no need to replace it. However, the 12th Light Dragoons (Lancers) changed their facings from yellow to a Polish-like crimson (Carman 1957: 106, 109).

Eventually light dragoons disappeared from the British Army. By 1914 (the last year the British Army wore full dress), the line cavalry of the British Army consisted of seven regiments of dragoon guards (numbered separately but considered line cavalry despite their designation as Guards), three regiments of dragoons with the remainder designated either hussars or lancers. The three regiments of dragoons, respectively English, Scottish and Irish, were numbered 1, 2 and 6. The remaining regiments with the date of their conversion to hussars or lancers are listed in Table 6. As can be seen, the process of dressing Britons as Hungarians or Poles was gradual but continuous one through the nineteenth century (see Plate 12).

## *Czapka* and *Kurtka* Circle the Globe

In 1833, the newly independent Greece provided new uniforms for its army and its cavalry were given lancer dress. While the *czapka* was crimson with a silver plate, the *kurtka* green with a crimson plastron, and the overalls green with crimson stripes, both the lancer girdle and the lance pennons used the national colours of white and light blue. This uniform was worn until Prince George of Denmark ascended the Greek throne in 1863 (Knötel et al. 1937: 191–2).

Sweden, in the 1850s, dressed its Royal Horse Guards as uhlans, although they were not armed with the lance. The *czapka* had a medium blue (lighter for officers) top piped white, a medium blue *kurtka* piped white with white epaulets and white metal buttons and medium blue overalls with white stripes and black leather reinforcement. The lancer girdle was Swedish yellow with blue stripes (Jansson 1973: 11)

The *czapka* was not a common item of dress in the United States Army, militia and volunteers. Indeed, it has been recognized as 'one of the few items of European military dress not widely adopted in the United States' (McBarron and Todd 1977: 58). An exception was the band uniform of a New York City militia organization, the Governor's Guard Battalion. Recruited among the élite of the city, its amateur soldiers spared little expense in purchasing fine uniforms to wear on parade down Broadway. The band wore *czapkas* with scarlet cloth tops edged in black velvet and topped by a white plume (McBarron and Todd 1977).

The National Lancers, not a Federal regiment but rather an élite Boston militia unit formed in 1836, wore a red *czapka* with a white plume, a red

**Table 6.** *Conversion of British Light Dragoons to Hussars and Lancers*

| Regimental title (as of 1914) | Date of Conversion |
| --- | --- |
| 3rd (King's Own) Hussars | 1861 |
| 4th (Queen's Own) Hussars | 1861 |
| 5th (Royal Irish) Lancers[1] | 1858 |
| 7th (Queen's Own) Hussars | 1805 |
| 8th (King's Royal Irish) Hussars | 1821 |
| 9th (Queen's Royal) Lancers | 1816 |
| 10th (Prince of Wales's Own Royal) Hussars | 1805 |
| 11th (Prince Albert's Own) Hussars | 1840 |
| 12th (Prince of Wales's Royal) Lancers | 1816 |
| 13th Hussars | 1861 |
| 14th (King's) Hussars | 1861 |
| 15th (The King's) Hussars | 1806 |
| 16th (The Queen's) Lancers | 1816 |
| 17th (Duke of Cambridge's Own) Lancers | 1822 |
| 18th (Queen Mary's Own) Hussars[2] | 1858 |
| 19th (Queen Alexandra's Own Royal) Hussars[3] | 1861 |
| 20th Hussars[4] | 1861 |
| 21st (Empress of India's) Lancers[5] | 1897 |

*Source:* Barthrop 1984: 61, 182–4; Barnes 1954: 325–6.

1. The 5th or Royal Dragoons of Ireland had been disbanded in 1799. A new regiment of Lancers, raised in 1858, was given the number 5.
2. Converted to Hussars in 1807, the 18th was disbanded in 1821. It was raised again as Hussars in 1858.
3. Converted to Lancers in 1816, the 19th was disbanded in 1821; a regiment of the Honourable East India Company took up the number upon joining the British Line as Hussars in 1861.
4. Formerly part of the army of the Honourable East India Company, joining the British Line as Hussars in 1861.
5. Formerly of the Honourable East India Company, the regiment joined the British Line as Hussars in 1861; the regiment converted to Lancers in 1897.

double-breasted jacket and blue trousers with a red stripe. This full dress was worn until 1869 (Katcher 1989: 41, Plate A1). A *czapka* survives in the Old Sturbridge Village Collection with the label of John B. Baker, a Boston Manufacturer active from 1837 to 1855. The red top, made of card covered with cloth, is bound with black tape. It has been speculated that it was made for the Boston Light Infantry Company (Curtis and Guthman 1971: 38–9), however, it would seem possible that it was made for the National Lancers or even the Governor's Guard Battalion of New York.

If the *czapka* was rare in the US, even less common was the use of the lance by cavalry. There was one well-known Civil War unit of lancers, the 6th Pennsylvania Volunteer Cavalry (Rush's Lancers), formed in August 1861, who carried lances only until May 1863, fighting the rest of the war as conventional cavalry. They were carrying their lances when sketched by artist Winslow Homer in May 1862. In dress they were indistinguishable from the rest of the Union cavalry (Larter and Todd 1982).

Canada never had a regiment of lancers. This is peculiar, given the fondness of Canadian Militia units for aping pretentiously the titles and dress of regular regiments in the British Army. Despite the large number of hussars who were found along with dragoons, guards, light horse and other cavalry units, no formation in Canada bore the title 'lancers' nor did any wear the *czapka*. The lance was occasionally in use, such as by a small ceremonial escort for a distinguished person or for the demonstration of horsemanship in a musical ride, the latter most frequently seen in the musical ride of a Canadian paramilitary organization, the Royal Canadian Mounted Police.

The *kurtka*, however, did find its way into the Canadian military closet, albeit briefly. From 1903 to 1929 the Non-Permanent Militia contained the Corps of Guides, whose duties were to provide knowledge of local topography in the event of the need to repel an invasion of Canada. The full dress uniform of the Corps of Guides included a splendid khaki *kurtka* with scarlet plastron, collar, cuffs and piping as well as a khaki and scarlet lancer girdle. This was worn with a white universal pattern spiked helmet and a khaki and scarlet puggaree – a folded cloth band about the base of the helmet (Summers and Chartrand 1981: 123–5). It would seem possible that the dress of Queen's Own Corps of Guides of the Indian Army (important in Chapter 8, below) had its influence on the choice of colours in the uniform of the Canadian Corps.

Australia also adopted the *kurtka* but not the *czapka* of the uhlan. In 1885 the Sydney Light Horse Troop became lancers adopting the uniform of the 5th Royal Irish Lancers but with white metal buttons and a dragoon helmet. Lances did not arrive in time for their first parade, so they substituted fishing rods with pennons attached! In 1889 the colour of the *kurtka* was changed from blue to red-brown with a red plastron, piping and cuffs. The collar became red in 1903 by which time the regiment was known as the New South Wales Lancers. Drab trousers with red stripes were tucked into black boots. Initially a white helmet was worn but this was replaced in 1890 by a drab felt hat with a red puggaree, the brim turned up on the left side and ornamented with black cock's feathers and a white metal regimental badge (Wiseman 1974).

Even India witnessed the spectacle of horsemen in Polish dress. Prior to the Indian Mutiny, officers of the Bombay Lancers wore a *czapka* with a red cloth top, laced gold, and a black leather skull and peak. Their lancer girdle was gold with two crimson stripes. Unfortunately there is little evidence as to the dress of the rank and file of this unit. The regiment reverted to ordinary Light Cavalry in 1862 (Carman 1961: 149–54). The Dutch also sent the *czapka* to India in a colonial venture. Officers of the Dutch Bengal Lancers in the 1830s wore a red *czapka* and *kurtka* with a dark blue plastron. The only apparent concession to the climate were white overalls with a double red stripe. Locally recruited other ranks wore a red turban with a white plume, a white jacket or shirt and baggy white trousers and a short-sleeved over jacket of red. Their lances had red, white and blue pennons (Crescent Books 1973: 46).

Polish styles continued to have considerable influence on the dress of the Army of India under British colonial rule. It is notable in the dress of the Governor General's Bodyguard as authorized in 1897. Sowars (the term for Indian Army cavalrymen) and native officers wore a scarlet *alkhalak*, a frock coat which reached to the bottom of the knee. It had a distinctive lancer appearance, because it was worn with a scarlet plastron piped blue and a gold lancer girdle with two red stripes. A blue and gold turban was worn on the head. This unit continues, maintaining a mounted squadron for ceremonial event, as the President's Bodyguard in the post-independence Indian Army. As has already been mentioned, British officers in the unit wore scarlet hussar tunics laced gold until 1921 (Bowling 1971: 5–6).

For other cavalry regiments in the Indian Army, the sowars did not exhibit elements of Polish dress, although the *kurta* (not to be confused with the lancer tunic, the *kurtka*) was sometimes piped in the facing colour along the seams of the sleeves and the back in the fashion of the lancer tunic. The *kurta* is a loose coat, buttoning from the waist to the neck, but which does not open below the waist, meaning it must be put on over the head.

As Indian Army units underwent frequent changes in title and changes in uniform (not to mention the complexity of the various orders of dress) anything less than a multi-volume study is open to the charge of superficiality. For simplicity, this discussion utilizes the numbers of titles of regiments as reorganized in 1903 and considers uniforms in this last decade (before 1914) when full dress was regularly worn. In several regiments when the troops paraded in full dress the British officers did not wear Indian dress but rather wore a lancer uniform with a white helmet rather than the *czapka*. In many other regiments British officers wore turbans and Indian dress when parading in full dress with their men but had a dismounted full dress uniform with the lancer tunic, lancer girdle and white helmet (see Table 7).

The lance was an important weapon in Latin American armies, but seldom was its use associated with the dress of the uhlan. An interesting hybrid uniform worn by a unit that does not seem to have used the lance is that of the National Guard Hussars of the Brazilian Empire in 1840. As one might expect of hussars, officers wore a gold-laced red dolman and a blue pelisse similarly laced gold. On their heads, though, these Hussar officers wore the *czapka*, with black leather bottom, a red cloth top edged in gold and a gold sunburst plate with the imperial arms in silver. The trumpeter of this unit wore neither the *czapka* nor the dolman and pelisse but rather wore a bearskin and red coat with a blue plastron laced gold (Balaguer and Girado 1972; see Haythornthwaite 1977: 138)

Table 7. *Lancer Dress worn by British Officers, Indian Army*

| Worn on parade with troops | Worn as dismounted full dress |
|---|---|
| 4th Lancers | 1st Duke of York's Own Lancers (Skinner's Horse) |
| 14th Murray's Jat Lancers | 2nd Lancers (Gardner's Horse) |
| 26th Light Cavalry | 7th Lancers |
| 27th Light Cavalry | 8th Lancers |
| 28th Light Cavalry | 9th Hodson's Horse |
| | 10th Duke of Cambridge's Own Lancers (Hodson's Horse) |
| | 11th Prince of Wales's Own Lancers (Probyn's Horse) |
| | 13th Duke of Connaught's Lancers |
| | 15th Lancers (Cureton's Multanis) |
| | 16th Cavalry |
| | 17th Cavalry |
| | 18th Tiwana Lancers |
| | 19th Lancers (Fane's Horse) |
| | 20th Deccan Horse |
| | 29th Lancers (Deccan Horse) |
| | 30th Lancers (Gordon's Horse) |
| | 31st Duke of Connaught's Own Lancers |
| | 32nd Lancers |
| | 37th Lancers (Baluch Horse) |

*Source:* Bowling 1971

Mexico dressed a regiment of lancers, the Jalisco Lancers, as uhlans in 1843. The *czapka* had a black leather bottom and brass bound peak, a brass sunburst plate, a red cloth top and yellow cords and plume. The red jacket was single-breasted, rather than being a *kurtka*. A white leather belt was worn rather than a lancer girdle (Hefter 1958: 45, 73; Hooker 1972).

The French took the Polish *czapka* with them into Algeria. On 17 November 1831, the Chasseurs d'Afrique were formed. While it has been truthfully said that 'the Chasseurs d'Afrique bore the lance and the chapska more in principle than in practice' (Richard 1992: 223), the *czapka* was officially for full dress until as late as 1846. A print dated 1840 depicts a Chasseur with slung lance wearing a *czapka*, a sky-blue frock coat with collar and cuffs of regimental colour and the full red trousers with false leather boots from mid-calf to ankle of the style adopted generally by the French cavalry some 14 years later (Thorburn 1969: 79).

The plastron also made its way into the uniforms of sub-Saharan Africa. Nigeria's Presidential Mounted Guard wore a dark green *kurtka* with a dark green plastron piped red. This was worn with a red cap wrapped in a white turban (D'Ami 1968: 58; Cassin-Scott and Fabb 1973: Plate 48).

## Post-Napoleonic France and Russia

Given the glory they had won in the French service, it is ironic that lancers were abolished in the French line cavalry with the restoration of the monarchy in 1815. The new Royal Guard did have one regiment of lancers, dressed in green *kurtkas* with crimson plastrons. Overalls were originally green with two white stripes but were changed to crimson in 1823. The crimson *czapka* was replaced by one of white in 1832 (Thorburn 1969: 34). With the exception of the Carabiniers, the entire cavalry of the line was reorganized, creating 'new organizations [which] had no past, no traditions, no reputation, and precious little self-respect' (Elting 1988: 670). In 1831, under the government of Louis-Philippe, lancers were re-established. The first five regiments of Chasseurs à Cheval were converted to that arm (Thorburn 1969: 67). At the same time Louis-Philippe abolished the Royal Guard, and the Lancers of that corps became the 6th Orléans Lancers (Thorburn 1969: 14, 34). These six regiments were dressed in the red of the old *Lanciers rouge* of the Imperial Guard. However, on 28 February 1837 this was changed to a royal blue *kurtka* and *czapka* with the first four regiments wearing yellow plastrons and second four regiments (two more had been raised in 1836) wearing *garance* (red) plastrons (Margerand 1945: 37–8; Haythornthwaite 1976: 126–7). Napoleon III included a regiment of lancers in his Guard, and in January

1858, half the lancers in his escort were wounded by a bomb in an attempt to assassinate him. These Guard lancers wore a magnificent white *kurtka* with pale blue piping and plastron, but for service, when war broke out with Prussia, they donned single breasted blue jackets. This lead to at least one occasion to their suffering casualties, being mistaken for Prussian Uhlans (Shann and Delperier 1991: 11, 43).

In that conflict, it is reported 'the French soldiers and country people stood aghast at the uhlans' and that 'the cry "les uhlans, les uhlans," was sufficient to strike terror everywhere' (Sigel 1989: 46). Possibly because of this, following the Franco-Prussian War the *czapka* vanished as an item of dress in the French army, although French dragoons carried lances in World War I.

Russia also abolished her uhlans during the reign of Alexander III, as the Tsar pursued a programme of 'Russification' of the army. Dress followed a style developed for an earlier independent Caucasian Corps before the Crimean War and was based on peasant dress. All line cavalry were converted to dragoons wearing double-breasted tunics fastened with hooks and eyes rather than buttons and a fur headdress with a cloth top. The army was clothed in its new uniform in time for the coronation of the new Tsar in 1882. Uhlan (and hussar) parade dress returned to the Russian line cavalry under the reign of Nicholas II, in 1907 (Mollo 1979: 36, 43, 139, 144).

## The German Empire

Uhlans flourished in the new German Empire (Plate 13), and by 1910 there were 26 regiments of uhlans in the German army; these included three in the Guard, sixteen Prussian regiments in the line, three Saxon regiments, two Würtemberg regiments and two Bavarian regiments (Caton 1969). Major General von Specht provides at least one reason for the ruthless reputation of the uhlans. 'The lance will prove to be the real weapon of the battlefield, whose thrusts a prostrate enemy, though out of reach of the sabre, cannot escape' (quoted in Sigel 1989: 44). John Keegan has called attention to the readiness with which cavalry generally attacked defenceless men on foot: 'That much of this wounding was by mounted men of infantrymen or unhorsed cavalrymen prompts one to speculate if some "extra-specific" factor were not at work – if men on horseback may not feel superior to and different from men on the ground, and so feel a reduced compunction about killing them out of hand' (Keegan 1976: 200).

Despite the varied designations (cuirassiers, hussars, dragoons, and so forth) and uniforms of regiments of German cavalry, by 1900 they were similarly trained and armed. Sigel (1989: 43) has noted 'the principle of unity in the cavalry is absolutely followed in the German army and is exemplified by their arms, of a uniform pattern, consisting of the lance, with a small flag showing the provincial colors, the carbine, sabre, and long sword – the heavy straight sabre of the cuirassiers.' The decision to arm all cavalry with the lance in 1899 is reported to have been made by Kaiser Wilhelm II, 'himself a splendid cavalryman [who] ... recognized the importance of the lance as the "queen" of weapons' (Von Specht quoted in Sigel 1989: 43).

If the uhlans of Germany no longer had a distinctive weapon when they marched off to war in 1914, they still signalled their historic role as lancers with their *czapkas*, which they continued to wear albeit with a light khaki cover. The *kurtka* was also worn, but without the plastron and in field grey, but with collar, cuffs and piping in the distinctive regimental colour (Mollo 1978: 122–4).

## The *Czapka* and the Great War

It was not just the German army in which the *czapka* was worn on the expectation of old-style cavalry action in 1914. Keegan and Holmes (1986: 94) argue that it is 'probable' that in that year the number of cavalry mobilized for combat far exceeded the number ever fielded before. The two sides had in the order of 355,000 men and horses ready to confront barbed wire, artillery, machine guns and magazine rifles. While its infantry went to war in uniforms of pike-grey, Austro-Hungary sent its Uhlans off to the Great War in single-breasted light-blue tunics faced and piped in red, madder red trousers, and a *czapka* with a grey-cloth cover (Mollo 1978: 98). Belgium's five regiments of lancers wore the *czapka*, a dark blue double-breasted tunic with a collar and piping in regimental colour and blue-grey trousers (Mollo 1978: 104, 184).

Poland was not independent during World War I, but Poles formed independent national units that fought on both sides in the conflict. The most remarkable uniform was the privately purchased full dress of the 1st Lancers of the Polish Legion in the Austrian service (the use of the lance in the regular Austro-Hungarian Army, despite the regiments of uhlans recruited in Poland, had been discontinued in 1888 [Lucas 1987]). In Austrian pike-grey faced and piped in crimson, it featured a *czapka* of classic Napoleonic style (Mollo 1978: 68, 155–6, 203–4). These troops would have looked at home riding with Poniatowski's lancers at the side of Napoleon. In 1917, France raised and clothed a Polish army, basically in horizon blue cut in French style but with horizon blue *czapkas* for all ranks. For officers and all ranks of the lancers and artillery this had a peak and chin strap, but it was without a peak for the infantryman (Mollo 1978:153–4). Among the recruits for this unit were Poles who had served in the German and Austrian forces but had been captured by the allies. It also included Americans of Polish ancestry who volunteered prior to the US entry into the conflict.

Full dress passed almost entirely out of existence in the aftermath of the machine guns and gas of World War I. The *czapka* on occasion does appear on parade worn by musicians or selected individuals in lancer regiments of the British Army, but the *czapka* is also commemorated in the forage cap worn by these regiments with four welts – front, back, left and right – on the round forage cap recalling the piping on the edges of its square-topped predecessor (Barthorp 1984: 170).

## Horsemen of the Steppe: The Cossacks

To the non-specialist, the literature on Cossacks consists of a frightening array of ethnonyms. The term has been used for a variety of frontier peoples of the Eurasian steppe (of diverse origin and history) as well as for refugee populations seeking the freedom provided by distance from figures of authority. Many 'original' Cossacks were not the horsemen of legend but rather river pirates on those streams flowing southward to the Black Sea and the Caspian. However, warfare with the Turks of the Ottoman Empire, with the Tatar nomads of the steppe and with fellow Cossacks created a skilled body of mounted fighting men, a resource that the ambitions of the Tsar in Moscow could not ignore. (On Cossack origins and ethnic history see Seaton 1985.)

Initially, under Peter the Great (1686–1725), the Russian or Don Cossacks, of the River Don, and the Ukrainian Cossacks of the River Dnieper fought under their own organization and leadership (Mollo 1979: 3). Catherine the Great (1762–1796), as one of her first acts upon assuming power, incorporated two *sotnias* (each the equivalent of a squadron of cavalry in the regular army) of Cossacks into her Guard. She also expanded the irregular cavalry on the Turkish frontier and at her death these included the Don, Ural, Grebenski, Terek, Volga, Orenburg, Slobdski, Ukrainian, Zaparogski, Stavropol, Kalmuk, Astrakhan, Azov and Bachmut Cossacks (Mollo 1979: 17–18).

Cossack mounts were almost as prone to elicit comment as the conduct of their riders. One English observer noted:

> The men are robust and fit for service; their horses appear completely the reverse; mean in shape, and slouching in motion, every limb speaks of languor, and every movement you expect to see them drop down dead under their heavy burden; but so false are these shows, that there is not a more hardy animal existing; it will

travel incalculable journeys, and remain exposed to the heat or cold, day and night, without manifesting any sense of inconvenience. (Sir Robert Ker Porter quoted in Seaton 1985: 120–1)

Another writer described them as 'small and thin, incapable of great effort, but utterly tireless' and added 'having been raised on the steppes, they are indifferent to the rigour of the climate, and used to putting up with thirst and hunger – pretty much like their masters' (quoted in Duffy 1981: 162). Major-General Sir Robert Wilson praised the ability of the Cossack pony 'that could walk at the rate of five miles an hour with ease, or dispute the race with the swiftest', despite being 'a very little, ill-conditioned horse' (quoted in Seaton 1985: 121).

With respect to the Cossacks themselves, observers presented views that conformed to common stereotypes of the frontier warrior. One spoke of 'unspoiled human nature' and a 'heart of gold' but it was more common to find references to cruelty and the practice of looting. Although described as being able to endure the hardship of scarce food, their gluttony also received comment. One observer claimed that drinking alcohol in great excess had no effect on them, while another reported that after doing so, they could hardly stand, yet became model soldiers upon climbing on their horses. They were said to flee from disciplined troops in formation, yet when they charged they did so with a shout 'more frightful and terrific than the war-whoop of the Canadian savages'. Major-General Sir Robert Wilson assessed their performance: 'there is no cavalry more serviceable or formidable if suitably directed' (Haythornthwaite 1987: 24, 33).

Cossacks played an important role in the struggle of Alexander I with Napoleon. The Don Cossacks alone supplied some 40,000 cavalry to the Russian forces facing the *Grande Armée* (Mollo 1979: 129–30). By this time the Cossacks were becoming regularized, with a uniform based upon their traditional dress, and trained to act in a battle role as well as a screen for the army (Plate 14). Their role in harassing the disintegrating *Grande Armée* on its retreat from Moscow is the stuff of legend. Even at this date there appears to have been little attempt for the Cossacks to dress in a uniform fashion while on campaign, with many wearing clothing obtained from the retreating *Grande Armée*. A British observer noted 'some of them appear like Hamlet's grave-digger when taking off their coats – generally four or five, one over the other according to size' (Haythornthwaite 1987: 33–4). Uniform regulations generally called for a colback-like headgear or a peaked forage cap, a *kaftan* or coat, which might reach anywhere from mid-thigh to the top of the ankle (in summer a demi-kaftan or waist length short jacket was worn) and voluminous trousers, often with a broad stripe. No spurs were worn since the knout, a short whip with a weighted end, was used to urge on the Cossack ponies. Many Cossack units did not use pennons on their lances, although those from some areas did use pennons of a distinctive colouring.

Cossacks did not have the same impact on the dress of light cavalry in metropolitan armies as did hussars and uhlans, although for a brief period Prussia incorporated units designated as Cossacks in its forces. The *Garde-Kosaken-Eskadron* was formed in 1813 as was a squadron designated *Garde-Volontär-Kosaken-Eskadron*. The latter wore a dark blue uniform and a fur cap with a red bag (Knötel et al. 1980: 152). These appear to have been absorbed in the Guard Uhlans in 1815. Napoleon also had for little more than a year a unit of Lithuanian Tartars in his Imperial Guard. Created on August 24, 1812, surviving members of the Lithuanian Tartars became part of the 3rd Regiment of *Éclaireurs de la Garde* in December, 1813 (Lachouque 1961: 508). Michal Sadeq Pasha Czajkowski raised the 1st Cossack Regiment from Slavs as part of the army of the Ottoman Empire in 1854. In 1857 it became part of the Ottoman Cossack Brigade of the Guard along with the 2nd Regiment of Ottoman Dragoons. This brigade served until 1865 when the 1st Cossack Regiment was disbanded and the 2nd Ottoman Dragoons were sent to Lebanon. There were other units, usually recruited from among Poles, bearing the name Cossack in the Turkish army and in 1877 the Guard Corps at Constantinople included a Cossack brigade of eight squadrons (Roubicek 1978: 16, 21–2).

Despite this relative dearth of Cossack units in metropolitan armies outside Russia, the broad Cossack trouser came to dominate military fashion for half a century. Ironically, it is probably a flamboyant French cavalry officer who initially brought the Cossack trouser to the attention of military tailors; this was the remarkable General of Division, le Comte Charles Lasalle. Among Napoleon's officers, it has been judged that 'next to Kellerman, Lasalle was the most gifted horse general in the French army, a dashing opportunist with an infallible *coup d'oeil*' (Johnson 1978: 60). Born in Metz in 1775, Lasalle's aristocratic heritage allowed him to become an infantry officer at the tender age of eleven. A slightly more mature Lasalle transferred to the 24th Regiment of Cavalry in 1791. Because of the Revolution, he found himself an ordinary trooper in the 23rd Chasseurs in 1796, but soon he was promoted to squadron commander. In the Italian campaign he captured the heart of the Marquisse de Sali (Hourtoulle 1979: 25) and at Rivoli he captured an Austrian battalion. He commanded the 22nd Chasseurs à Cheval in Egypt, distinguishing himself at the Battle of the Pyramids. His military career was probably not helped, however, by another event of the summer of 1798. Lasalle had fallen in love and taken as a mistress a married woman in France. His letter to her from Egypt was captured by the British and published in the London press. The woman's husband, who then divorced her, was the brother of Louis Berthier, chief of Bonaparte's general staff and future Marshal of France (Hourtoulle 1979: 46–8). For four years Lasalle commanded the 10th Hussars, and then went on to command cavalry brigades. Among his legendary accomplishments was the capture of the garrison and fortress of Stettin with a brigade of hussars (the 5th and 7th – known as 'la brigade infernale'). Napoleon wrote to Marshal Murat, his commander of cavalry, 'I compliment you on the capture of Stettin; if your light cavalry can take fortified cities I can disband my engineers and melt down my siege artillery' (Hourtoulle 1979: 107; translation mine). Having fought in Spain, Lasalle commanded a division at Wagram, where, in the closing phase of that two-day battle, he was shot through the head by a Hungarian grenadier (Young 1976: 131–2).

Lasalle is usually depicted wearing the green dolman and pelisse[3] of the 7th Hussars. This regiment, part of 'la brigade infernale', wore tight red breeches in full dress. Instead Lasalle wore baggy red Cossack trousers with leather false boots on the bottom. So he is shown in the famous painting by François Flameng (see Young 1976: 131), in a 1912 painting by Edouard Detaille (Richard 1992: 177) and in the illustrations prepared by Jack Girbal for the most recent biography of the famous cavalier (Hourtoulle 1979). Vernet depicts Lasalle wearing such trousers when receiving the surrender of Stettin (Plate 15).

One should also not underestimate the visual impact the Cossacks had on Parisians where they formed part of the allied army occupying that city following the defeat of Napoleon (see Lachouque 1961: Plate 151). The heterogeneous mixture of the army of occupation led to copying aspects of each other's dress as well as a general competition to impress the local population, the tourists who had flocked to Paris, and each other with respect to appearance. Mollo (1972: 133) notes that 'gradually everyone became smarter and stiffer, and their uniforms tighter'. The fact that the allies anticipated a period of peace encouraged such 'smartening' of uniforms at the expense of practicality. However, the adoption of the voluminous Cossack trouser ran counter to this trend towards stiffness and tightness. Tightness above the waist was balanced by the elegant fullness of the Cossack trousers adopted by some. Britain, converting light dragoons to lancers, put these troops in Cossack trousers, as Austria did with her lancers (see Haythornthwaite 1976: Plate 9b). In the French army the nether-wear of all branches of the cavalry became increasingly baggy, with hussars leading the way. By the Second Empire all French cavalry were clad in red baggy trousers (the horse artillery wore the same style in blue) with leather bottoms (see Shann and Delperier 1991).

## Conclusion

When the lance reappeared on European battlefields in the late eighteenth century, it was most frequently in the hands of cavalry recruited in Poland. The prominent role played by this Polish cavalry in the army of imperial France fixed in European military minds the association between the weapon and the dress of the Polish soldier. The *czapka* and *kurtka* became common elements in the dress of cavalry armed with the lance.

The Cossacks, who also used the lance, were less influential on the world's military uniforms. Still, the full trousers first worn by these horsemen of the Russian steppes became a widely copied style for mounted troops for much of the nineteenth century.

# 5

# 'Ladies from Hell'

And wild and high the 'Cameron's Gathering' rose,
The war-note of Lochiel, which Albyn's hills
Have heard, and heard, too, have her Saxon foes;
How in the noon of night that pibroch thrills
Savage and shrill! But with the breath which fills
Their mountain pipe, so fill the mountaineers
With the fierce native daring which instills
The stirring memory of a thousand years,
And Evan's, Donald's fame rings in each clansman's ears!

Lord Byron<br>Waterloo

## The Scots Military Tradition

Britain recruited its first exotic warriors from its northern frontier. Scotland had long been a source of fighting men for the continent, both before and after union with the English Crown. Scottish archers first served as bodyguards to the French monarch in 1440. In the Thirty Years War, Swedish King Gustavus Adolphu's employed some 20,000 Scots, while opposed to Gustavus Adolphus were some 10,000 Scots serving in the army of France (Wood 1987: 13). The oldest infantry regiment in the British Army, now known as The Royal Scots (The Royal Regiment), was recruited from among these mercenaries. In 1633 it was raised by John Hepburn for the French service from Scottish veterans of Gustavus Adolphus's Green Brigade and Gray's Regiment which had been in the forces of the King of Bohemia. It finally passed to the British payroll some 45 years later. The regiment glories in its nickname, proclaiming its antiquity – Pontius Pilate's Bodyguard (Henderson 1993: 40–5).

Those who were recruited from the Lowlands of Scotland wore conventional military dress, but a portion of these troops were Highlanders and wore the belted plaid that was to characterize the Highland soldier in the next century. A German print (Plate 16) depicts Highlanders in the service of Gustavus Adolphus in Highland dress, armed with bows as well as muskets. These Highlanders were often at company strength and attached to a regiment of conventionally dressed Lowlanders. Both the Earl of Mar's Regiment (later the 21st Foot – the Royal Scots Fusiliers) and Lord Leven's Regiment (later the 25th Foot – the King's Own Scottish Borderers) had Highland Companies (Lawson 1940–67, Volume 1: 66). Even the Scots Guards had a Highland company from 1704 to 1714 (Henderson 1993: 27). These companies seem to have been limited to home service and did not follow their parent regiment out of the Highlands for service in England or overseas.

Intense hostility divided the peoples of the Highlands along tribal lines. To the long history of violence between the clans were added divisions of religion and conflict over succession to the throne of the kingdoms of England and Scotland. From a London perspective, the Highlands were seen as being a region of outlaws and bandits, largely owing allegiance to the Stuarts overseas. It became imperial policy to use the animosity and divisions that existed within the Highlands to help pacify them; a native police force (or 'watch') was created to bring order to the region. It was these independent companies that led to the formation of a regular regiment of Highlanders in the British Army. The government in London had been reluctant to take the step, but found that it could not enforce law in the Highlands using 'lumpish Redcoats, English or Lowland Scots, who were more at sea north and west of the Tay than they were in Flanders'. For practical reasons, the Crown was forced to seek 'the help of bilingual savages whose motives were, at best, uncertain' (Wood 1987: 29).

It was Charles II who first used Highlanders to preserve order among their neighbours, who might be friends or enemies. In 1667, he commissioned the Earl of Atholl to enlist men to form a 'watch upon the braes' (Prebble 1975: 24). However, these independent companies gained a reputation for pursuing private ends rather than those of the Crown and of filling their own pockets (or sporrans, the purse worn on the front of the kilt) rather than the treasury of the government. Two years following the revolt of many clans in the Jacobite Rebellion of 1715, the independent companies of the Watch were disbanded.

The Commander-in-Chief for North Britain, General George Wade, himself of Irish Protestant origin, soon saw the need to revive the independent companies recruited among presumably loyal Highlanders. He authorized their formation on 15 May 1725, and stipulated their dress:

> That Officers commanding companies take care to provide a plaid clothing and bonnet in the Highland dress for the non-commissioned officers and soldiers, belonging to their companies, the plaid of each company to be as near as they can

of the same sort or colour; that besides the plaid clothing to be furnished every two years, each soldier is to receive from his captain a pair of brogues every six weeks, a pair of stocking every three months, a shirt and cravat every six months. (Quoted in Lawson 1940–67, Volume 2: 54–5).

## Highland Dress

A few terms relative to Highland dress as well as its development in the eighteenth and nineteenth centuries deserve comment. Plaid does not refer to a pattern woven into a cloth but rather to the garment itself. The pattern of the cloth, created by a repetitive series of threads in the warp matched by the same sequence coloured thread in the weft, is known as a tartan or a sett. One can define a tartan or sett very precisely by indicating the number of threads of each colour in the pattern moving from left to right. However, the pattern repeats itself in reverse after the last warp in the defining sequence has been threaded on the loom. If sett runs from $C_1$ to $C_n$, then the threads in the warp would run $C_1, C_2, C_3, \ldots C_{n-2}, C_{n-1}, C_n, C_{n-1}, C_{n-2}, \ldots C_3, C_2, C_1, C_2, C_3, \ldots C_{n-2}, C_{n-1}, C_n, C_{n-1}$, etc. The cloth so woven could be (and is) used to make any number of garments, but the plaid (or sometimes, the belted plaid) is perhaps the simplest of these. It was a broad piece of woollen cloth, at least as long as the height of its wearer. To don it, a belt was placed on the ground and the plaid placed over it, the belt being about the distance from the bottom edge as the wearer's waist was from his knee. When the belt was fastened, the lower portion of the plaid ideally covered the wearer from his waist almost to his knee, and the upper part of the plaid was allowed to bunch around the hips, with the top end fastened by a pin or brooch to the left shoulder. In foul weather the entire upper body could be wrapped in the plaid to keep out the wet and cold. One of General Wade's officers provided his impressions of a Highlander wearing a belted plaid:

> [It was] set in folds and girt round the waist to make it a short petticoat that reaches half-way down the thigh, and the rest is brought over the shoulders and then fastened before . . . so that they make pretty near the appearance of the poor women in London when they bring their gowns over their heads to shelter them from the rain . . . [Its length was] so very short that in a windy day, going up a hill, or stooping, the indecency of it is plainly discovered. (Edward Burt quoted in Trevor-Roper 1983: 20)

The kilt, which continues to mark the status of the Highland soldier, was derived from this garment, but is quite different. The best evidence suggests that the kilt (or *felie beg*, often written as philibeg) was invented sometime during the second quarter of the eighteenth century by an English Quaker, Thomas Rawlinson (Trevor-Roper 1983: 21; but for a contrary view see MacKinnon 1970: 50–5). The kilt is simply a skirt, with pleats sewn permanently at the back and whose front overlaps and is secured by a buckle or buttons at the top and a brooch, a blanket pin, or a rosette at the right side (for males – when women adopted the kilt they fastened it on the left). Somewhat confusingly, a voluminous scarf worn about the body under the right arm and over the left shoulder, fastened there with a brooch, and trailing from the shoulder to the back of the knee and worn with the kilt, came to be called the plaid. A simple scarf attached to the left shoulder is called a fly plaid. Either the plaid or the fly plaid might be worn with the kilt or with trews (however, trews will come into this story later).

## The Creation of the Black Watch

It is clear that when the independent companies were recruited in 1725, and when they were incorporated into the regular army as the 43rd Regiment of Foot in 1739, the idea of associating clans with tartans had not yet occurred to Highland Scots (Trevor-Roper 1983). Thus the oft-repeated story that these independent companies and the regiment they founded were given a special 'government' tartan to disassociate their dress from that of any clan is apocryphal. However, we have noted General Wade's call for as uniform a tartan as possible, and it seems likely that wool dyed green and blue from dyes derived from heather and the blaeberry (also known as the bilberry) dominated the plaids they wore. It is very possible that the dark appearance of this tartan when viewed in anything but the brightest light and from anything but the closest distance led to these independent companies being called *Am Freiceadan Dubh* or the Black Watch. Then again, the name may reflect the negative opinions held by those whom the Black Watch were policing. On a more positive note, it has been said the name may derive from the role played by the Black Watch in stopping 'blackmail', as the practice of extortion was known in the Highlands. There may be some truth in all these hypotheses (Prebble 1975: 27).

In 1739, the six independent companies of the Watch were joined by four newly raised Highland companies to form the Earl of Crawford's Regiment of Foot. Their distinctive uniform – as the 43rd, or Lord Sempill's (Highland) Regiment of Foot – appeared in the 1742 *Cloathing Book* (Plate 17) which depicted most of the then extant regiments of the British Army. With the disbanding of Oglethorpe's Regiment (which had been the 42nd Foot) in

1749, the Highland Regiment became the 42nd Foot, and in 1758 they were granted the title 'The Royal Highland Regiment', but throughout their history they have been known, first unofficially and later officially, as the Black Watch (Grant 1971: 8–10).[1]

It was William Pitt, Wood notes, who claimed to have initiated Westminster's recognition of the Highlanders as a 'hardy and intrepid race of men' whose military potential could be tapped by the British Army. Wood (1987: 42) sees the Highland Scots as setting the pattern for the continued development of the empire:

> This identification of suitably warlike, or martial, races was to characterize the Imperial policing policy of the British Empire throughout the nineteenth century as other equally martial races were discovered, beaten and then induced to put on British uniform. It had been developed with the Highlander, it was perfected with the Gurkha, the Pathan, the Sikh and Kikuyu.

The novel dress of the 43rd (Highland) Regiment of Foot is said to have tweaked the interest of the Hanoverian monarch of Britain. George II asked that representatives of the regiment come visit his court. A pair of Highlanders made the trip to London and demonstrated Highland dancing to the King. George II showed his pleasure in their performance by giving each a guinea. As the recruits to the Black Watch were from among the élite of Highland society, accepting payment for the dance was beneath their dignity, and so the two soldiers gave the King's gratuity to the doorman as they left the room (Carman 1957:75).

In addition to the belted plaid, the 43rd Foot wore other elements of Highland attire. The blue bonnet was worn instead of the cocked hat, although the Grenadier Company of the regiment wore a grenadier cap rather than the bonnet. In place of the long coat of the regular infantryman, the short Highland jacket was worn, but in the red of the British Army. Originally this exhibited cuffs and collar of buff, but when the 42nd Foot became the Royal Highland Regiment in 1758 it conformed to the British Army practice of wearing the blue facings which were the privilege of 'Royal' regiments. Hose of a red, pink and white pattern reached nearly to the knee. The *Cloathing Book* does not show the sporran or purse, but other illustrations depict it as being of plain leather, closing at the top with a brass clasp much like that of a pocketbook or change purse, and it was ornamented with leather thongs and tassels (Reid 1993: 12–13). All ranks were armed with the basket-hilted Scottish sword, and initially many carried the all-steel Scottish pistol and the targe, a circular brass-studded shield. Cartridges for their Brown Bess muskets were carried in a black leather box attached to the front of their black leather waist belt. The sword was suspended from another black leather belt, worn over the right shoulder. Brass-buckled brogues were the regimental footwear.

It seems probable that many who enlisted in the regiment thought service would only be in the Highlands, as had been the case with the independent companies. However, Britain was involved in a war on the continent, so in 1743 the regiment marched south to London to be sent on service outside Britain. Many Highlanders believed they were being sent to the West Indies, which was proving to be a graveyard for British garrisons. Over 100 mutinied, and started to march north. The mutineers were for the most part captured and three were executed in the Tower of London by a firing squad from the Scots Guards. The remaining mutineers were dispersed among other regiments, some to the West Indies and to the new colony of Georgia in North America (Prebble 1975: 13–87). The Black Watch was sent to Flanders and fought at the Battle of Fontenoy in 1745. At this battle they earned the praise of the British commander, the Duke of Cumberland, for charging with their traditional swords and targes at the French fortifications before the village of Fontenoy and for later covering the allied retreat. The over-weight commander of the Black Watch, Lieut.-Col. Sir Robert Munro, is reported to have required rescue by his men when he became wedged in a narrow French entrenchment, and the casualties for the 43rd Foot were some thirty officers and men killed and three times that number wounded (Grant 1971: 6–8).

That same year, Charles Edward Stuart made a final attempt to regain the throne taken from his grandfather by William of Orange, but on the field of Culloden that dream, and a large number of Charles's Highland supporters, perished. There were, however, Scots on both sides at Culloden, including Highlanders. James and John Chisholm were officers in the 1st Foot (The Royal Regiment, now The Royal Scots) while their brother Roderick was with the Jacobite army (Wood 1987: 32). Among the casualties of the brutal repression following the rising in 1745 was the national dress of the Highlanders, or rather, its use was forbidden to all except for men in the Royal Army. Wearing 'plaid, philibeg, trews, shoulder-belts ... tartans or particoloured plaid or stuff' was illegal until 1782; Dr Johnson and Boswell found the wearing of the tartan or plaid had been completely suppressed when they toured Scotland in 1773 (Trevor-Roper 1983: 24). However, men of the 42nd (Royal Highland) Regiment of Foot and other regiments raised in the Highlands were able to dress in a fashion that, if worn by civilians, would lead to six months imprisonment. Thus the opportunity to wear traditional Highland attire is said to have been an inducement for enlistment (Barnes 1956: 60).

## The Shift to 'Stylized Native' Dress

As with other military uniforms, the dress of the Highland soldier began to evolve almost from the first. Mr Rawlinson's philibeg or 'little kilt' was recommended for wear by Brigadier George Augustus Viscount Howe, who was to die, along with many of the Black Watch, in the British campaign against Fort Ticonderoga in what is now northern New York State. A contemporary observer noted: 'The Highlanders have put on Breeches and Lord Howe's Filabegs' (Ray and Elting 1974a: 4). It has been suggested, however, that it was not breeches which the 42nd wore under the philibeg in North America, but rather Indian leggings, made of blue woollen cloth as per regimental order (Reid 1993: 38). By the 1780s the philibeg had become normal dress for the Highland soldier; although officers may have worn the belted plaid for full dress for another two decades (Reid 1992: 10, 34). Originally the philibeg was made from the worn-out belted plaid, and there was sometimes material enough left over to make a Highland scarf or fly plaid. In any case, the scarf or fly plaid came to be worn frequently, particularly by officers and pipers (again, more on bagpipes below).

The 43rd Foot initially wore a short jacket, and in time both Highlanders and those designated as Light Infantry (initially one company per battalion) wore almost identical jackets, cut off so they just covered the buttocks, as opposed to the coats of the ordinary infantry (and grenadiers in other than Highland regiments), which reached to the back of the knee. Later, in 1797, the skirts on the coats for the entire army were shortened (Lawson 1940–67, Volume 5: 1). Highland regiments then adopted the same pattern jacket as the rest of the army, but other aspects of their dress became elaborated and stylized in the same manner that the exotic dress of other colonial troops became elaborated and stylized once they became part of regular imperial forces.

One of the first items of dress to be stylized was the sporran. Originally a functional purse, to compensate for the lack of pockets in the belted plaid, it became merely decorative – so much so that as early as the Napoleonic wars it was not worn on campaign. The original plain leather was replaced by leather with the fur or hair intact, and the tassels on the original leather drawstrings on the purse became decorative elements, known as 'bells', on the front of the sporran (Reid 1992: 13–14). The goatskin sporran issued to the men in Highland regiments became known as the 'hairy purse' (Lawson 1940–67, Volume 4: 98). With the Black Watch, the adoption of a white goatskin purse is said to have coincided with the replacement of red waistcoats by white ones in 1768 (Carman 1957: 100). In its fully evolved form, the outward appearance of the sporran reminded one more of a whisk broom than a purse, and has been described as 'a large confection of Regimental design weighing anything up to 2 lb' (Walton 1986: 87). Many modern sporrans are covered or faced with a splay of horse-hair (MacKinnon 1970: 64).

The blue Highland bonnet was sometimes decorated with feathers on the left side above the cockade. These feathers 'grew' through time until by 1810 or so they covered the bonnet entirely. Soon after, and continuing to this day, the Highland bonnet consisted of black ostrich feathers over a wire frame,[2] a form felt to have evolved from those few feathers originally worn at the side of the bonnet. A case for the influence of North American Indians on this headdress is made below in Chapter 8. By the time Highlanders returned from active military service among North America native peoples, at the end of the eighteenth century, the foundation had been laid for the fully developed feather bonnet that has adorned the heads of Highland soldiers from the earliest years of Queen Victoria's reign.

The Highland steel pistol and the basket-hilted broadsword were abandoned for other ranks by the time the Black Watch set off to America to fight in the American Revolution, although the basket-hilted sword continues to be carried by officers in Highland (and now, also Lowland) Scottish regiments on ceremonial occasions. Some two decades earlier the targe had fallen into disuse. In equipment the Highland soldier came to resemble his comrades in the British line. Thus, the Highlanders who fought under Wellington at Waterloo were distinguished by their kilts, hose, and bonnets – otherwise they were dressed and armed as British line infantry (see Plate 18).

Lagging behind the rest of Europe, Britain finally moved to clothe its infantry in tunics in 1855.[3] Highlanders did not don the tunic, however, but instead received the doublet that had the peculiar flaps, four in number, which have come to be known as Inverness skirts. The doublet had been worn by some pipers before its general adoption in Highland battalions. A print by B. Clayton of the 93rd Sutherland Highlanders dated 1854 shows officers and other ranks in coatees but the piper wearing a single-breasted doublet with Inverness skirts. Clayton's representation of a piper of the 42nd Highlanders of the same date shows him wearing a coatee (Nevill 1909: 61, 67). The doublet initially adopted for Highland regiments was double breasted, but within a year it was replaced by a single-breasted doublet. Each Inverness flap was decorated with three buttons and white piping, with those of officers were also edged with gold lace (Carman 1957: 144). This Victorian invention of doublet with Inverness skirts has become a universal component of Scottish dress, both military and civilian (see Plate 19).

An issue in Scots military uniform remaining to be addressed is that of trews. Trews appear to have been a ancient Highland garment, contemporary with the belted plaid. Indeed, there is some association between trews and the aristocracy of the Highlands, for as one great enthusiast for the orthodox wearing of the kilt noted, 'if there is one pursuit for which the kilt is completely unsuitable, it is riding a horse' (MacKinnon 1970: 51–2). Hence the wearing of trews was associated with equestrian activity and most common among the upper classes. But ancient trews differ from the modern garment which is called by that name, as the original trews were 'skin-tight' woollen tights, complete with feet, made of tartan cloth, 'cut on the cross . . . The sett of the tartan was smaller than usual and the seams were nicely arranged so as to preserve the sett' (MacKinnon 1970: 56).

These trews passed into disuse with the belted plaid, or possibly even predeceased their lower-class cousin. However, some Highland corps wore 'tartan pantaloons' – ordinary trousers made of tartan cloth, which soon came to be known as 'trews' and continue to be so designated. The 97th (Inverness-shire) Regiment, raised in 1794, served briefly as marines before being disbanded, and were issued tartan pantaloons or trews (Reid 1992: 14, 22, 37), for presumably the sight of Highlanders scrambling up ratlines to assume positions in the ship's crow's nest would have been too traumatic for their Royal Navy shipmates had the regiment worn kilts. Other regiments, including the 1st or Strathespay Fencibles – whose claim to fame is having mutinied twice in the space of 16 months (March 1794 and June 1795) – wore trews rather than the kilt (Reid 1992: 36; Prebble 1975: 261–391). In the Peninsula campaign, a number of men of the 42nd Regiment had their kilts made into trousers when they had the opportunity (Lawson 1940–67, Volume 5: 40). At New Orleans in 1815, the 93rd (Sutherland) Highlanders wearing trews charged against Americans under the command of Andrew Jackson (Reid 1992: 22). One student of Highland dress has dismissed this form of nether garment as ' "drain-pipe" trousers' (MacKinnon 1970: 56). Similarly, in 1804, Allan Cameron of Erracht, Colonel of the 79th Foot, scorned tartan trews as 'buffoon tartan pantaloons' and 'a harlequin tartan pantaloon', which would deprive the Highlander of 'that free congenial circulation of that pure wholesome air (as an exhilarating native bracer) which has hitherto so peculiarly benefited the Highlander for activity and all the other necessary qualities of a soldier' (quoted in Reid 1992: 14–15).

The story of the Highland regiments is a complex one, and Horse Guards (as British Army Headquarters was and is known) perceived that kilts discouraged recruitment among other than Highlanders. It should be noted that even regiments designated as Highlanders had a portion of recruits of English and Irish origins (see Table 8). Officers might also have origins other than in the Highlands. Arthur Wesley, later (after the family name had been changed to Wellesley) the Duke of Wellington, briefly served in 1787 as an ensign in the 73rd Highland Regiment (Reid 1992: 34). Because they wished to attract recruits outside the Highlands, the military bureaucracy determined that some Highland regiments who had once worn kilts should be dressed in identical fashion to the rest of the British line infantry, whereas others were ordered to wear trews. The 71st Foot, although officially a kilted regiment, had adopted trews upon return from Argentina in 1807 (Reid 1992: 16). They officially lost both kilt and trews in 1809 when they were converted to light infantry, but in 1834 they replaced their grey trousers with trews of Mackenzie tartan (Carman 1957: 114; Barthorp 1982: 69). The 71st (Highland Light Infantry) were the second regiment officially to wear trews. In 1823, the 72nd Foot, which had also lost its kilt in 1809, was authorized to dress in feather bonnets and trews of the Charles Edward Stuart sett, a variant of the Royal Stewart tartan (Henderson 1993: 131).[4] Two other de-kilted regiments, the 74th and the 91st, were later also granted the right to wear trews (Carman 1957: 136, 144).

Table 8. *Origins of Men of Highland Regiments*

| Regiment | Dates | Scots | English | Irish | Foreign |
|---|---|---|---|---|---|
| 42nd Foot | 1807–12 | 1980 | 84 | 201 | – |
| 78th Foot | 1811 | 1019 | 8 | 9 | – |
| 79th Foot (1 Bat.) | 1800–15 | 1735 | 257 | 172 | 5 |
| 79th (2nd Bat.) | 1804–08 | 1558 | 1698 | 152 | 6 |
| 92nd Foot | 1811–25 | 716 | 51 | 111 | – |
| 93rd Foot | 1811 | 1014 | 18 | 17 | – |

*Source:* McKay 1993

## Turning Lowlanders into Pseudo Highlanders: The 1881 Army Reforms

Although bagpipes had long been part of the unofficial establishment of Lowland Scots regiments, the clothing for the rank and file of these regiments did not differ – beyond the usual regimental distinctions – from other units in the British line. This was to change after 1881, constituting an example of the diffusion of 'hinterland' dress. The line infantry in the British Army underwent a major reorganization in 1881 known, because of its chief architect, as the Cardwell reforms (see Farwell 1981: 153–64). One goal of the reorganization was to ensure that each regiment of the British line infantry had at least two battalions – hence formerly independent regiments were amalgamated as first and second battalions of a new regiment. This reorganization created six Highland regiments, five of them kilted. The five kilted regiments were the Black Watch (incorporating the 42nd and 73rd Foot), the Seaforth Highlanders (formerly the 72nd and 78th Foot), the Gordon Highlanders (75th and 92nd Foot), the Queen's Own Cameron Highlanders (the 79th Foot, which later had a second battalion added), and the Argyle and Sutherland Highlanders (formerly 91st and 93rd Foot). The Highland Light Infantry (formerly the 71st and the 74th Foot) remained dressed in trews, the only Highland regiment so dressed. Three of the four Lowland regiments already had two battalions, so they were not forced to undergo amalgamations with other regiments as was the case for most of the British infantry. However, in the 'rationalization' that took place with this reorganization, it was decided to distinguish the uniform of English line regiments from those of Scotland, so the Lowland Scots were issued a uniform derived from that of their wild cousins to the north. All four Lowland Scots regiments (The Royal Scots, the Royal Scots Fusiliers, the King's Own Scottish Borderers and the Scottish Rifles) who had previously worn the 'civilized' dress of the rest of the British line, were dressed in the by now 'traditional' Highland doublet and trews (Plate 20). Originally these trews were the government or Black Watch tartan. However, as a result of the early nineteenth-century 'Celtic revival', a plethora of tartans had been invented and associated with common surnames in both Lowland and the Highland Scotland. Soon each of the four Lowland regiments were given permission to wear trews of a tartan which was anachronistically associated with the name of an early commanding officer. As one student of Scottish dress cynically noted, 'one cannot but reflect how astonished these [early commanders of Lowland regiments] would be to see their men so strangely habited' (Hesketh 1961: 80).

One should also note that two regiments in the Territorial Army (part-time soldiers who serve as a reserve to the regular British Army) and who are recruited not in Scotland but rather in England wear Highland dress with doublet and kilt. These are the London Scottish and the Liverpool Scottish. The former wear a distinctive uniform of Hodden Grey, including both doublet and kilt. The full dress of the Liverpool Scottish was a 'drab' or khaki doublet with red collar, cuffs, shoulder straps and piping. They wore kilts of Forbes tartan (Barnes 1956: 312–13).

## The Kilt and Modern War

When the British Army discarded the traditional red coat as being impractical in the field (see Chapter 7 below for a discussion of khaki), the skirts of the new service dress jacket were cut to accommodate the sporran and kilt. However, in the Boer War, the sporran was abandoned while on service and the front of the kilt was covered with a 'kilt apron' of khaki, which came equipped with a pocket to replace the sporran. The kilt apron initially covered only the front half of the kilt, but Highland units in the Great War of 1914–18 wore a second apron to cover the rear of the kilt. The London Scottish found no need to cover their Hodden Grey kilts with a kilt apron as the first territorial unit to enter the Great War, suffering nearly 400 casualties at Messines on 31 October 1914 (Barnes 1956: 312). It was in this war that Highland soldiers were dubbed by their German foes as 'the ladies from Hell'.[5] For the most part the kilt was not worn in combat in World War II. Officially this was said to be because of fears of damage to the bare nether parts of Highlanders from mustard gas. Chappell has observed, however, that 'despite official orders to the contrary, men of the 6th Battalion, Highland Light Infantry [the only kilted battalion of the regiment], were caught by the camera wearing the kilt in battle during the 2nd BEF period, June 1940' (Chappell 1994: 59; see also Wood 1987: 125). On occasion, individual officers and pipers wore it close to the action; a painting by Michael Stride depicts a kilted piper of the Queen's Own Cameron Highlanders piping them into battle amid shells and searchlights at El Alamein (Grant 1977: between pp. 72–3), while the Gordon Highlanders turned out in kilts as the guard for the Headquarters of the 51st (Highland) Infantry Division for Field Marshal Montgomery's inspection (Grant 1977: 123) and German officers surrendering at Bremerhaven in 7 May 1945, did so to Highland officers in kilts (Grant 1977: 152). Wood (1987: 128) has noted how as part of 'a propaganda war', the image of the Highland soldier 'dressed in khaki Battledress blouse above his kilt and boots and short puttees' was useful. As he points out: 'The archetypal figure of the Scottish Highland piper appeared regularly at Victory parades in North African villages, Sicilian towns, Italian cities (and all of their equivalents in northern Europe) whenever good newsreel coverage of the fighting soldiers was required.' Despite the fact it is no longer worn on the battlefield, the kilt remains the distinguishing element in the dress of the Highland soldier.

Clearly, the employment of Highland Scots in the British Army constitutes an example of the use of hinterland warriors in the wars of empire.[6] As in other cases, the 'native' dress became stylized upon the 'regularization' of the units of hinterland warriors, and it had its influences on the dress of other units in the imperial forces (Lowland Scottish regiments).

*'Ladies from Hell'*

## Highland Units in the British Empire and Beyond

Military units in both hemispheres and on four continents beyond Europe have dressed as Highlanders. In some cases these were units composed of emigrant Scots, many veterans of service in British Highland regiments. In other cases a large population of emigrant Scots and their descendants supported the raising of kilted regiments. Enlistment in these units was not restricted to those with Highland ancestors, and it was not unknown to see kilts on soldiers of Asian or African background (see Plate 21).

This propensity to dress up in kilts followed Highlanders to all areas of settlement in the British Empire and had an impact on the dress of the armies of the British Commonwealth. Of these Canada will be the first to be discussed, although the complexity of the organization of Canada's military, both regular army and militia, since the birth of the Canadian confederation in 1867, dictates the superficiality of the discussion. I therefore present a brief summary of the current status of Highland Dress in the Canadian Forces, the status as it existed in the 1950s, and as it existed in the Great War of 1914–18, the only major conflict where large numbers of Canadians wore kilts into battle.

The infantry component of the contemporary regular Canadian Forces contains no battalions that wear the kilt in any order of dress. There had been a kilted battalion, the Black Watch (Royal Highland Regiment) of Canada, but this battalion was disbanded in 1968. Canada has long maintained only a small number of regular, full-time soldiers but has a tradition of militia (now known as the Reserves) to be mobilized in times of crisis. It is in the contemporary Reserves that the Highland tradition is assiduously preserved. A recent Special Commission on the Reserves (Canada 1995) lists 51 infantry units within the Land Force reserves, although most of these are currently little more than company (or even platoon) strength. They do, however, carry the traditions of battalions that fought through the two world wars, the Anglo-Boer War, the Northwest Rebellion of 1885, the Fenian raids and even in some cases the War of 1812. Of these, fifteen have a Highland ancestry, although the frequency with which they parade in kilts and other aspects of Highland dress is not known. Over the past three decades, on free weekends, I have attended parades where the Toronto Scottish, the Lorne Scots, and the 48th Highlanders of Canada paraded a large body of their members in kilts.

In the mid-1950s there were an even greater number of regiments in the Canadian Army who were entitled to wear the kilt, and Barnes (1956: 319–31) lists nineteen kilted regiments. In addition, two or three regiments were authorized to wear the doublet and trews. The military tartans of the British army were most commonly used (although no regiment is recorded as wearing the Gordon tartan). Two tartans worn as trews by Lowland Scots regiments in the British Army, the Leslie and the Douglas, were worn as kilts by Canadian units, the former by the New Brunswick Scottish and the latter by the Perth Regiment. Five regiments wore kilts of the Black Watch tartan (or as it is sometimes known, the Sutherland); three wore Mackenzie tartan kilts; two wore the Cameron of Erracht tartan of the Queen's Own Cameron Highlanders. A wide variety of other tartans were worn. The Lorne Scots, for example, wore Campbell of Argyll; the Nova Scotia Highlanders wore Murray of Athol; the Essex Scottish wore MacGregor and the Lake Superior Scottish wore McGillivary.

The only war in which Canadians went into action wearing kilts was the First World War. Some 260 infantry battalions were recruited for the war. Of these, only fifteen were kilted battalions. This figure is somewhat misleading, however, because of the initial 17 battalions (with a date of organization of 6 August 1914) of the Canadian Expeditionary Force (CEF), four were kilted and three of these served as part of the First Canadian Division in Flanders from February 1915, until the Armistice. The 15th Battalion wore the badges and Davidson tartan of the 48th Highlanders of Canada, a Toronto militia regiment. Four members of the 16th Battalion, recruited in British Columbia, were awarded the Victoria Cross. The men of the 16th Battalion wore kilts of the Mackenzie tartan while its pipers were dressed in the Lennox tartan, including Piper James Richardson who received a posthumous VC (on the CEF see Stewart 1970).

Australia boasted five Highland regiments in the 1950s. Each was affiliated with one of the five kilted Highland regiments then in existence in the British Army, and wore the tartan of the affiliated regiment. The five regiments were the Victoria Scottish Regiment (Gordon tartan); the Cameron Highlanders of Western Australia (Cameron of Erracht tartan); the South Australian Scottish Regiment (Mackenzie tartan); the New South Wales Scottish Regiment (Black Watch tartan); and the Byron Regiment (Sutherland tartan). At this time South Africa was still part of the Commonwealth and its army included four kilted regiments. These were (with their tartan) the First City (Graham of Montrose), the Queen's Own Cape Town Highlanders (Gordon), the Transvaal Scottish (Murray of Atholl) and the Pretoria Highlanders (Hunting Stuart). New Zealand had but a single kilted regiment, the New Zealand Scottish, formed in 1939.

In other areas of the Empire, emigrant Scots formed units such as the Calcutta Scottish (Army Auxiliary Force, India), a Scottish Company of the Bombay Volunteer Rifles, a Highland Company of the Rangoon Volunteer Rifles, a Highland Company of the Shanghai Volunteer Corps, a Scottish

Company of the Hongkong Volunteer Defence Force, a Scottish platoon in the 2nd Selangor Battalion Federated Malay States Volunteer Force and a Scottish Company in the Singapore Volunteer Corps (Barnes 1956: 332–44; Carman 1969: 87–9).

It was not just in the outposts of the British Empire that Scots formed kilted military units. The 79th New York Volunteers, formed in 1859, shared a regimental number and Cameron of Erracht kilts with the 79th Foot of the British Army. According to Haythornthwaite (1975: 150) they wore the kilt with a doublet of blue piped red with red cuff slashes and a red and light blue collar. Other authorities (Severin and Todd 1982; Katcher 1989: Plate C3) show a blue coat cut away to accommodate the sporran (white horse hair with a black cantle and three black tassels) rather than a true doublet. When the kilt was not worn, it was replaced by either trews of Cameron of Erracht tartan or conventional sky-blue trousers. In this dress the 79th New York marched off to help save the Union, and there is some evidence that the kilt and trews were worn in battle, at least in the very early stages of the war (Haythornthwaite 1975: 149–51). On the Confederate side, the Highland Company of the Charleston, South Carolina, Militia entered the war in red jackets and kilts of the MacDonald tartan (MacLeod 1959: 102).

The kilt was used in Africa in a colonial context. Funds from the estate of a former officer, Major R. H. Leeke, provided for the formation of a band for the 4th Battalion of the King's African Rifles at the end of the First World War and, from its inception, the band was dressed in kilts (Moyse-Bartlett 1956: 695). Barnes pictures a drum major in the twilight of the colonial era (dated 1957) dressed in a rifle-green kilt, a white tunic cut in the Highland fashion, a brown leather sporran and a red fez (Barnes 1960: 316, Plate VI[15]). The 4th King's African Rifles was recruited in Uganda, and after staging a coup in 1971, Idi Amin, the rather erratic dictator of that newly independent nation, briefly put his army in kilts of the Royal Stewart tartan (see Campbell 1975: 20).

## Scots, Bagpipes and Martial Dress

The above cases indicate that the kilt had some minor impact on the dress of the world's military. The troops recruited from the Highlands had a greater impact on martial dress around the world, albeit for dress worn on ceremonial occasions, in another area. This influence accompanied the adoption of the bagpipe as a musical instrument in regimental bands whose pipers wore elements of Highland dress, or Highland dress as it had evolved through the nineteenth century.

The bagpipe is not, of course, a musical instrument confined to the Highlands of Scotland. Indeed, it is misleading to speak of '*the* bagpipe', for it is rather a class of instruments. Historically, in one variety or another, bagpipes have been widely distributed about the Mediterranean and north and east into large parts of Europe and Asia, so that bagpipes form part of folk music traditions from India to Ireland, from Tunisia to Finland. The Pitt Rivers Museum at Oxford is credited with having 'probably the finest extant *systematic* collection of this most important of our folk wind instruments' (Baines 1960: 13) largely acquired through the labours of Curator Henry Balfour from 1883 to 1939. Baines' analysis of bagpipes from this collection included specimens from Algeria, Auvergne, Berry, Bohemia, Bosnia, Brittany, Crete, Egypt, Gwalior, Greece, Hungary, Ireland, Italy, Macedonia, Madras, Northumbria, Rumania, Spain and Tunisia, as well as Scotland.

Some of the differences among these bagpipes are readily apparent to an observer with no musical background. Most bagpipes contain three principal components in addition to the bag. One of these is the chanter, which the player fingers with both hands to produce the melody. The second is one or more drones, which produce a continuous sound to accompany the melody. The third is the source of air to fill the bag. This source can be either a blow pipe or an arrangement with bellows. Bagpipes differ from each other in the form of the chanter, in the presence and number of drones and in the mechanism (bellows or the player's lungs) used to inflate and maintain pressure within the bag. The modern Highland bagpipe, whose use will be shown to have had an impact on military dress, is mouth blown with three drones – one bass drone and two tenor drones.

It is not appropriate here to enter into the history of the bagpipe around the world, and this, in any case, is far from being crystal clear. In Britain the first form of the bagpipe, the *chorus* which lacked drones, seems to have been replaced by a bagpipe with a single drone in the fourteenth century (Collinson 1975: 84). This latter was probably used by one of the most famous of literary pipers, the Miller of the Canterbury pilgrims of Chaucer. Chaucer wrote:

A Baggepipe / wel koude he / blowe and sowne
And ther with al / he broghte vs out of towne (Chaucer 1979: 30)

Bagpipes, then, are not exclusively Highland instruments, even in Britain, although it is among Highlanders that they early on became associated with war. Collinson (1975: 140) quotes a French military officer, part of a force aiding the Scots against the English in 1549:

fourteen or fifteen thousand Scots, including the savages accompanying the Earl of Argyll arrived ... and while the French prepared for combat ... the wild Scots [*les Eccossois sauvages*] encouraged themselves to arms by the sound of their bagpipes.

In Collinson's view, this is 'the first eye-witness account of the use of the Great Highland bagpipe in battle – from a Frenchman!'

Following the Jacobite rebellion of 1745, the military importance of the bagpipe became part of British law. James Reid, who had been captured at Carlisle by the forces of the Duke of Cumberland, was put on trial at York. His defence was that he did not take up arms against the Hanoverian monarch, since he was a piper. The court, however, observed that 'a Highland regiment never marched without a piper' and concluded 'therefore his bagpipe, in the eye of the law, was an instrument of war' (Collinson 1975: 170–1).

It is worthy of note that, from their beginnings, units recruited in the Lowlands had pipers on their establishment. The earliest illustration of pipers in the regular British Army shows, appropriately, pipers of the senior infantry regiment of the British line, the Royal Scots. They appear in 'The Destruction of the Mole at Tangier 1684' by Stuyp (Henderson 1993: 52). Their dress is that of the ordinary infantryman, with a red coat, grey breeches and stockings and a broad-brimmed black hat and their pipes have two drones (Cochrane 1987: 19). Several paintings depict another Lowland regiment, the 25th Foot (now the King's Own Scottish Borderers), while stationed at Minorca in 1769. In these, while officers, men, fifers and drummers are depicted in the dress of ordinary members of the British line, there is a piper wearing the reversed colours of a musician (that is the coat of the facing colour of the regiment, yellow in this case, with lapels and cuffs of red) with a belted plaid which is likely to be the government or Black Watch tartan (Lawson 1940–67, Volume 3: 62, Plate I).

The twentieth century has seen the adoption of pipe bands in highland dress by some British Army units with no particular Scottish connection. The Royal Tank Regiment dates from the invention of the tracked armoured fighting vehicle in World War I. In 1971 the 4th Royal Tank Regiment formed a pipe and drum band that was officially recognized in 1979. Its members wear black doublets and kilts and shoulder plaids of the Hunting Rose tartan. Pipers wear black glengarries and the drummers and drum major wear the feather bonnet with a blue-and-white diced band. The pipe bag is dark blue and pipe ribbons are of Hunting Rose tartan (Asquith 1997b: 15–18, 61). Territorial units (militia or part-time soldiers) in the British Army located in Scotland sometimes boast a pipe band even though the parent unit in the regular army does not. The Royal Army Ordnance Corps (Territorial Army) had two pipe bands, each formed in 1957. That of 12 (General Stores) Company was based in Edinburgh and wore kilts of the Lamont tartan while pipers of 51 Ordnance Field Park, based in Glasgow, wore the Mackenzie tartan. Both pipe bands were discontinued in 1967 (McKenzie 1998). The Scottish Transport Regiment (Volunteers), part of the Royal Logistic Corps, includes a corps of pipes and drums, wearing kilt and shoulder plaid of the MacDuff tartan (Asquith 1997a: 57–61). Several volunteer units of the Royal Artillery have kilted pipe bands. These include the 204th (Tyneside Scottish) Battery, the 19th Regiment Royal Artillery (The Highland Gunners), the 40th Regiment Royal Artillery (The Lowland Gunners), the 103rd Regiment Royal Artillery (The Lancashire Artillery Volunteers), the 104th Regiment Royal Artillery (Volunteers) and the 105th Regiment Royal Artillery (Volunteers) (Gibbs 1998: 48). The Royal Air Force, or rather No. 602 (City of Glasgow) Squadron Auxiliary Air Force, also boasts a pipe band, wearing kilts of the Grey Douglas tartan (Steel 1998).

The association between the Scottish soldier and the bagpipe was such that several military units about the world adopted the bagpipe as an instrument to provide martial music for their troops on parade. In almost all cases (there are a few exceptions) when the bagpipe is heard in a military setting it is the great Highland bagpipe that is being played. As dress, rather than music, is the focus of this study, what is significant to the matters being considered here is that military musicians who play bagpipes around the world usually wear elements of Highland dress.

One need not, of course, adopt the dress of a Highlander to play the bagpipe. One interesting example of a military pipe band that did not utilize any items of Highland dress is that of the 1st Canadian Mounted Rifles, raised in Brandon, Manitoba, for the Canadian Expeditionary Force in World War I. That they wore ordinary Service Dress tunics and trousers rather than kilts is perhaps understandable since the entire band of twelve piper and eight drummers was mounted on horses, which they broke and trained to march, while their rider played the pipes. The pipe bag and the pipe ribbons were of the Royal Stewart tartan (Stewart 1970: 110–11).

A battalion raised for the Great War but independent of the Canadian Expeditionary Force was Princess Patricia's Canadian Light Infantry (PPCLI). Raised privately by the Montreal millionaire, Andrew Hamilton Gault, it served initially with the British Army in France and Flanders, but eventually joined the 3rd Canadian Division on the Western Front. The regiment took its name from the daughter of the Duke of Connaught, then serving as the Governor General of Canada. The officers and men wore the ordinary service dress of the British and Canadian infantry, but, even though there was no overwhelmingly strong Scottish component in the unit, the regiment maintained a pipe band. Its members wore a dark blue Glengarry with black cock's feathers and a kilt of Hunting Stewart tartan and the Highland pattern Service Dress jacket. The regiment is now a regular infantry regiment in the Canadian Forces.

It has been already mentioned that Canada raised fifteen kilted battalions as part of the 260 battalions of the Canadian Expeditionary Force (CEF). All of these kilted battalions had kilted pipe bands that frequently wore different headgear, special sporrans, and other elements of what had come to be considered Highland dress. Most wore the same tartan as the battalion, but some followed the custom of the pipers and wore a different tartan from the riflemen. The Lennox tartan of the pipers of the 16th Battalion has already been mentioned; the Pipes of the 15th Battalion (raised from the 48th Highlanders of Canada) wore Stewart of Fingask tartan. The wearing of a distinctive 'music' tartan may be related to the eighteenth-century practice of dressing drummers in distinctive uniforms. Drums were used to communicate orders to the rank and file, so it was important that drummers be easy for officers to find and order to beat the appropriate command. This distinctive uniform was often the reverse of the ordinary uniform of the battalion and drummers often had distinctive lace.[7]

Despite the small numbers of kilted battalions in the Canadian Expeditionary Force, a large number of battalions had pipe bands, mostly in kilts with other elements of Highland dress. In addition to the 15 kilted battalions of the CEF, another 31 battalions had pipe bands. Details of dress are not always readily available, but at least 25 of these were kilted pipe bands. Thus 46 of the 260 battalions of Infantry in the CEF maintained pipe bands (Stewart 1970 provides details of dress, if known, for all these pipe bands in the CEF). In addition to these, there were the pipe bands of the 1st Canadian Mounted Rifles and the PPCLI already mentioned, and a pipe band for the Canadian Forestry Corps and another for the 1st Pioneer Battalion.[8]

Pipe bands have also appeared in the armed forces of the United States. The Second Army had a pipe band wearing kilts and a plaid of the Hamilton tartan, khaki Eisenhower jackets (a waist-length jacket resembling that of British Battle Dress) and a white scarf or ascot about the neck. Pipers and drummers wore a black glengarry, and the drum major wore a feather bonnet with a white plume (MacLeod 1959: 101–2). The United States Sixth Army also had a pipe band, organized in May 1950, and disbanded eight years later. It wore kilts and plaids of the Royal Stewart tartan and doublets that were a close copy of, if not identical to, those worn by the pipers of the Scots Guards. The drum major wore a feather bonnet and the pipers and drummers wore blue tam-o-shanters with red hackles (Bard and Craver 1960).

The 62nd United States Army Band at Fort Bliss in Texas currently has pipers dressed in shell jackets and kilts (Gibbs 1998).

The United States Air Force also boasts a pipe band. Originally the pipers simply wore the uniform of the band of the United State Air Force (MacLeod 1959: 101), but in 1960 they acquired full Highland dress ordered from Scotland and picked up by the band while on a tour of Britain. The band wore kilts and plaids of the Mitchell tartan in honour of General 'Billy' Mitchell who was a pioneering advocate of air power in the US military. Their doublets were dark blue piped white and they wore a dark blue glengarry with a red tourie and the badge of the US Air Force Band. The drum major wore the feather bonnet with a white plume and ironically, this representative of the US republic carried a mace topped by crown surmounted by a lion – the British Royal Crest. The band also had a kilted evening dress, substituting a black mess jacket for the doublet (Spicer and Elting 1967). The Pipes and Drums of the United States Air Force Reserve carries on the tradition of this band, but with some variation in the uniform. They wear an official US Air Force tartan, which was created in 1987.

The Pipes and Drums of the United States Military Academy (West Point) also wear an official tartan registered with the Lord Lyon, King of Arms, in Scotland. This sett incorporates the grey, black and yellow associated with the USMA. When formed in 1972 they wore the red McQueen tartan, but assumed their own tartan in 1985. With the kilt and plaid they wear a modified form of the grey cadet jacket, with skirts shortened and rounded at the front to accommodate the kilt and sporran. Pipers wear a black glengarry with a red tourie and the brass badge of the Academy on the left side; the glengarry of the drummers is diced grey and gold (Jones and Milligan 1991).

The above examples clearly relate to the ethnic heritage of the population from which the armies drew their personnel. However, not all military bagpipers are found in units with Scottish ancestry. Given the widespread use of bagpipes outside Scotland, it is perhaps not surprising to find military bagpipers elsewhere in the world, but an examination of the dress of these pipers reveals that many have received the concept of military piping from the Scots inhabitants of England's northern frontier who were incorporated into the British Imperial Army.

At least since 1875, pipers have played an important ceremonial role in the army of India. In 1875, it is said that Coke's Rifles (1st Punjab Infantry) initiated the use of pipes among Indian units (Carman 1969: 204). Although pipers were established under British Imperial rule and the influence of Scottish members of the officer corps, they have continued to be important in both India and Pakistan since independence. At the height of the Raj, the Indian Army constituted the largest volunteer army in the world. It was a

## 'Ladies from Hell'

highly complex institution, recruited from Hindu and Moslem, members of diverse castes, and residents of widespread regions. Its complexity daunts the non-specialist but fortunately there have been a few works published that outline the history of martial dress in India, and these make clear the influence of Scottish soldiers and their pipers.

The Northwest Frontier under the Raj has become a locale of romance and legend. In these hills the British imperial forces made effective use of Mountain Artillery, with their mule-borne screw guns.[9] The Mountain Artillery (or at least five batteries of this important branch of the Indian Army) had pipers. The batteries known to have possessed bagpipes were the 21st Kohat, 22nd Derajat, 23rd Peshawar, 24th Hazara and the 27th Mountain Battery. The 22nd had bagpipe covers and pipe ribbons of the Graham tartan. Scots who were posted in the Egyptian desert during the First World War heard pipe music, and discovered it came from pipers of the Indian Army's 22nd Mountain Battery (Carman 1969: 46). After independence, the Pakistan Artillery continued the piping tradition, wearing a tartan shoulder plaid with the dark blue full dress uniform and white gaiters (D'Ami 1969: 70).

From the fragmentary evidence, it is not clear if these artillery pipers affected any aspect of Highland dress, but many other Indian Army pipers, while not going so far as to dress in the kilt, did wear the plaid. For example, the 125th Napier Rifles (formerly the 25th Bombay Native Infantry) wore a plaid of the Urquhart tartan. This dark green tartan with its red overstripe matched well the rifle green uniform, piped red down the front of the tunic and around the cuffs. A red cummerbund was also worn, and the shoulder straps were red. The turban was rifle green with the regimental bugle horn badge and wrapped about a red 'kullah', a conical hat that rises above the turban or puggaree. White gaiters were worn, reinforced with black leather (Carman 1969: 181). The 1st Battalion, 6th Rajputana Rifles, had also adopted the Urquhart tartan when it formed a pipe band in 1927. Pipers of this battalion wore a white tunic (Carman 1969: 234).

The piper of another rifle regiment wearing the shoulder plaid was photographed in 1914. He was from the 130th King George's Own Buluchis (Jacob's Rifles). This regiment, since 1883, had worn rifle green uniforms faced red, and red trousers. The piper has a rifle green turban and white gaiters. It has been suggested that his shoulder plaid, pipe bag cover and pipe ribbons are of Royal Stewart tartan (Barthorp 1979: 33). Given the royal connection in the regimental title, this seems likely.

Other infantry pipers wore the shoulder plaid in the Imperial Indian Army. The 38th Dogras wore a plaid of the Campbell tartan (Carman 1969: 119). The 42nd Deolis wore a plaid of the MacDonald tartan. Their pipe bags and ribbons were also of MacDonald tartan (Carman 1969: 123). The pipe band of the 2nd Bombay Native Infantry was formed in 1896 but did not gain official approval until 1925. It wore shoulder plaids of the Old Stewart tartan, but carried Mackenzie tartan pipe ribbons on its pipes (Carman 1969: 177). Pipers of the Madras Pioneers in 1901 were authorized to wear the Old Stewart tartan (Carman 1969: 67). Pipers of the 14th Ferozepore Sikhs did not wear a tartan but wore blue doublets with white braid on the Inverness skirts (Carman 1969: 110).

The pipers of the 40th Pathans certainly provide one of the most interesting of uniforms of Indian Army pipers. Instead of wearing a shoulder plaid of Scottish tartan, they draped a Kohat lunghi (a long, wide scarf or sash of local manufacture) around the body, pinned and falling from the left shoulder in the same manner as a Scottish plaid. The lunghi seems to have been fastened by a large regimental badge. A painting by Chater (c. 1895) depicting a piper shows him wearing a green puggaree or turban with a silver or white fringe and a green kullah. His drab or khaki tunic has green collar and cuffs, and his full khaki trousers are wrapped in khaki puttees. The pipe bag and ribbons are the same green as the facings and turban (Glover 1973: 80–1, Plate 23; Carman 1969: 120–1).

The Indian Army underwent a major reorganization in 1922 with previously independent regiments being joined together as battalions of very large regiments. Many of these battalions had pipe bands and a record exists of the tartan shoulder plaids they wore. Pipers of the 5th Battalion, 1st Punjab Regiment, wore shoulder plaids of the Maxwell dress tartan (Carman 1969: 230). The 2nd Battalion of the 4th Bombay Grenadiers featured pipers wearing the Mackenzie tartan between the world wars (Carman 1969: 232). In the 9th Jat Regiment pipers wore a tartan of green, blue and yellow, but the name of the sett, if any, is not known (Carman 1969: 36). Following World War I, both the 1st and 10th Battalions of the 10th Baluchs had pipers wearing Robertson tartan (Carman 1969: 235). Pipers for four of the battalions of the 12th Frontier Force Regiment wore different sett. The 1st and 4th wore Mackenzie, the 3rd wore Ferguson, while the 5th (Queen Victoria's Own Corps of Guides) because of its royal connection wore the Royal Stewart. Clothing Regulations of 1939 permitted the 13th Frontier Force Rifles to wear a red and green tartan (Carman 1969: 240). The first battalion of this regiment was descended from Coke's Rifles, credited as being the first unit in the Indian Army with a pipe band. Pipers of the 1st Battalion of the 14th Punjab Regiment wore the Hay tartan (Carman 1969: 238). The pipers of the 3rd Battalion of the 15th Punjab Regiment wore the Rose tartan. Pipers of the 1st Battalion of the 17th Dogra Regiment wore the Mackenzie tartan while those of the regiment's 2nd Battalion wore Sutherland tartan shoulder plaids. The sombre rifle green worn by the pipers of the 18th Royal

Garhwal Rifles was complemented by their Black Watch tartan shoulder plaids (Carman 1969: 239).

I have been unable to find evidence that some regiments wore a shoulder plaid, but the regiments in question did use tartans as pipe bag covers and/or pipe ribbons. These included the 22nd Bengal Native Infantry with Black Watch tartan (Carman 1969: 115), the 27th Bengal Native Infantry who used the Rose tartan (Carman 1969: 116) and the 37th (The Prince of Wales' Own) Dogras using Mackenzie tartan (Carman 1969: 119). In yet other cases, while the regiment or battalion had a pipe band, it did not make use of tartan pipe bag covers or pipe ribbons. These included the 47th Sikhs (Carman 1969: 128), the 4th Bombay Native Infantry (Carman 1969: 177), the 26th Bombay Native Infantry (Carman 1969: 182), the 1st Sikh Regiment of the Punjab Frontier Force (Carman 1969: 221), the 4th Battalion of the 2nd Punjab Regiment (Carman 1969: 230) and 106th Hazara Pioneers (Glover 1973: 116–7, Plate 34).

The Indian Army under the Raj also provided another unusual example of the use of bagpipes. The 17th Bengal Lancers boasted a small mounted pipe band (c. 1900) consisting of five or six pipers and a kettle drummer. The drum banners bore a crescent and star and probably the number 17 to the left of the crescent and the letters 'B C' (for Bengal Cavalry – the regiment's official title until 1900) to the right of the star (see photograph in Harris 1979: 31).

Since independence, Indian Army regiments have carried on the use of pipers, with the uniform modifications reflecting Highland dress. Military bands are ephemeral creatures, subject to budget cuts and such demands, but some idea of the importance of pipe bands in the Indian Army is indicated that a list of regimental marches for 27 regiments of infantry indicates 23 of them have pipe bands (see Table 9).

## The Gurkhas

Perhaps the strongest associations of pipes with soldiers of the Indian Army are with the battalions of Gurkhas. Gurkhas have been recruited from the India's neighbouring state of Nepal since Britain engaged in a brief war with that kingdom in 1815. Britain was so impressed by the quality of the foe that it faced that it recruited into its own service prisoners of war from that conflict, and, through diplomacy, secured rights were to recruit in Nepal. The mountain kingdom has been the source of perhaps the world's most famous and most respected mercenaries ever since, as part of the Indian Army under the Raj and in the service of Britain and India since Indian independence

Table 9. *Regimental Marches for Indian Army Pipe Bands*

| Indian Army infantry regiment | Marches for pipe band |
|---|---|
| Brigade of Guards | Back of Banachie |
| The Parachute Regiment | Hundred Pipers |
| The Punjab Regiment | Hundred Pipers |
| The Madras Regiment | Swadharma Kirth |
| The Grenadiers | Back of Banachie |
| The Maratha Light Infantry | Singarh |
| The Rajputana Rifles | Varies with the individual battalion |
| The Rajput Regiment | Jhan Jhani Maina |
| The Jat Regiment | Back of Banachie |
| The Sikh Light Infantry | Hundred Pipers |
| The Dogra Regiment | Dikhi Le Dogra Desh |
| The Garhwal Rifles | The Barren Rocks of Aden |
| The Assam Regiment | How Beautiful is My Land |
| The Mahar Regiment | Deshon ka Sartaj Bharat |
| The Jammu Kashmir Rifles | Chal Shiboo Meriye |
| The Jammu and Kashmir Light Infantry | Kadam Kadam Badhaye Ja |
| 3 Gorkha Rifles | Cock O' the North |
| 5 Gorkha Rifles | Highland Laddie |
| 8 Gorkha Rifles | Bonny Dandy |
| 9 Gorkha Rifles | Atholl Highlanders |
| 11 Gorkha Training Centre | Hundred Pipers |
| Ladakh Scouts | Hundred Pipers |

*Source:* Das 1984: 217

in 1947. Despite the fact he fights for pay rather than from patriotism, the Gurkha has enjoyed remarkably good press throughout his service both to the British Crown and to the Indian Republic.

To organize the materials relative to pipers in Gurkha battalions, I will group the information according to the ten regiments of Gurkhas that were in existence at the time of Indian independence. Although they, like other regiments in the Indian Army, went through many name changes over time, they have been known as the 1st through the 10th Gurkhas for most of this century. It was with these designations that they fought in many theatres through the two world wars. In 1947, upon independence, the 1st, 3rd, 4th, 5th, 8th, and 9th Gurkhas entered Indian service, and the 2nd, 6th, 7th, and

## 'Ladies from Hell'

10th Gurkhas became part of the British Army. Officially, the Indian Army changed the spelling to 'Gorkha' and dispensed with titles that indicated a regimental association with the British Crown, however the Indian Army retained the old numbers and aspects of the regimental titles not tied to the old empire. The Gorkha regiments in the Indian service have seen a great deal of active service and increased in strength; an additional regiment, the 11th Gorkha Rifles, was raised in 1949 (see Chappell 1993). Those regiments remaining in British service retained their old regimental numbers and titles,[10] but, although playing an active role in British military operations over the past fifty years, have seen their regimental strength diminish to single battalions as various British governments pursued economy measures. Recently, these four historic regiments have been amalgamated into a single regiment.

John Masters joined the 4th Prince of Wales's Own Gurkha Rifles in 1935 and his recollections of his pre-war experiences frequently mention the role of pipers in the life of the regiment. He had finished his first meal in the officers' mess when the double doors were thrown open and

> the noise burst upon us and overwhelmed us, and with it one behind another in single file, came the four bagpipers who were causing it. The leader swung his shoulders and began to march around the table; the others followed. All wore rifle-green full dress. Silk banners hung from two of the pipes, one green, one pale silver. (Masters 1956: 97)

After the pipers had played and marched out, the president of the mess half-filled a small silver bowl with Scotch and called the pipe-major (the senior piper in the regiment) back in. This bowl with small handles on each side was known as the quaich. It was given to the pipe-major.

> The pipe-major raised the quaich in front of his face with both hands, looked round us over the brim, and shouted '*Taggra rahos!*' ('Good health!'). He poured the whisky down his throat in one easy motion till it was all gone, and went on turning over the quaich until he could kiss the bottom with a loud smack. Then he reversed it again, bowed his head, and handed it back to M.L. All the officers cried out, '*Taggra raho!*' raised their glasses and drank to the pipe-major. (Masters 1956: 99)

Masters describes the pipe band leading the regiment in November as it marched off on manoeuvres (Masters 1956: 109), and the lone duty piper marching among the tents rousing the encampment playing 'Hey Johnny Cope' (Masters 1956: 123).

One day, the duty piper, attending too intently to his task, split the bag of his pipes. According to Masters (1956: 283) this resulted in 'such uncannily impertinent noises' that the unfortunate piper found himself under arrest because he 'did play his bagpipe in an insolent manner'.

The Hindu festival of Dussehra at which the Gurkhas sacrificed a buffalo, ideally cutting off its head with a single blow of a *kukri*,[11] was closed with the pipe band playing the regimental march. Then, 'the pipes wailed more slowly to another tune, and the Gurkhas broke ranks to follow the band, shouting and throwing flowers' (Masters 1956: 174). On 11 March, Regimental Day for the 4th Gurkha Rifles, the bugles, pipes and brass bands of the two battalions of the regiment combined to beat Retreat. This massive military musical ensemble consisted of forty buglers (twenty-four of whom also played drums), forty pipers, and a fifty-strong brass band (Masters 1956: 179). Clearly pipers played a significant role in the life of the 2nd Battalion, 4th Prince of Wales's Own Gurkha Rifles.

Before launching into the Highland influence on the dress of Gurkha pipers, a few words about the nature of Gurkha uniform is appropriate. All ten Gurkha regiments were designated 'Rifles' and, in common with other rifle regiments in the British service, they had full dress uniforms of rifle-green, a shade verging upon black. This had collar, cuffs and piping in a facing colour, either black or red. Full dress headdress for men and Gurkha officers (as opposed to British officers of Gurkha regiments) was the 'Kilmarnock cap'. This was a round 'pill box' style hat, often worn cocked slightly to the right. It was ornamented by the regimental badge at the front and a 'tourie' – a small tuft – at the centre of its circular flat top. Buttons were black.

Both battalions of the 1st King George V's Own Gurkha Rifles (The Malaun Regiment) – to use their final title, granted in 1937, prior to their coming under the authority of an independent India – boasted pipers. Those of the first battalion originally wore plaids of a tartan known as the 'Childers' sett. This in fact was the government or Black Watch tartan, but the Childers sett received its name because it was pattern used for the trews of the Lowland regiments when the British Army was reorganized by the Secretary of War, H. E. Childer. This was replaced around 1907 by a specially designed tartan, possibly green with a red stripe. Pipers wore the Glengarry instead of the Kilmarnock, complete with a cock's feather in the Highland fashion. Instead of the tunic a rifle green Highland doublet with black piping was worn, and trousers were tucked into black gaiters. A photograph of a piper of the 2nd Battalion in 1892 also shows a Glengarry with the regimental badge below a feather. He too wears a doublet, but it is piped white. The shoulder plaid is said to be of Mackenzie tartan. The trousers are tucked into tartan stockings and white gaiters are worn. The pipe and drums appear in similar dress in a photograph of the 2nd Battalion taken in northern India in 1897 (Chant 1985: 62). This elaborate uniform of the late nineteenth and early twentieth centuries later became simplified – wearing of the plaid ceased in 1920 (Carman 1969: 201–2; Marrion and Fosten 1970: 10). The 1934 report by Adam (Nicholson 1974: 40) that the 1st Battalion of the 1st Gurkhas wore a shoulder plaid of the 'Childers' tartan and that the 2nd Battalion wore one of Mackenzie may reflect earlier usage.

I have found no record that The 2nd King Edward VII's Own Goorkhas (the Sirmoor Rifles) ever enjoyed music played by their own pipers, and the absence of a pipe band at any point in its history makes this regiment unique among the Gurkha regiments formed during the Raj. However, the unit as a whole had a Scottish dress distinction whose origins predate their actions at the siege of Delhi during the Indian Mutiny in 1857. This is the black and red dicing which circles the bottom of their Kilmarnock bonnets, much like the dicing circling the bottom of Highland bonnets (Chant 1985: 33; Chappell 1993: 46).

The 3rd Queen Alexandra's Own Gurkha Rifles had a pipe band that, in 1894, wore a doublet and shoulder plaid. The 2nd Battalion of the 3rd Gurkha Rifles took their pipers and pipes with them to France, where in the spring of 1915 six pipers were photographed playing for the troops and local civilians. The pipers wore unadorned service dress and what appear to be knitted caps (Chant 1985: 73). A 1934 photograph shows a drummer of the pipes and drums in a uniform of khaki drill with a shoulder plaid (Carman 1969: 204).

The pipes of the 4th Prince of Wales's Own Gurkha Rifles have already been described relative to the experiences of John Masters in the 1930s. Their pipe band was instituted in 1885 by a Colonel Hay and has erroneously been identified as the first pipe band in an Indian Army regiment (Carman 1969: 204). In 1887 the 2nd Battalion pipes were recorded as wearing a Glengarry with a Highland doublet and plaid and trews of the Mackenzie tartan (Marrion and Fosten 1970: 20). The 1st Battalion had worn the tam-o-shanter from the inception of the pipe band, but by 1890, the hat was adorned with a black cock's feather and these pipers wore a Highland doublet with dark braiding and a shoulder plaid, probably of rifle-green cloth (Carman 1969: 204–5). A photograph of the pipe major found in Masters (1956), dating from his service in the regiment in the 1930s, shows normal full dress with the addition of a dark (presumably rifle-green) shoulder plaid. Adam in 1934 indicated neither battalion of the 4th Gurkhas used a tartan (Nicholson 1974: 40).

In the 1890s, pipers of the 5th Gurkha (Rifle) Regiment, later the 5th Royal Gurkha Rifles (Frontier Force) wore glengarries with black cock's feathers, a rifle-green doublet piped black, a shoulder plaid of government tartan and rifle-green trousers tucked into short white gaiters or spats. Pipe bag and ribbons were also of the government tartan (Chappell 1993: 7, 49, Plate C4; Carman 1969: 207–8). In 1934 pipers of this regiment continued to use the government tartan for shoulder plaid, pipe bag covers and pipe ribbons (Nicholson 1974: 40).

Early in its history the 6th Queen Elizabeth's Own Gurkha Rifles had a pipe band, but that of the 1st Battalion was soon disbanded. The 2nd Battalion created a pipe band in 1904 but it was also disbanded in 1914 (Carman 1969: 209). A piper of the 6th, photographed in 1912, wears the uniform of khaki shorts and jacket, which had been adopted as warm weather dress by many Gurkha battalions. His hat is the Kilmarnock bonnet and his legs are wrapped to below the knee in dark (probably rifle-green) puttees. He wears a shoulder plaid of rifle-green pinned at his left shoulder with a silver circular brooch. Over his right shoulder he wears the broad shoulder belt with a large silver buckle (Marrion and Fosten 1970: 27). Pipe bands were formed again in 1923, again wearing shoulder plaids not of tartan but of rifle-green (Carman 1969: 209). Adam reported in 1934 that the Black Watch tartan was used for pipe bags and pipe ribbons only (Nicholson 1974: 40). Both Barnes (1960: 308–9) and D'Ami (1969: 74) depict pipers of the 6th Gurkhas wearing shoulder plaids of the Black Watch tartan, with Barnes dating his as 1955. The pipers wear the black Kilmarnock bonnet, a white drill uniform consisting of a coat with a standing collar and shorts, black belts (including a large one over the right shoulder), dark green hose tops with red garter flashes and short white gaiters or spats. The use of tartan shoulder plaids may have been a short-lived practice with the 6th Gurkhas or the illustrations may be in error. An undated, but more recent photograph of a piper of the 6th shows him in a Kilmarnock cap and No. 1 dress, which was a tunic and trousers of rifle green. He wears a shoulder plaid and the broad shoulder belt, and, as the photograph caption notes, 'no tartan is worn'. Even the pipe bag is plain rifle green (Chappell 1993: 59).

Through a complex process the 7th Gurkha Rifles were formed in Burma in 1902. In Burma the regiment had a pipe band wearing glengarries with black cock's feathers and shoulder plaids of government tartan. Gaiters were worn. This pipe band ceased to exist in 1909 but was reconstituted in 1922. Puttees replaced gaiters, but the shoulder plaid of Black Watch or government tartan was reintroduced (Carman 1969: 209). A photograph of a pipe major of the regiment in 1953 showed him wearing battle dress, as adopted by the British Army for active service in 1940, with no Scottish distinctions. His headgear was the slouch hat with light khaki puggaree edged at the top by a thin rifle green line (Marrion and Fosten 1970: 29). A photograph of the Pipes and Drums of the 1st Battalion of the 7th Gurkhas taken in Kuang, Malaya, in 1956 shows them with a black Kilmarnock, white jacket and shorts, shoulder plaids (Douglas tartan), dark green hose tops and white gaiters. The Drum Major does not wear a shoulder plaid and his hose tops appear to be of the Douglas tartan (Chappell 1993: 49). More recently, for parade, the pipers of the 7th Duke of Edinburgh's Own Gurkha Rifles have worn a white tunic with a standing collar, and the skirts were rounded at the front in the Highland fashion.[12] The tunic for the pipers had rifle-green wings edged white. Rifle-green trousers were worn with white spats. Headdress was the black Kilmarnock with the regimental badge, and a shoulder plaid of the Douglas tartan was worn (Thompson 1985: 158). The drum major wore trews of Douglas tartan (Marrion and Jones 1992: 34; Chant 1985: 150). The 7th Duke of Edinburgh's Own Gurkha Rifles was one of two regiments to take bagpipes on the Falkland campaign in 1982 (the Scots Guards was the other).

The 8th Gurkha Rifles did not wear the shoulder plaid, but had pipe bags and ribbons of the Black Watch tartan. An illustration dated 1914 shows a piper of the 1st Battalion wearing a plain black Kilmarnock cap, rifle-green trousers tucked into black puttees, and a dark green doublet piped white on the Inverness skirts, up the front and around the bottom of the collar (Plate 22). In the 1930s the Kilmarnock bonnet was ornamented with two bands of white lace, the top narrower than the bottom. Khaki tunic and shorts were worn. The pipe major wore a small gorget (a small metal crescent, worn horizontally, points upward) below his throat (Carman 1969: 210; Marrion and Fosten 1970: 34). Gorgets were badges of rank for officers in the eighteenth century but for the most part passed out of use by 1850; I know of no other pipe major who wore a gorget as a badge of rank.

The pipe band of the 9th (Gurkha Rifles) Regiment of Bengal Infantry, as it was then officially known, was formed in 1895. Pipers wore the Kilmarnock, but with no badge. They wore green serge trousers, black puttees, the Highland doublet, and a plain-green shoulder plaid (Carman 1969: 211; Marrion and Fosten 1970: 36). The pipe band of the 2nd Battalion was formed in 1910, and in 1914 Colonel Sir Beauchamp Duff provided funds for shoulder plaids of the Duff tartan. As the 1st Battalion was mobilized before these could be purchased, only the pipers of the 2nd Battalion wore them until they too were mobilized for war. After the war, the wearing of Duff tartan plaids was not resumed because 'certain Highland regiments' objected, on the grounds that Duff (who had since died) was not Chief of Clan Duff and hence had no right to authorize his regiment to wear the tartan. Pipers of this regiment in the 1930s wore a dark-green plaid with the regimental plaid brooch, a rifle-green doublet with silver diamond shaped buttons, rifle-green trousers and green puttees and black boots. Belts were of black patent leather (Mains 1997: 140).

The first pipers of the 10th Gurkha Rifles had been trained by pipers of the Royal Scots, so the association of this Gurkha regiment with the senior regiment of the British line is recognized in their shoulder plaids. These are of the Hunting Stewart tartan, the same tartan worn as trews by the Royal Scots. I am uncertain as to the date when the Hunting Stewart tartan was adopted by the 10th Gurkhas. The pipe band of the 1st Battalion was founded in 1895, and though the Royal Scots played a role in this, at that time the Royal Scots were still wearing the government tartan, not adopting the Hunting Stewart until 1901 (Thorburn 1973: 3). Perhaps it was after the Royal Scots trained the pipers of the 2nd Battalion, in 1910, that the shoulder plaid of the Hunting Stewart tartan was adopted by the 10th Gurkha Rifles. Pipe bags, lower pipe ribbon and hose tops are also of the Hunting Stewart tartan, but the Royal Stewart tartan is used for the upper pipe ribbon (Carman 1969: 211; Marrion and Fosten 1970: 39; Chappell 1993: 55–6, Plate F2).

Two additional Gurkha pipe bands were formed to represent units created within the British army after Indian independence. The Queen's Gurkha Signals were born on 23 September 1954, and formed a pipe band the next year. Pipers wear a black Kilmarnock bonnet with a blue tourie. Dark blue trousers with a wide scarlet stripe were worn. The white tunic has straight skirts rather than the curved Highland pattern. The pipers wear a shoulder plaid of the Grant tartan and the pipe bag and ribbons are also of the Grant sett, reflecting the unit's affiliation with the 51st Highland Division Signal Regiment, which had utilized the Grant tartan for its pipers since 1920. The Gurkha Transport Regiment was formed in 1958. Its pipers wear a dark blue Kilmarnock cap with a tourie of the same colour. The white tunic has rounded skirts in the Highland fashion and dark blue trousers with a double white stripe are worn. The pipe bags, pipe ribbons, and shoulder plaids are all of the red MacDuff tartan (Anderson 1989).

## Scots Bagpipes in the Middle East

Bagpipes are an indigenous instrument in the Middle East (see Baines 1960). However, when Middle Eastern armies recently adopted the bagpipe, it was not the indigenous bagpipe but rather the Highland bagpipe that was used. There is evidence for at least two separate formations of pipe bands in Middle Eastern armies, only one of which was under direct British influence. In neither case, though, were elements of Highland dress adopted.

Perhaps the best known of Middle Eastern pipe bands were those of the Arab Legion. The Arab Legion was formed in 1920 to preserve order in the British-supported monarchy of Transjordan (now Jordan), organized by a

British Captain, Frederick G. Peake. In 1930, Peake was joined by another remarkable officer, John B. Glubb, who assumed command of the Arab Legion in 1939 upon Peake's retirement. Glubb commanded the Arab Legion through World War II (during which the Jordanian monarch offered the use of the force to the British) and the later conflicts with the new state of Israel. Glubb was dismissed as commander in 1956 and the Arab Legion officially became the Jordan Arab Army (Young 1972; Laffin 1982).

The Arab Legion in the 1950s had not one but three pipe bands, known by the colour of the epaulets and aiguillette that adorned the British Battle Dress they wore as the red, blue or green bands. Pipe bags were the same colour. It is said the first pipers in the Arab Legion were taught to play by the pipers of the Black Watch. White gaiters were worn with the battle dress, and all pipers wore the red and white *shemagh*, or Arab head scarf, which was standard Legion wear (see D'Ami 1969: 60–1). There is also a photograph of pipers of the Arab Legion wearing what appears to be British Service Dress and the peculiar spiked helmet that Peake is said to have introduced (Young 1972: 21). In the summer of 1955, the massed bands of the Arab Legion toured Britain, beating retreat at Horse Guards' Parade and the pipe and drums parading down Princess Street in Edinburgh (Glubb 1957: 384).

Pipers have also served as part of the establishment of the Palestine Liberation Army, a force distinct from the Palestine Liberation Organization and formed originally in Egypt by President Nasser, before becoming associated with the Syrian army. Like the rank and file of the Palestine Liberation Army, its pipers wore a camouflage uniform with a red beret and their pipe bag bore the colours of the Palestinian flag – black, red, white and green (Laffin 1982: 29, 36, Plate F1).

## Conclusion

It is clear that the most distinctive feature of the dress of the Scots warrior, the belted plaid and its later manifestation, the kilt, has largely been confined to units raised in a variety of settings from emigrant Scots and their descendants. Of much greater influence was the more widely adopted Scots bagpipe with accompanying elements of Scots dress – shoulder plaid, doublet, trews and headdress – among the armed forces of the world. In this chapter I have not considered instances where the bagpipes are from indigenous traditions, such as the use of Irish pipes or Northumberland pipes in the British Army or Breton pipes by the French. Even in the first instance, though, one observes, among Queen Elizabeth's Irish Guards at Buckingham Palace, the three drone Scottish war pipe rather than the two drone Irish variant. It is clear that the fighting abilities of the Scot and the music that inspired him have had a lasting impact on military traditions far beyond the highlands of Scotland.

# 6

# North African Mameluks and Zouaves

The zouaves . . . have certainly proved that they are what their appearance would indicate, – the most reckless, self-reliant, and complete infantry that Europe can produce. With his graceful dress, soldierly bearing, and vigilant attitude, the zouave at an outpost is the beau-ideal of a soldier.

Major-General George B. McClellan

## Napoleon and his Mameluks

When a Colonel Barthélémy arrived in France in 1801 with some 150 Mameluks from Egypt, asking to serve Napoleon, their services were accepted and they were eventually incorporated into his Imperial Guard, attached to Napoleon's favourites, the *Chasseurs à Cheval*. These mounted Egyptians introduced the dress of North Africa into the French military establishment. Napoleon ordered Jean Rapp, a soldier of no small ability and reputation, to organize the squadron, and in January 1802, they became officially part of the Consular Guard, ancestor to the Imperial Guard (Lachouque 1961: 30–1).

Contemporary illustrations of the Mameluks show considerable variation in dress, so the following is only an approximation of their appearance (see Plate 23 for a contemporary representation of a Mameluk of the Guard). A white turban was wound about a red, yellow or green low cylindrical, shako-like headgear (*cahouk*), ornamented with a brass Islamic star and crescent and with a large, cloth-covered button in the centre of the top. A short jacket, coloured either green, blue, yellow or violet was decorated with black braid on the sleeves and a sleeveless waistcoat of red embroidered black was worn over this. Very full, crimson trousers (*charoul*) extended from the waist to the ankles, and the boots which peeked out from beneath the trousers might be black, fawn, red or green. The waist was wound with a sash (colours seem to have varied) into which was tucked a dagger and a holster containing two pistols. A blunderbuss (or, in the later years of the Empire, a carbine) was suspended from a green pouch belt over the left shoulder, and a curved oriental sabre with a Mameluk hilt hung from red cords passing over the right.

As Napoleon's wars dragged on, the original Egyptian members of the troop were replaced by men recruited in metropolitan France, but Egyptian dress was retained. It is said that when the squadron finally disbanded in 1814 on Napoleon's first abdication only 18 men were of Egyptian birth (Windrow and Embleton 1974: 16–17, 24). This unit did not have a profound influence on the dress of light cavalry[1] (perhaps that branch of the military had already been saturated with examples of weird and wonderful costume), but it did lay the groundwork for the acceptance of infantry dressed in North African fashion when France developed colonial aspirations in Algeria fifteen short years after Napoleon's defeat at Waterloo. Indeed, as Lachouque (1961: 31) has observed, 'uniforms of foreign troops on their soil, whether friends or foes, have always captivated the French' and as a result 'oriental fashions became the rage. Imitating Madame Bonaparte, the ladies doted on turbans, while every self-respecting officer – even in the light infantry – carried a Turkish scimitar.'

This squadron of the Imperial Guard was part of the French army occupying Madrid on *Dos Mayo* (2 May 1808) when the local population rose up to violently express their displeasure at Napoleon's attempt to place his brother Joseph on the throne of Spain. The Mameluks were a special focus for Spanish hatred, given the earlier struggles between Moslem and Christian for control of the Iberian Peninsula, and the French dead and wounded on this violent day included every Mameluk officer (Lachouque 1961: 121–2). Witnessing the violence was the artist Francisco Goya, whose painting *Dos Mayo* features the brutal confrontation between the Mameluks and the young men of Madrid (Keegan and Darracott 1981: 50–1).

Napoleon also had a personal Mameluk orderly, Roustam, who served him from 1800 through the days of the empire, always wearing Mameluk dress. Almost invariably he is pictured among the staff surrounding the Emperor in the battle art celebrating Napoleon and his victories. Roustam was constantly in attendance to Napoleon, sleeping on a pallet outside the Emperor's bed chamber within the large tent Napoleon used on campaign (Elting 1988: 74).

## France and Algeria

The dress of North Africa, in stylized form, thus was familiar to the French public when a French army landed at Sidi-Ferruch, near Algiers, in June 1830.

The nominal cause of the invasion was a dispute between the French Consul and the Turkish Governor of Algiers. Eric Wolf (1969: 211) argues that although 'begun as a military operation abroad in order to divert French attention from the growing unpopularity of the regime of Charles X at home, the occupation of Algiers soon became an end in itself.' By August some 500 indigenous men, said to be Berbers of Zouaoua origins and to have been previously employed by the Turks, were recruited for French service (Heggoy and Haar 1984: 39).

On 1 October 1830, a *bataillon des Zouaves* came into official existence (Dutailly 1978: 43), and shortly thereafter a second battalion was raised. The first battalion was commanded by a Captain Maumet of the General Staff and the second by a Captain Duvier of the Engineers. The Zouaves were soon in action, coming under fire on 28 November as part of the Medeah expedition. In their first year of existence their uniform was described: 'Jacket with sleeves and waistcoat closed in front, without sleeves, in blue cloth. Moorish pants in wine-colored cloth . . . Belt [sash] of blue cotton cloth . . . Turban and red riding breeches. Shoes, legging in leather. Knapsack. Turkish cartridge box. Distinguishing marks for officers and non-commissioned officers are the same as in the Hussars service' (Richard 1992: 190).

From the first, all officers and even most of the non-commissioned officers were French (Dutailly 1978: 45), and increasingly the rank and file were of French rather than indigenous North African in origin. In 1835 a third of the Zouave companies were French; in 1841 reorganization stipulated that eight of the nine companies of each battalion were filled with French rather than North African personnel (McAfee 1991: 9). Their dress, however, continued to be North African. It was in this dress that Zouaves won glory in the capture of Constantine in 1837. Of the 300 Zouaves participating in the attack, 71 were killed and another 76 wounded (Richard 1992: 193). Four years later the Zouaves were expanded to three battalions, one in each of France's Algerian provinces, and these became regiments in 1851. All three regiments, each with two battalions of eight companies, departed in May 1853, to join the Anglo-French force fighting the Russians in the Crimea, where all three regiments distinguished themselves at the battle of Alma and the world became aware of the Zouave.

Shann and Delperier (1991: 44) note: 'The uniform worn by the Zouaves first made its appearance in 1833, and was fixed definitively in 1853. From that time on it scarcely changed and could still be seen in parades as late as 1962, when the Zouaves were finally disbanded.'

It should be noted that although Europeans had replaced North Africans in Zouave units of the French army, other colonial units, locally recruited, also wore a Zouave-style uniform. The *Tirailleurs algériens* (commonly known as Turcos) wore dress of an identical cut (but of a somewhat more subdued colouring) to that of the Zouaves. The North African Turcos also fought in the Crimea, but were ignored by the (racist?) world press focussed on the actions of Zouaves in that theatre. McAfee (1991: 15) notes 'they never gained the popular acclaim of their European counterparts'. The Spahis, a locally recruited cavalry unit, also wore North African dress, much of it also identical in style to that of the Zouaves. However, because of the attention received by the Zouaves, what was a common North African style of dress became known as a Zouave uniform.

The Zouave uniform can be broken down into a number of elements. A fez (*chechia*) was worn on the head, red with a blue tassel in the original form. For parades this was wrapped by cloth turban, red until 1852, then green until 1870, and thereafter white. The fez and turban combination is similar in appearance to the *cahouk* and turban worn by Napoleon's Mameluks. Over a collarless vest was worn a short jacket, open at the front, decorated with tape or braid. Originally simply edged in red, by 1833 the front of the jacket was decorated on each side with a loop of tape ending in a trefoil known as a *tombeau*. A wide sash was worn about the waist. Very baggy red 'trousers' (*serouel*) lacked separate legs, being two squares of cloth sewn together with an opening and waistband at the top and two openings at the bottom for the soldier's legs. These fastened above the mid-calf and white gaiters covered the remainder of the leg to the boot. In some orders of dress the upper half of the gaiter was covered by a leather greave or *jambiere* (McAfee 1991: 20–2). In summer and for undress a white *serouel* of identical cut to the red trouser was worn (Plate 24).

The *Tirailleurs algériens* (Turcos) wore similar uniforms, but of light blue cloth (both jacket and *serouel*) with yellow trim. Again white trousers (or *serouel*) replaced those of full dress when on service in warm weather. During the reign of Napoleon III a regiment of Zouaves was incorporated in the Imperial Guard, dressed as their counterparts in the regular forces, save that yellow trim replaced the red on their dark blue jackets.

An important aspect of this Zouave dress lies in the contrast it provided at the time of its introduction (the 1830s) to the prevailing European military fashion, which most notably included a tight coat (often called a coatee), cut square across the waist, with tails at the back and a high standing collar with a leather stock (the origin of the nickname 'Leathernecks' for the US Marines – presumably applied by the more comfortably attired crews of the ships on which they served). The collarless vests and short jackets of the Zouave were without a doubt more comfortable to wear, for as the American observer George B. McClellan (who later commanded the Army of the Potomac in the American Civil War) reported, 'the men say that this dress is the most convenient possible, and prefer it to any other'. He noted that it left the neck 'unencumbered by collar, stock, or cravat' and that the jacket was cut to 'allow free movement of the arms' (McClellan 1861: 61).

## Elmer Ephraim Ellsworth, Zouaves and the American Civil War

The Zouaves of the French army had established an outstanding military reputation for themselves by the time the issue of slavery came to threaten the union of American states. Playing soldier was an American pastime in the mid-nineteenth century, and for many it was the glory of dressing up for parade that was the attraction. Local units took grandiose titles and were attired to suit the tastes of their volunteer membership. It was in these theatrical parade uniforms that many men from both the north and the south marched off to fight the American Civil War. Some formally or informally called themselves Zouaves, and these joined the army to save the Union (or to dissolve it) in uniforms derived from North Africa. One can see little modification of the French/Algerian uniform in that of the Louisiana Zouaves of 1861 or Duryée's Zouaves from New York (Todd 1954: Plates 17 and 21).

One must concede that in this example of the diffusion of the costume of hinterland warriors to distant places, certain historical factors played an important role. Elmer Ephraim Ellsworth, a handsome young law clerk, met a veteran of the Crimea who had served with the Zouaves. The two of them recruited a company of amateur soldiers, calling it the United States Zouave Cadets and using the drill and dress of French Zouaves (Plate 25). They took the unit on a tour of the eastern United States in 1860, their itinerary including West Point, which provided 'their severest test' (Cunliffe 1980: 120). In August they performed their spectacular drill on the lawn of the White House (Haythornthwaite 1975: 154). Todd reports this as 'an epoch making trip' and notes 'everywhere it was greeted with wild enthusiasm' (Todd 1954: Plate 17).

Ellsworth went on to provide a tragic footnote to Civil War history. Upon the outbreak of the Civil War in 1861, Ellsworth recruited a battalion from among New York City firefighters and dressed them as Zouaves (the 11th New York Volunteer Infantry, known as the New York Fire Zouaves – see Plate 26). This battalion has been characterized as 'one of the most notoriously undisciplined and unsatisfactory regiments in American history' (McBarron, Todd and editors 1982: 14). On 24 May 1861 Ellsworth's regiment crossed into Alexandria, Virginia. Ellsworth saw a Confederate flag flying over the

Marshall House, a local inn. He scampered up to the third floor and hauled it down, but descending the stairs he was confronted and killed by the inn's proprietor, James W. Jackson. One of Ellsworth's men killed Jackson (Botkin 1960: 39–42). These two were among the first to die in America's Civil War (Ketchum 1960: 71). Despite this brief and undistinguished career, another New York Zouave regiment, the 44th New York, adopted the 'rather theatrical' name of 'Ellsworth's Avengers' (Todd 1954: Plate 21), while the 19th Illinois Volunteers bore the name Ellsworth's Zouave Cadets (Haythornthwaite 1975: 154).

Documentation exists of numerous Zouave units on both sides of the conflict; however, ephemeral nature of many of these units makes it impossible to compile a complete listing of units who either called themselves Zouaves or wore Zouave-like uniforms. Although whole battalions and regiments dressed as Zouaves, it was also not uncommon in the initial stages of the war for only one or two companies of a regiment to wear Zouave dress. Many of these varied from those of their North African prototypes, as did the uniforms of the troops commanded by Ellsworth. As McAfee notes, the 'exotic and colorful' uniforms of the Zouaves and Turcos of the French army 'were far surpassed by the imagination shown in designing uniforms for American Zouaves' (McAfee 1991: 90). He feels 'quasi-zouave uniforms' were more common than 'fully-rigged Zouaves such as the Philadelphia Zouave Corps'. Possibly the most notable deviation from the original uniform was use of baggy trousers (with two legs) instead of following the pattern of the original *serouel* of North Africa. Following the model of Ellsworth's United States Zouave Cadets it was also the case that many regiments wore a kepi rather than a fez, although for Union troops the kepi was often red rather than the blue of conventional Union regiments.

An example of a modified 'Zouave' uniform is that of the 11th Indiana Regiment commanded by Lewis Wallace, who later served as governor of New Mexico at the time of the reign of terror of William Bonney (Billy the Kid) and who also authored *Ben Hur*. Wallace's Zouaves wore standard issue US Army light blue trousers and a red (later blue) cap rather than the fez. Their Zouave status was indicated by their jacket, however. The short black jacket, cut in Zouave style, had attached in the front two blue panels that buttoned, providing the wearer with a false vest (McAfee 1991: 60, 91).

It is sometimes asserted that certain regiments were not 'actually' or 'in fact' Zouaves but rather were 'chasseurs'. Such an assertion has been made about the 14th New York State Militia (Woodbridge and Grube 1982: 60; Windrow and Embleton 1973: 98–9), popularly known as the 14th Brooklyn. They wore a red kepi and a jacket, false vest combination, similar to that described above for the 11th Indiana, with both front edges of the blue jacket

## North African Mameluks and Zouaves

bordered with a row of functionless bullet or bell buttons and a scarlet false vest closed with a similar but functional row of buttons. It should be mentioned that Ellsworth's original United States Zouave Cadets had similar rows of brass bullet or bell buttons ornamenting both edges of their Zouave jackets (see Plate 25). The 14th Brooklyn seems to be imitating this American Zouave style. The baggy red trousers of the 14th Brooklyn were worn with white leggings. It may be because the waist belt was worn over the jacket rather than under it and because the jacket had a small, stand-up collar unlike the usual collarless Zouave jacket that some authors have insisted this unit was chasseurs, not Zouaves. Woodbridge and Grube (1982: 60) do concede that 'almost all contemporary accounts refer to the men as "Zouaves" or "red legged Zouaves."' Whether Zouaves or chasseurs, they wore their baggy red trousers throughout the war, winning distinction on such fields as Bull Run, Antietam and Gettysburg.

Other Zouave units more closely approximated the North African model of dress (see Plate 27). Duryée's Zouaves (the 5th New York Volunteer Infantry) wore a uniform closely approximating that of the original French units. It has been suggested that this orthodoxy was inspired by the enlistment of Felix Angus, a veteran of the 3rd Zouaves in the French service, who wore his 3rd Zouave uniform when he enlisted (Smith 1996: 52).

It is sometimes stated that the Zouave uniform was an artefact of the beginnings of the war and that the flamboyant costume eventually gave way to a more sober, standardized dress (see Todd 1954: Plate 21). However, as indicated above, the 14th Brooklyn wore their full red trousers in combats throughout the war, until disbanded in 1864. Other regiments raised late in the conflict assumed Zouave (or modified Zouave) dress. The 33rd New Jersey Volunteer Infantry wore Zouave dress for its first year in combat, as part of General William T. Sherman's army in Georgia and the Carolinas in 1864. The men wore baggy dark-blue trousers with red knots decorating the front tucked into black leather leggings, a dark-blue shirt edged red and closed with closely spaced bullet buttons and a dark blue jacket decorated with red lace or piping. A red sash was worn about the waist and a dark blue kepi with red piping was worn. Only in September 1864, was this Zouave dress replaced by the regulation uniform of US Infantry (Ray, Strurcke and McAfee 1982).

The 114th Pennsylvania (Collis Zouaves) imported the cloth for their uniforms from France in sufficient quantities to ensure they were dressed as Zouaves from their formation, in August 1862, until the end of the war. In 1864 they became the provost guard for the Army of the Potomac (the force which spent the war fighting Robert E. Lee's Army of Northern Virginia in the Civil War's major theatre) and its band served as the official band of the

Army of the Potomac's headquarters. The regiment was dressed in true Zouave fashion adopting a red fez with a yellow tassel, a white turban, a dark blue Zouave jacket with light blue cuffs decorated with red tape including *tombeaux*, a broad light blue sash, red trousers ( not the true *serouel*) and white gaiters (Todd and editors 1982). The regiment also followed French fashion in recruiting a *vivandiere*, a sutleress who carried a keg of spirits to refresh the troops. The *vivandiere*, Mary Tobee (or Mary Tippee), wore red trousers, a blue skirt with a red stripe, a light blue sash and the regiment's Zouave jacket, and was armed with a very large pistol in a holster on her waist belt (see Plate 28).

The 146th New York received its Zouave uniform in time to wear it at Gettysburg (1–3 July 1863) and it continued to wear it through the remainder of the war. With the baggy trousers, shirt and jacket all light blue trimmed yellow, the dress was very close to that of the Turcos or *Tirailleurs algériens*. A red fez with a red tassel (some sources suggest a yellow tassel) was worn, wrapped with a white turban for full dress (McAfee and Grube 1982). Serving in the same brigade with the 146th New York were the 140th New York and the 155th Pennsylvania, both of whom also acquired Zouave uniforms, with jackets and baggy trousers of dark blue, trimmed in red for the 140th New York and yellow for the Pennsylvanians (McBarron and Todd 1982b; Smith 1996: 62–3).

On the Confederate side, the most famous (or in the words of some commentators, most infamous) Zouave unit was Wheat's Tigers. The son of a Virginia Episcopalian (Anglican) minister, Wheat had earlier fought in Mexico, Cuba, Central America, and with Garibaldi in Italy and the red shirts of Wheat's Tigers were said to recall the dress of Garibaldi's liberators of Italy. They were issued conventional blue Zouave jackets, but with such poor quality dye that they faded to a brown hue. Denied the elegance of scarlet trousers, they wore *serouel* of bed-ticking – a course white cloth with pinstripes of blue. Some wore a red stocking cap with blue tassel, at least reminiscent of the original Zouave head gear, but others adopted a straw hat (Smith 1996: 45–7, 58–9).

### The Pontifical Zouaves

While America was divided by her Civil War, an army of foreigners was being raised to defend the interests of the Papacy in another war engulfing Italy. The composition of this international force included soldiers from France, Germans and Austrians, Swiss, Dutch and Belgians, in addition to Canadians and a smattering of men came from other countries around the world (Lodolini 1976: 74–5), The largest and most famous unit in this army was the Pontifical Zouaves. More than 300 of its 2900 strength came from the heavily Francophone and Catholic Canadian province of Quebec. When the first contingent of volunteers departed from Montreal to join the Pontifical Zouaves in 1868, it is reported that 20,000 gathered to see them off. The entire city had a population of only 100,000 at this time, of which 60,000 were French-speaking Catholics. The cost of transporting the volunteers to Rome was borne by the Church in Quebec, $112,000 was raised (Chartrand 1995: 200).

The vast majority of the Pontifical Zouaves had been recruited in France, and after Rome fell to forces of the Kingdom of Italy in 1870 (an attack by Garibaldi had been beaten back in 1867), the French members of the corps were sent back to France, which was then at war with Prussia. After the fall of Napoleon III, Lieut.-Colonel de Charette offered his Zouaves to the new republic and these were accepted under the title of Voluntaires de l'Ouest, still wearing the uniform of the Pontifical Zouaves, a grey Zouave jacket and trousers, trimmed red, a kepi with grey top and red band and piping, red sash and white gaiters. Officers also wore Zouave dress, unlike their counterparts in the old Imperial Army, but sky blue in colour, trimmed black. In this dress the unit fought at Brou, Loigny and Le Mans before being mustered out of service in August 1871 (Norman 1972b: 10–1).

## Zouaves and the British Empire

The British Empire was not beyond the influence of this North African uniform style popularized by the French. Queen Victoria herself is credited with expressing a desire to see Imperial troops dressed as Zouaves (Kieran 1992: 119), although, interestingly, the British did not clothe men of the regular army as Zouaves, but did conclude that such dress was suitable for troops raised in the colonies. Most notable is the dress of the West India Regiment, whose uniform was depicted with some detail and accuracy, even if the illustration is an example of Victorian racist caricature, in 'Major Seccombe's' *Army & Navy Drolleries* (Plate 29). Seccombe provides a verse and a caricature for each letter of the alphabet, and the West India Regiment appears under 'Z for Zouave' although the name was never applied to that particular unit. The uniform continues in use, worn by the Jamaica Military Band, a post-colonial successor to the band of the West India Regiment (Marrion 1987: 616). Major R. M. Barnes reflects the stereotype that led to the adoption of the uniform in his characterization of it as 'entirely satisfactory – smart, colourful, picturesque, and suited to the climate and the people for whom it was designated' (Barnes 1960: 215). The Zouave-style dress was adopted in 1858, after the British experience fighting alongside Zouaves in the Crimea (Kieran 1992: 119). Seccombe depicts a Zouave jacket, but other illustrations of the dress of the West India Regiment show that it differed from the 'classic' Zouave pattern of uniform in that it consisted of a red sleeveless jacket edged with yellow tape and decorated with yellow cord, fastened at the neck and worn over a white shell jacket laced yellow (Wilkinson-Latham 1970: 154). This differed from the shirt and short jacket worn by Zouaves but was reminiscent in style of the dress of Napoleon's Mameluks mentioned above.

Similar dress was worn by the contingent of the Gold Coast Constabulary (later the Gold Coast Regiment, West African Frontier Force, and still later, the Ghana Regiment), which attended the diamond jubilee of the Queen-Empress in London in 1897. It was entirely navy blue, trimmed in red, with a red fez. The source consulted does not indicate that the turban (puggaree in British military terminology) was worn (Barnes 1960: 176). A photograph of Captain Davidson Houston of the Gold Coast Hausas shows him wearing a Zouave uniform with his medal from the Ashanti War of 1874. He wears a dark shell jacket with a dark, elaborately braided vest. His trousers are hardly full, but are tucked into Zouave style gaiters (Haythornthwaite 1988: 58). Eventually the baggy Zouave trousers were discontinued in British West African military dress, being replaced by khaki shorts, but the 'Zouave' style jacket continued as the full dress of Britain's West African troops through the colonial era (Plate 30).

## The Indian Army

Elements in the dress of the Indian Army under the Raj may also have Zouave roots or origins, although the resemblance to French Zouaves is less clear than is the case for the West India Regiment or the Gold Coast Constabulary. Prior to the Indian Mutiny (see Chapter 7 below) the native regiments in the armies of the Honourable East India Company had worn the tight red coatee (complete with bars of lace across the chest in the style of Wellington's infantry at Waterloo) and the trousers of the regular army. On their heads they wore the shako until 1847 and the Kilmarnock cap after that (Wilkinson-Latham 1977: 35–6). Prior to the Mutiny, a British officer preaching reform in the dress of the British Army, wrote

> There are many parts of the dress of the royal army exceedingly inconvenient to the English soldier... To the native of India, then, accustomed from infancy to a

light and loose clothing, the tight European dress, when worn for the first time, must be disgusting; there are parts of it, indeed, to which he never becomes reconciled.

He notes that in April 1842, the 2nd, 16th and 28th Bengal Native Infantry captured the heights before Kojuck Pass, only after discarding their 'pantaloons', finding it impossible to scale the precipice while wearing them (Luard 1852: 115–16). After the Mutiny (1857-9), reforms led to a less European appearance for the Indian Army. In Bengal and Madras this led to the adoption of the 'Zouave' tunic adopted in Bengal in the 1860s and in Madras in 1883. This was a red tunic with collar and cuffs of the regimental facing colour and with a front panel of the facing colour piped white running down the front of the tunic (Barthorp 1979: 38). This pattern probably received its name because the garment gave the appearance of buttonless outer garment (like the classic Zouave jacket) over a buttoned vest of a contrasting colour and to some extent it apes the pseudo-Zouave garments worn by some troops in the American Civil War described above. The front of the tunic (the cloth panel of the facing colour) was originally cut diagonally from the last button to the edge of the panel at the skirt, possibly increasing its pseudo-Zouave appearance. To this 'Zouave' tunic were added trousers cut as nearly as full as those worn by the West India Regiment and even baggier than many worn by American units who chose to call themselves 'Zouaves' during the American Civil War. The 'Zouave' tunic was worn in full dress until replaced by a garment of Indian origin, the kurta made of red or rifle green serge, in 1903 (Barthorp 1979: 38–9).

## Other Zouaves

In Brazil in the 1860s the *Zuavos da Bahia*, recruited from among the black population, were included among the *Voluntario da Patria*. With yellow tape and *tombeaux* ornamenting the jacket, their uniform was nearly identical to that of the Zouaves of the Guard of Napoleon III (Barroso 1922: 62, 97, Plate 118).

France herself uniformed Senegalese and other West Africans in baggy trousers and the fez, similar to that of the original Zouaves. The issue of the fez by both the British and the Germans to sub-Saharan African colonial troops probably also had Zouave origins.

The original Algerian Zouaves had been employed by the Turks before offering their services to the French invaders of North Africa. It is therefore ironic that after Turkey lost control of most of her North African empire, the modernization (or better a 'Europeanization') of the Turkish Army led to the creation of Zouave units in the late nineteenth century. The Zouaves of the Guard wore uniforms nearly identical to those of the Imperial Guard of Napoleon III (see Roubicek 1971: Plate 19). In 1898, when the Turkish line infantry consisted of 75 regiments of four battalions, there were two Zouave regiments of two battalions each (Roubicek 1971: 20). Other Turkish units, such as the Gendarmes and the Albanian Guards, wore Zouave jackets if not the full Zouave uniform (Roubicek 1971: Plates 18, 22).

## Conclusion

In this chapter I have tried to show the impact of a particular colonial experience, that of the French in North Africa, on a wider military culture. There are interesting paradoxes here in the use of indigenous auxiliaries in the colonial experience, including the role played by the indigenous population in its own subjugation, and also the recognition of military merit among the conquered by the conquerors and their sister colonial states. This recognition takes a material, and very visible, form in the adoption of the dress of the colonized by the colonial military establishment and in the diffusion of that dress to other nations participating in the wider military culture of the colonial powers.

# 7

# Khaki – 'Not a Bad Colour for Work'

With that he whistled his only son, that dropped from a mountain-crest –
He trod the ling like a buck in spring, and he looked like a lance in rest,
'Now here is thy master,' Kamal said, "who leads a troop of the Guides,
'And thou must ride at his left side as shield on shoulder rides . . .'

Rudyard Kipling
The Ballad of East and West

## Lumsden of the Guides

Conflict on the frontiers of India led to an innovation in military dress that was to have an impact upon all armies of the world: the invention of the khaki uniform.

In 1846 a Corps of Guides, initially consisting of a single troop of cavalry and two companies of infantry, was raised on the border between the Punjab and Waziristan by Lieutenant Harry B. Lumsden. Lumsden had been born on 12 November 1821, on the *Rose*, a ship belonging to the East India Company sailing in the Bay of Bengal. His father, Thomas Lumsden, an officer in the Bengal Horse Artillery, was returning to India, bringing his new wife whom he had married while on leave for two years in Aberdeenshire. The young Lumsden was sent from India to Aberdeenshire for his education in 1827 and returned to India as an ensign in the 59th Bengal Native Infantry in 1838 (Lumsden and Elsmie 1899: 1–2).

The complex history of the British in India and their creation and organization of an Indian Army defy easy explanation. Regulars from the British Army served in India dating from the 1754 arrival of the 39th Foot on the subcontinent (Harris 1979 :3). From the first, British regulars in India were greatly outnumbered by locally raised troops, officered, at least in part, by the British. Until the Indian Mutiny (1857), these were the forces of the Honourable East India Company (popularly 'John Company') consisting of three armies, Bengal (seventy-four regiments of infantry; ten of light cavalry), Madras (fifty-two regiments of infantry; four of light cavalry) and Bombay (twenty-nine regiments of infantry; three of light cavalry). In addition, there were numerous supporting troops such as artillery (both horse and foot) as well as engineers, sappers and miners (see Fosten 1969). The Honourable East India Company's mercantile army also included a few European (principally Irish) regiments.

France was the first European power to recruit native troops in India, but the Honourable East India Company soon began to do so to match French numbers in the contest for control of South Asian markets. At first locally raised French and British forces dressed in native fashion with the addition of European military coats and European arms (Chartrand 1991: 34–5; Haswell Miller and Dawnay 1966–70, Volume 1: Plates 184–9, Volume 2: 36–7). Gradually, though, the dress of the John Company's Indian troops became increasingly European in appearance. In the early nineteenth century, Indian infantry wore impractical styles, with a tight coatee with long tails, a tall collar and stock, and a high, bell-topped shako. If anything, the Indian army shako was less functional than its counterpart in the British Army as it lacked a peak to protect the face from the sun. Among the regular cavalry, it is reported they 'wore uniforms so tight that they could hardly get on their horses without splitting their overalls' (Wilson 1974: 11).

In addition to the 'regular' establishment of the East India Company, 'irregular' troops and companies were frequently raised, and Lumsden's Corps of Guides was such a unit. The idea of the Guides came from Sir Henry Lawrence, who was later to die in the siege of the residency at Lucknow during the Indian Mutiny, but it was the young Lieutenant Harry Lumsden who moulded them into their legendary image.

In a letter to his father dated 6 February 1847, Harry Lumsden, then a 25-year-old subaltern, indicated he was 'to commence to recruit my new corps . . . to consist of 1 Resaldar, 1 Resaidar, 2 Jemadars, 2 kote duffadars, 12 duffadars, a trumpeter, and 80 sabres in the Cavalry, with 2 Subadirs, 2 Jemadars, 18 havildars, 18 naicks, 4 buglers, and 146 Infantry Sepoys'[1] (Lumsden and Elsmie 1899: 34–5). He asked his father for some items necessary to wage war or maintain peace on the mountainous frontier, 'the very best telescope you can set your hands upon. I do not mind it being a trifle heavy, provided it is a first-rate one, nor paying the price for it, so long as it is good enough for the Officer commanding "the Guides"' and two pistols to carry in his belt 'to keep up with the fashions of the place and make myself on equal terms with my neighbours in my wanderings' (Lumsden and Elsmie 1899: 35–6).

The Guides reached full strength in March 1848, and in some respects the story of Lumsden's recruitment of frontier warriors rivals fiction (Lumsden and Elsmie 1899: 44). Sir Henry Daly, who commanded the Guides at the siege of Delhi, noted 'on the enrolment of the Guides each man's personal history was known to Lumsden' (Lumsden and Elsmie 1899: 66). Lumsden desired 'men accustomed to look after themselves, and not easily taken aback by any sudden emergency' (Lumsden and Elsmie 1899: 67). Dilawar Khan, a notorious outlaw who made his fortune by robbing and kidnapping wealthy travellers, was such a thorn in the side of the government that 2000 rupees (approximately £200) were offered for his head, but to Harry Lumsden he seemed a potential recruit for the Guides. Lumsden sent Khan a safe-conduct and the two men talked of their past encounters, the subaltern arguing that Khan would eventually be caught and hanged. Why not, Lumsden suggested, join the Guides instead? Dilawar Khan laughed at the idea, but said he would think about it and slipped off into the hills. Six weeks later, with no safe-conduct to protect him, he reappeared to enlist. He served in the Guides for two decades, commanding a platoon as a Subadar, and froze to death while on a secret mission in Afghanistan for the Government of Queen Victoria in 1869 (Mason 1976: 339; Lumsden and Elsmie 1899: 67–73).

The brothers Fateh Khan and Rasul Khan were also clearly the sort of men Lumsden wanted for the Guides. The former was a Risaldar in the cavalry and the latter a Subadar of infantry. At the siege of Multan in the Second Sikh War, when raiders stole camels from the British camp, Risaldar Fateh Khan and 70 Guides immediately set out to attempt to recover the stolen animals. Instead they encountered some 1200 Sikh cavalry. Khan and his men charged, driving a wedge through the body of Sikh horsemen. Khan then halted (it is much more difficult for a commander to stop a cavalry charge than to start one), wheeled and charged the Sikhs again. Again Khan and his men halted, and they charged a third time when the Sikh cavalry broke and fled to the safety of the fortress of Multan (Mason 1976: 329; Lumsden and Elsmie 1899: 53–4).

His brother, Subadar Rasul Khan, with 140 men, was once sent to scout and gather intelligence a day's march ahead of the main force advancing on the Sikh fortress of Gorindghar. After his men had removed any badges that would betray their origins, Khan took advantage of the existing ambiguity of loyalties to suggest to the fortress commander that he and his men were on the Sikh side. The commander of the fort wisely did not let Khan and his men enter, but three of Khan's men masqueraded as prisoners who, on Khan's suggestion, were placed in the fort's prison. Khan then asked the commander to allow some of his men into the fort to guard the prisoners. That night Khan's men inside the fort overpowered the Sikh sentries and let in the remainder of the Guides, who had camped outside the front gate of the fort.

Khan and his Guides made prisoners of the sleeping garrison and when the main body of the army arrived they found the Union Jack flying over Gorindghar (Mason 1976: 330–1). Subadar Rasul Khan received a sword and 1000 rupees for the capture of Gorindghar (Lumsden and Elsmie 1899: 63).

It was decided by Lumsden to dress his Guides in lose-fitting khaki coloured uniforms – 'khaki' comes from Urdu and means 'dusty'. The initial dress of the Guides is not clear, but a regimental tradition maintains that, from the outset, the unit wore mud-coloured clothing from the local bazaar (Cadell 1953: 132). Another version, from Sir George Younghusband, has Lumsden purchasing white cloth from the bazaar at Lahore and having it 'dyed' by soaking it in water and rubbing mud into the cloth (Whitehorne 1936: 181). When the corps was authorized to triple its size (to three troops of cavalry and six companies of infantry) in June 1849, Lumsden had his new second-in-command, W. S. R. Hodson, order cloth from Britain for the Guides – 'We must do them all brown!!!' (quoted in Cadell 1953: 132).

This cloth had not arrived when the Guides were engaged in December of that year. They were, however, dressed in clothing the colour of mud, a colour in wide use in the Punjab and the Northwest Frontier when Lumsden adopted it for the Guides. In what is often described as its very first use in action, at Sangao on 11 December 1849, khaki clothing almost led to the Guides attracting friendly fire. The Guides with the 60th Rifles (from the regular British Army – dressed in rifle green, which was often black because of the instability of the dye), the 1st Punjab Infantry (also in rifle green) and a detachment of artillery marched to punish villages that had been resisting paying annual tribute in 1849. The artillery was about to fire on the Guides (mistaking them for the enemy) when a gunner recognized their khaki uniforms. 'Lord! sir; them is our mudlarks!' (Lumsden and Elsmie 1899: 80).

In early 1850, Lumsden and his Adjutant, Henry Newdick Miller, appeared in khaki before the Commander-in-Chief for India, Sir Charles Napier. Lumsden wrote of the meeting to Hodson. 'He looked at us both for a minute and then remarked, "Yes, it's not a bad colour for work".' Shortly after, Lumsden reported with pride that 'Sir Charles says "The Guides are the only properly dressed Riflemen in India"' (quoted in Cadell 1953: 133).

The Guides were soon joined by other units dressed in khaki. In 1849 Punjabi units were raised as the Transfrontier Frontier Brigade, renamed two years later the Punjab Irregular Force, and in 1865 becoming the Punjab Frontier Force. Four regiments of Punjab infantry dressed in khaki, faced black for the 2nd, green for the 3rd and 5th and blue for the 4th. As has been mentioned, the 1st Punjab Regiment dressed in rifle green. The Guides themselves became part of the Punjab Irregular Force in 1851 (Carman 1969:

213–4). A number of other units associated with the Piffers, as the Punjab Irregular Force was known among the British officer corps, adopted khaki. Of four regiments of Sikhs, the 2nd was clad in green while the other three were originally clad in red with yellow facings. In March 1852, the 1st Sikhs dyed their white summer uniforms khaki. The 3rd Sikhs adopted khaki dress in 1855. The 4th Sikhs abandoned red for khaki in 1856 (Carman 1969: 221–3).

## The Indian Mutiny

Khaki was widely used in the tragic and brutal episode known as the Indian Mutiny, in which the Bengal army revolted, while the troops of the other two Presidencies remained loyal. This war was marked by religious and racial hatred and contempt in which both sides summarily executed prisoners and slaughtered non-combatants. It is not a war to raise one's evaluation of the nobility of the human condition (although it is probably correct to observe that all wars contain incidents that lower that evaluation).

Rumour had been rampant within the Bengal Army that the English were systematically causing troops to violate the complex variety of taboos that reinforced Hindu ideas of religion and caste as well as the Muslim prohibition against eating pork, and hence make it easier to force them to convert to Christianity. The famous cartridge for the Enfield Rifle, which was being adopted for the army in India, was feared as another British attempt to subvert the religious practices of the subcontinent, for the cartridge consisted of a paper wrapping a bullet and powder in a neat package. In normal drill in the use of the Enfield, this cartridge was bitten open before the charge and bullet were rammed down the barrel. The cartridge was greased with tallow, and though their officers tried to convince the sepoys and sowars that the tallow did not contain the fat of cows or pigs, and that they could tear the cartridge rather than bite it, the troops simply did not believe their British officers. Some disagreement exits as to the facts about the actual production of the cartridge, but Mason (1976: 265) is firm in his conclusion: 'There cannot be any reasonable doubt that the tallow used on the new cartridges, whether prepared in England or in India, contained the fat of cows; those from England certainly, and those from India probably, contained the fat of pigs.'

Although there had been incidents in the immediate past, the revolt of the 3rd Bengal Light Cavalry at Meerut precipitated the conflict. Eighty-five sowars, who had refused to use the cartridge and had been court marshalled, put in irons, and sentenced to ten-years' hard labour, were freed by their comrades on 10 May 1857, and most of the Indian troops in the garrison joined the mutiny. The British portion of the garrison, the 60th Rifles, the 6th Dragoon Guards and the Royal Artillery, failed to have any significant impact on the mutinous sepoys and sowars. Meerut was only a hard day's march from the old capital of the Mogul Empire, Delhi, where the entire garrison revolted on the 11 May, when a 3rd Light Cavalry trooper brought news of the previous day's actions at Meerut. The entire subcontinent fell into the long and bitter conflict.

At the outbreak of the Mutiny, the British 52nd Regiment of Foot (Oxfordshire Light Infantry) had been dressed in the normal summer uniform – white drill jackets, trousers, and forage cap covers. Upon being ordered on 25 May to join the Punjab Movable Column marching to recapture Delhi, its commander, George Campbell, decided to dye the summer uniforms khaki. The colour proved so popular that the men themselves dyed their flannel shirts. A bugler serving in the 52nd at the time remembered its appearance.

> Instead of the jacket, nearly all wore the loose flannel shirt outside the trousers with waist turban and belts outside. Our head-dress consisted of the old forage-cap, with khaki cover... The ... shoulder-belt plates for rank and file were abolished during the latter part of, or immediately after, the Crimean War, but we retained them until after the Mutiny ... Many of our men used in 1857 a common lemonade bottle, leather covered, and a strap over the shoulder ... The khaki curtains to the cap-cover were quilted... In the khaki clothing the N.C.Os. were distinguished only by the chevrons worn on both arms; these were of white worsted lace on buff cloth, fastened on by small hooks and eyes. Officers had no distinction whatever in their dress, only their small gilt buttons (Sumner 1941).

Colonel Campbell of the 52nd later observed that a motive in adopting khaki was that a white uniform proved difficult to keep clean and the time taken to clean trousers meant that five pairs of white trousers were required whereas two pairs of khaki trousers were sufficient (Whitehorne 1936: 181).

As the 52nd were dyeing their uniforms before leaving Sialkot to join the British forces at Delhi, the 61st Foot (South Gloucestershire) lost their regimental silver in the Officers' Mess at Ferozepore when three Native battalions mutinied and burned the Mess to the ground (Asquith 1998:39). Prior to marching to confront the mutinous battalions at Delhi, they dyed their white uniforms 'a sort of bluish brown called out here "karky"' (Fosten 1969: 15). Like the 52nd Light Infantry, the 61st Foot claims to be the first British unit to adopt khaki (Asquith 1998: 39). Whitehorne (1936) gives honours to both, saying the two 'simultaneously adopted khaki in the Mutiny'.

## Khaki

So many British regiments adopted khaki during the mutiny that the claim to priority of the 74th Highlanders is often ignored, although six years earlier they had fought in the 8th Kaffir War in South Africa in drab (resembling khaki) smock-frocks (sometimes referred to as 'Holland boat coats' because they were issued to wear on board ship to save wear and tear on the regular uniform) rather than their scarlet coatees. They continued to wear their trews of Mackenzie tartan and a dark-blue peaked forage cap with a red, white and black diced band (Barthorp 1982: 77–8). Mollo (1972: 211) credits this as the first time a regular British regiment wore khaki.

According to an officer of the Bengal Engineers present at the siege of Delhi, the British force 'contained a strange mixture of uniforms and faces, which showed the motley nature of the force that had been scraped together in this desperate crisis of the Empire'. He noted that most of the European regiments 'had dyed their coatees [meaning jackets or shirts?] the well-known khakee (or dust colour)'. He describes this as 'a sort of a grey drab, varying very much in tint'. While Coke's 1st Punjab Infantry and the Sirmoor Battalion (later 2nd Goorkhas) wore rifle green, 'almost every other regiment (cavalry, artillery and infantry), Native and European, turned out in the aforesaid khakee, but it was of so many different shades – puce colour, slate colour, drab, &c. – that a delightful variety was exhibited... I am quite sure no two men were dressed alike in the whole camp' (quoted by Steele 1958).

At about the same time that many of the troops attacking Delhi were dressing in khaki, a column of the 70th Regiment of Foot marched to Mardan to attack the mutinous 55th Bengal Infantry. They are reported to have used mud to stain their white summer uniforms as they were particularly worried that white uniforms would reveal their position on moonlit nights (Shandy 1937: 59).

The 3rd Bombay Europeans, a regiment in the employ of the Honourable East India Company, were part of Sir Hugh Rose's campaign in Central India. Dressed red like the other soldiers on the expedition, they obtained sufficient stone-coloured cotton to make both trousers and blouses for themselves, and dyed their puggrees[2] a similar colour. At least one author finds it 'tempting to believe that the 3rd Europeans were the first British regiment ever to fight in khaki' although 'it is possible and even probable that the inspiration came from the uniform of the Guides' (Hill 1936: 151). After the Indian Mutiny, the 3rd Bombay Europeans became part of the British Army as 109th Foot, later the 2nd Battalion, the Prince of Wales's Leinster Regiment, an Irish regiment disbanded upon the creation of the Republic of Ireland in 1922 (Barthorp 1982: 151).

Many other British regulars wore khaki during the Mutiny, including the King's 8th, the 13th Foot (Somerset Light Infantry), the 29th Foot, the 32nd

Foot (Duke of Cornwall's Light Infantry), the 35th Foot (Royal Sussex), the 75th Foot and the 91st Foot (see Norman 1972a; Fosten 1969; Barthorp 1982). The 71st (Highland Light Infantry) on leaving Bombay dyed their uniforms with curry powder! It was in khaki that the 93rd Foot (Sutherland Highlanders) won seven Victoria Crosses in twenty-four hours at Lucknow. Their 'brown holland tunics' were essentially khaki in tone, with red collars and cuffs. Kilts, sporrans, diced hose and white gaiters were worn along with the feather bonnet. In a concession to the climate, this last had its lining removed and was equipped with a quilted movable peak for protection from the sun (Barthorp 1982: 87–8; Wilkinson-Latham 1977: 38–9). Other cases of the wearing of khaki by British infantry on campaign in the Indian Mutiny have in all likelihood occurred but have failed to have received documentation in the historical record.

Several regiments of regular British cavalry also saw service in India during the Mutiny. Some failed to appreciate the advantages of khaki. Two Dragoon Guard regiments fought in brass helmets and coats or jackets of regimental colour: red for the 2nd (the Queen's Bays) and blue for the 6th (the Carabiniers). Contemporary observers were critical. 'The poor Carabiniers looked dreadfully heavy and oppressed in their blue clothing and overalls.' 'There are the Queen's Bays, who look, in their scarlet coats, as if they had come out for the express purpose of catching the rays of the sun' (Fosten 1969, Part I: 15). Exposed to the sun, the helmets became so hot they blistered the skin of any body part that came into contact with them. Some of the Bays created make-shift covers for their helmets from 'filthy "chuders" taken from drovers' (Fosten 1969, Part I: 15) while in the latter portions of the campaigns the 6th Dragoon Guards adopted the forage cap with a white cover (Barthorp 1988: 44).

Other cavalry were more sensibly clad. The 3rd Light Dragoons wore both coat and trousers of khaki (Fosten 1969, Part I: 15). Troopers of the 7th Hussars wore khaki coats over dark blue booted overalls with khaki puggaree bound about their peakless forage caps (Barthorp 1988: 38). Although the 17th Lancers originally wore their blue *kurtkas*, with the lapels buttoned over to conceal the white plastron front, they eventually adopted khaki jackets which were piped blue along the seams of the sleeves and back in lancer style (Fosten 1969, Part I: 17). The 9th Lancers were notable among the forces before Delhi in that they did not dye their hot weather dress khaki but rather continued to dress in white stable jackets, trousers and forage caps (Wilkinson-Latham 1977: 34).

Indian troops played a large role in defending besieged garrisons against mutineers and restoring British rule. At the start of the siege of the Residency of Lucknow, 45 per cent of its defenders were Indians; when Henry Havelock fought his way through to reinforce the garrison on 25 September 1857, the defenders had been reduced from 1,692 men to 979. Fifty-one per cent of the garrison's losses were sustained by the Indians (Mason 1976: 302).

Of the Bombay Army, only portions of the 26th and 27th regiments joined the mutiny. All of the Madras Army remained loyal to their employers. Interestingly, in the Punjab, the Sikhs who just ten years before had been fighting the British in what is known as the 2nd Sikh War, not only refused to mutiny but flocked to the British colours as new regiments were raised. Pertinent to this study is the fact that almost universally these units raised in the Punjab, both the regular Punjab infantry and the irregular Sikh infantry, wore khaki. Khaki was less popular in the cavalry. The 1st Punjab Cavalry wore dark blue and the 2nd Punjab Cavalry (Probyn's Horse) began the war in scarlet tunics (Wilkinson-Latham 1977: 22–6) although they later wore 'whitey-brown "khaki"' with blue turbans (Norman 1972a, Part II: 4). An irregular unit of mounted Sikhs, Hodson's Horse, initially wore white, then, for winter wear in 1857, were issued dark blue quilted coats and khaki 'pyjamas' or baggy trousers. The following summer they turned out in khaki faced red with red turbans (Norman 1972a, Part II: 4).

The full dress of the Honourable East India Company's Horse Artillery was certainly one of the most magnificent uniforms in the history of the British Empire. It consisted of a dark blue dolman, heavily laced in gold, with red collar and cuffs, light blue overalls, and a Romanesque helmet, resembling that worn by French cuirassiers, with a crimson horsehair plume flowing behind and a band of leopard skin about the base. However, the gunners were not long in the lines before Delhi when this was changed to a khaki jacket and trousers and a forage cap with a quilted khaki cover (Fosten 1969, Part II: 17; Barthorp 1988: 44).

## After the Mutiny

Following the Mutiny, the Crown replaced John Company in the administration of India and the control of its armies. The European regiments that had been in the service of the Honourable East India Company were incorporated in the regular British Army, not without objection from some of their personnel. The armies of the three Presidencies, each with its own numbering system, continued in existence until the Kitchener reforms of 1903, but major reorganizations with changes in regimental designation, confuse the nonspecialist attempting to trace a regiment's lineage backwards or forward in time.

The army of the Bengal Presidency underwent the most radical reorganization following the Mutiny. Since all the 'regular' cavalry had rebelled, their place was taken by formerly 'irregular' cavalry who had remained loyal. For example, the irregular squadrons brought into the British service by Lt James Skinner in 1803 became the 1st Bengal Cavalry (later the 1st Bengal Lancers) also known as Skinner's Horse. Thus, many regiments of the Bengal cavalry bore the names of the subalterns who originally raised them as irregular horse. Eventually there were nineteen regiments of Bengal Cavalry.

Those infantry regiments that did not mutiny continued in service, but were renumbered in order of their seniority. Thus the 21st became the 1st Bengal Native Infantry, the twenty regiments senior to it having participated in the Mutiny and the 31st became the 2nd Bengal Native Infantry. New battalions were also raised, so that by 1861 there were forty-four regiments of Bengal Native Infantry, and four regiments of Gurkhas included on the Infantry establishment of the Presidency. The Punjab Frontier Force (the 'Piffers') remained separate, with four regiments of Sikhs, six of Punjabis, one of Gurkhas, and the infantry component of the Guides. The infantry of Madras and Bombay remained much as they were prior to the Mutiny as was also the case of the units of the Hyderabad Contingent. In 1903 Kitchener instituted a major reorganization of the Indian Army, uniting the armies of the three Presidencies under one command and providing a common numbering system, except for the Gurkhas who were numbered separately (see Barthorp 1979).

This post-Mutiny infantry became more Indian in appearance, and as time went on the Army as a whole came to resemble Lumsden's Guides and other irregular forces raised in the Punjab at the time of the Mutiny. Turbans were authorized for wear by sepoys throughout the army in 1860. Clothing became looser, and 'Zouave' in style (see Chapter 6 above). This Indianization included the adoption of khaki as both service dress for most and as full dress for some (Plate 31), and khaki also increasingly became the working dress of the British troops stationed on the subcontinent.

Khaki, however, was not always accepted with great enthusiasm by British troops sent to India, or so at least one story goes. It has been claimed 'the new-fangled uniform positively drove the men of one regiment to drink' for they were so ashamed by the appearance of their white drill uniforms dyed khaki in the local bazaar that they refused to leave their barracks. Instead they took refuge in the regimental canteen leading to 'an alarming increase in drunkenness' (Hills 1936: 251). It is hard to conceive of an increase in drunkenness, however, given the importance of alcohol consumption in the culture of the Victorian soldier (Farwell 1981: 209–15).

**Plate 1.** A Hungarian hussar identified by Haswell Miller and Dawnay as the Regiment Karoly of the Austrian army. They attribute the unsigned painting to David Morier and feel he produced it while in Flanders in 1748–49 (Haswell Miller and Dawnay 1966–70, Volume 1: Plate 115; Volume 2: 20, 26). This identification is accepted by Haythornthwaite (1994: 38, 44) although he notes earlier and later descriptions of the regiment describe its dress as light blue rather than the green shown by Morier (see Table 2 in which the regiment is listed under the name of a new commander, Pàlffy). The colback is brown fur with a scarlet bag and cords and ornamented with a sprig of leaves. The dolman, pelisse and breeches are green laced red. The barrel sash is red and green. The pelisse, worn suspended over the back rather than the left shoulder, has brown fur. Boots are tan. The shabracque is dark green trimmed red with the arms of Hungary on the portion covering the pistol holsters. The Royal Collection © Her Majesty the Queen.

**Plate 2.** A second of David Morier's paintings of Austrian Hussars now in the Royal Collection. Haswell Miller and Dawnay (1966–70, Volume 1: Plate 119; Volume 2: 26) feel this may represent either the Beleznay Regiment (Bethlén on Table 2) or the Ghilany Regiment (Hadik on Table 2). This painting illustrates the wearing of the winged cap or mirliton. This is completely black in Morier's painting. Like the colback in Plate 1, the headdress is decorated with green foliage. The dolman is green laced yellow as is the pelisse which has brown fur. The breeches are scarlet and boots are tan. The shabracque is red trimmed yellow. The Royal Collection © Her Majesty the Queen.

**Plate 3.** A 'classic' hussar uniform – an officer of the 5th Hussars of France in the 1st Empire. The basic colours of the uniform are provided in Table 4. The black fur colback has a red plume and bag trimmed gold. The barrel sash is crimson with gold barrels. From *The Military Costume of Europe* (London: John Booth, 1822). Courtesy Anne S. K. Brown Collection, John Hay Library, Brown University, Providence, Rhode Island.

**Plate 4.** A 'Huzzar' of the Queen's Rangers and a light infantryman from the same unit, 1781. Water colour by Captain James Murray. These loyalists under the command of John Simcoe fought against American rebels during the American Revolution. The Huzzar wears a black colback or shako (it is not clear which it is) with a white metal crescent badge and a green bag tipped with a white tassel. Both jacket and breeches are dark green. The sabre scabbard is supported by a black belt over the right shoulder. The jacket is open to reveal the ruffle of a white shirt and a black cravat tied about the neck. The saddle cloth is dark green with white crescents and a pistol holster covered with black fur is attached to the front left of the saddle. There may be a matching holster on the right. He wears short black boots or shoes with black gaiters. The light infantryman wears a black felt or leather light infantry cap ornamented with white and green feathers and with a crescent badge on the front. He has a waist-length green jacket with white shoulder straps and wings (shoulder ornaments worn by grenadiers and light infantry as well as by musicians) and white trousers tucked into black gaiters. Courtesy John Ross Robertson Collection, Toronto Reference Library.

**Plate 5.** A dismounted Java Hussar with (left) the Governor General's Bodyguard and (centre) a sowar (native cavalryman) of the Bengal Native Cavalry, 1815. All three sowars wear hussar dolmans, but that of the Java Hussars is the same dark blue as the dolmans of the regular British cavalry. Collar and cuffs are red and the dolman is laced with white cording. The overalls are white and the turban headdress, cloth over a wicker frame, is red with white trim. The Bengal Native Cavalryman wears a French grey dolman laced white with orange collar and cuffs, has white breeches tucked into high boots and a blue turban with a brass ornament on top and white trim. The Governor General's Bodyguard is dressed like the Madras sowar except that his dolman is red laced white with dark blue collar and cuffs. The Governor General's Bodyguard earned 'Java' as a battle honour for their action there against the Dutch (Wilson 1970: 21). Print by C. Hamilton Smith. Courtesy of the Director, National Army Museum, London.

**Plate 6.** The 1st Life Guard Regiment of Hussars, Germany, c. 1900. This illustrates the hussar tunic and lacing adopted by Germany, Britain and other armies in the second half of the nineteenth century. Similar tunics were worn by many units in other branches also. These hussars wear a black tunic with white collar and lace (silver lace for officers) and dark blue breeches. The colback has a red bag, a black and white plume, a white and black cockade (for Prussia) and a death's head badge. The black tunic and the death's head badge date back to the hussars of Frederick the Great. From Siegel 1900. Courtesy the Toronto Reference Library.

**Plate 7.** A trooper of the *Régiment de dromadaire* in a hussar dolman and hussar breeches. These troops were part of the French force fighting in Egypt in 1800. The dolman is sky blue laced white with a red collar and shoulder straps. The hussar breeches are scarlet. In this illustration the trooper is wearing a black bicorne with a white plume. Other sources state the regiment also wore a shako, initially red and then replaced by one black in colour. From *The Military Costume of Europe* (London: John Booth, 1822). Courtesy Anne S. K. Brown Collection, John Hay Library, Brown University, Providence, Rhode Island.

**Plate 8.** A British officer of the 3rd Punjab Cavalry, ca. 1900. The tunic closes with hooks and eyes and five loose loops of cording pass over the chest fastening to toggles or olivets at each end. As can be seen these also pass over the pouch belt. This regiment wore blue tunics with red facings and gold lace. The loops were black. Courtesy of the Director, National Army Museum, London.

**Plate 9.** A uhlan (right) with an infantryman (left) and dragoon of the Austrian army in the late Napoleonic era. While the uhlan is identified as belonging to the regiment of Count Schwarzenberg, that regiment in fact wore a *czapka* with a green top. It was the Archduke Carl Regiment which wore the red-topped *czapka* (Knötel et al. 1937: 281; Haythornthwaite 1986: 36). The four regiments of uhlans were distinguished by the colours of the tops of the *czapka*. The *czapka* is the model adopted in 1801 to replace the original *konfederatka* (for the form of this latter headdress see the image of the 'Hulans britanniques', Plate 11 below). Otherwise they wore the same basic uniform - a dark green *kurtka* with red collar, cuffs and piping. The garment also had red lapels that could be folded back to form a plastron, or buttoned across for the double-breasted effect shown here. Dark green overalls with a red stripe and short black boots were also worn. The red piping on the front of the overalls is not supported by other authorities, nor is the quartered lance pennon. Austrian lancers are usually illustrated carrying a lance pennon with a broad black top, a narrow yellow stripe, a narrow black stripe and a broad yellow bottom. The Infantryman wears the white Austrian uniform with red collar, cuffs and turnbacks while the dragoon wears a similar uniform with blue facings. Print published 1822 by T. Goddard and J. Booth, London. Author's collection.

**Plate 10.** Dutch Lancer of the Imperial Guard, France, 1811. This splendid image is after a painting by General Baron Louis-François Lejeune, a staff officer who reached the rank of major-general in Napoleon's army. The lancer here wears the red *kurtka* with blue plastron, collar, cuffs and piping. The yellow aiguillette (the cords on the left shoulder) mark him as a member of Napoleon's Guard. His tight red pantaloons have two blue stripes. Especially well-illustrated is the *czapka* with its black leather base and peak, red cloth top edged yellow with yellow cords and its classic sunburst brass plate (compare it to the British *czapka* from later in the century, Plate 12). This illustration was originally published by *Carnet de la Sabretache* in 1904. Courtesy Anne S. K. Brown Military Collection, John Hay Library, Brown University, Providence, Rhode Island.

**Plate 11.** *Hulans britanniques*. Raised in 1793; disbanded 1796. This émigré cavalryman wears a white *czapka* piped yellow with a black fur base, a red coat laced yellow and green breeches also laced yellow. The Lance pennon is quartered red and yellow. Courtesy Anne S. K. Brown Military Collection, John Hay Library, Brown University, Providence, Rhode Island.

**Plate 12.** A British lancer officer as depicted in Major Seccombe's *Army and Navy Drolleries* (London: Frederick Warne, 1875). The source does not identify the regiment, but the scarlet plastron and cock's feather plume indicate his membership in the 12th (Prince of Wales's Royal) Lancers. Clearly shown in the caricature are the *czapka* with its scarlet top, the plastron and lancer girdle. The officer wears a blue tunic and his trousers have a double stripe in gold lace. Note the extensive cording from the *czapka* draped about the body. Author's collection.

**Plate 13.** German uhlans marched off to the Great War wearing their *czapkas*. This photograph is identified as a patrol in Belgium and the two dismounted uhlans in the foreground seem to have confiscated a local dog cart. From *Nelson's Portfolio of War Pictures*, Part 3, London: Thomas Nelson & Sons, 1914. Author's collection.

**Plate 14.** Cossacks as depicted by John Augustus Atkinson. Atkinson was in Russia from 1784 to 1802 where he received the patronage of Catherine II and where he collaborated with his uncle James Walker to produce *Picturesque Representation of the Russians* published in London in 1803–4 (Lachouque 1961: 522). Haswell Miller and Dawnay (1966–70, Volume 2: 52) comment: 'Atkinson was not essentially a military artist and had no special interest in drawing the details of uniform accurately, but his characterisation of the soldier on parade or at work combined with sensitive and artistic excellence, make his military work an important contribution to the history of the army of the time.' The Cossacks here wear blue jackets with red collars, pale blue full trousers with red stripes and fur caps with a white plume and a red cloth top. There seems to be a red sash about the waist and the serrated edge of a white undergarment appears below this. Noteworthy are the ponies serving as mounts. The dismounted figure at the left wears a blue great coat also with a red collar. His cartridge box is black (as is the pouch belt) and bears the cypher 'A' for Tsar Alexander. Author's collection.

Plate 15. Lasalle accepts the surrender of the fortress of Stettin, 30 October 1806. A drawing attributed to Horace Vernet. One can contrast the voluminous Cossack-style overalls of General le Comte de Lasalle with the tight breeches of the Prussian officer and the Hussar on the left. Courtesy Anne S. K. Brown Military Collection, John Hay Library, Brown University, Providence, Rhode Island.

Plate 16. A German print depicting Highland Scots (identified in the print as *Irlander*) in the service of Swedish King Gustavus Adolphus in 1631. All wear the Scots bonnet and the two on the right exhibit a reasonable depiction of the belted plaid. By permission of the British Library, shelfmark 1750.b.29.

**Plate 17.** The 43rd or Highland Regiment of Foot, from *A Representation of the Cloathing of His Majesty's Houshold and of all the Forces upon the Establishments of Great Britain and Ireland*, 1742. The regiment was renumbered the 42nd Foot in 1751, became the Royal Highland Regiment seven years later and since 1881 has born the title The Black Watch (Royal Highlanders). The artist has found the tartan and the diced hose too complex to deal with but has accurately reflected the bulkiness of the belted plaid gathered about the hips. The soldier is armed with a Brown Bess musket, a Highland basket-hilted sword and a dirk. The sword is suspended from a black belt over the left shoulder. The red waistcoat and coat are both collarless with the coat having buff slashed cuffs. Buttonholes have narrow white piping. A peculiar buff ammunition pouch is worn at the front of the waist. The bonnet is dark blue. By permission of the British Library, shelfmark 142.e.14.

**Plate 18.** Highlanders as part of the allied forces occupying Paris, 1816. By this time Highlander were wearing the 'little kilt' rather than the belted plaid. From the waist to the neck their dress was basically no different from that of any other British infantry, but like all other infantry, the coat exhibited regimental distinctions in facing colours and lace. The now elaborately feathered bonnet was a distinction of kilted regiments. The print suggests that the kilt made an impression upon the ladies of Paris. One can perhaps read too much into such an image, but the working-class French woman on the left appears much less happy with the encounter than her sisters, higher in the social hierarchy, on the right. Courtesy Anne S. K. Brown Military Collection, John Hay Library, Brown University, Providence, Rhode Island..

**Plate 19.** A soldier, piper and officer of Princess Louise's Argyll and Sutherland Highlanders. These represent the final stage in the evolution of the full-dress Highland uniform with the feather bonnet, doublet, little kilt, sporran, diced hose and gaiters. The red doublets have yellow collar and cuffs and the tartan is the Sutherland, a somewhat lighter variant of the government or Black Watch tartan. The piper wears a dark green doublet and a glengarry rather than the feather bonnet. Both the piper and the officer wear a plaid, the officer's being the simple fly plaid. The Officer's badger skin sporran is a regimental distinction. From a painting by Richard Simkin originally published as a supplement to *Army and Navy Gazette*, 4 July 1896. Courtesy the Toronto Reference Library, Toronto, Ontario.

**Plate 20.** In 1881 the regiments of Lowland Scots, who had worn the dress of ordinary British infantry for more than two centuries, were put into a pseudo-Highland garb with doublets and tartan trousers, which have come to be known as trews. Richard Simkin painted this representation of the dress of the Cameronians (Scottish Rifles) in 1882. The first battalion of the regiment was the old 26th Foot; the second battalion was the 90th Foot. Neither was a rifle regiment prior to the reforms of 1881, so they gave up their scarlet tunics for rifle green doublets. Later the rifle-green home service helmet was replaced by a shako and the government (or Black Watch) tartan trews were changed to the Douglas tartan. By 1914 the pipers of the regiment were wearing kilts and the glengarry bonnet, rather than trews and tam-o'-shanter shown here. From a postcard published by The Cameronians (Scottish Rifles), Hamilton, Scotland. Author's collection.

**Plate 21.** Detail of *The Conquerors* by Eric Henry Kennington. Depicted are men of the 16th Battalion, 1st Division, Canadian Expeditionary Force, in France during World War I. Of particular note is the obvious varied ethnic origins of these 'Highlanders'. The battalion, which bore the title 'Canadian Scottish', was raised in British Columbia. They wear kilts of the Mackenzie tartan. Curiously, the artist has failed to depict the kilt apron. Courtesy the Canadian War Museum, catalogue number 8968, copyright the Canadian War Museum.

**Plate 22.** Drummer and Piper, 1st Battalion, 8th Gurkha Rifles, 1914. Detail from a watercolour by Richard Simkin. They both wear the black Kilmarnock bonnet with a red tourie and the rifle green trousers and dark puttees of regiment's review order, but they also wear rifle green Highland doublets piped white. In addition to the Inverness skirts, the doublet exhibits the wings found on the doublets of pipers in Scots regiments. Courtesy of the Director, National Army Museum, London.

**Plate 23.** Captain of Mameluks of the Guard, France, during the Consulate or early Empire. Coloured engraving by Nicholaus Hoffmann. The Mameluk wears an orange jacket with half sleeves over a green, sleeved waistcoat. A pair of pistols are tucked into the white and gold sash about the waist. The baggy trousers are magenta as is the pistol holster on the saddle; the saddle cloth and bridle are bright blue trimmed gold. The turban is white flecked with gold and the red shako also is flecked with gold. The plume is white. The jacket is unusual with its half sleeves; Mameluks are usually depicted with a sleeveless over-jacket open to reveal the waistcoat. Courtesy Anne S. K. Brown Military Collection, John Hay Library, Brown University, Providence, Rhode Island.

**Plate 24.** *Zouaves in Camp.* Water colour by Carl Goebel, c. 1865. This camp scene shows the French Zouave uniform to advantage. All wear the short jacket with the red trim and the *tombeaux* on the front. Two of the seated figures are dressed for parade with their scarlet full dress trousers (*serouel*) and turbans wound about the *chechia* or fez. The third wears campaign dress with the white *serouel* worn for summer campaigns and the simple *chechia* without the turban. Courtesy the Anne S. K. Brown Military Collection, John Hay Library, Brown University, Providence, Rhode Island.

**Plate 25.** The United States Zouave Cadets, 1860. This is the unit, formed by Elmer Ellsworth in Chicago, which toured the eastern United States prior to the outbreak of the Civil War. The uniform deviated from the Zouave original, notably in the red trousers which, while baggy, are not the true *serouel* of the Zouave. The cut of the jacket is similar to that of the French Zouaves but it lacks the ornamental *tombeaux* and has added the ornamental ball or bullet buttons. A red kepi with a dark blue band is worn instead of the Algerian fez. The sash is red; the shirt under the jacket is pale blue. Originally published in *Frank Leslie's Illustrated Newspaper*. From Johnson, Lee, Ridpath, Morgan and Kilmer 1895, p. 40. Courtesy Dora Hood Rare Book Room, Dana Porter Library, University of Waterloo, Waterloo, Ontario.

**Plate 26.** Elmer Ellsworth raised the 11th New York Volunteer Infantry, also known as the 1st New York Fire Zouaves, to serve the Union cause at the start of the Civil War. New York City firemen provided the recruits. This member of the regiment photographed in 1861 wears a grey jacket and trousers. The jacket, trimmed in blue and red, has brass ball or bullet buttons. Pinned to the left side of his jacket is the badge of his fire company. Underneath his jacket he wears his red fireman's shirt, with its collar exposed. The kepi is red with a blue band. The 'A' on the front of the kepi designates his company and below that is '1Z' for 1st Zouaves. The leggings are light brown. He seems to have borrowed a musket with a sword bayonet attached for the photograph since his own bayonet is at his side in its scabbard. The black crepe tied to his left arm is probably in mourning for the death of Ellsworth. Courtesy United States National Archives, Still Pictures Branch, (NWDNS-111-B-6343).

**Plate 27.** This wounded Zouave from the American Civil War wears a uniform very similar to the French original. This is most noticeable in the cut of the trousers which in fact are a true *serouel*. Courtesy United States National Archives, Still Pictures Branch (NWDNS-111-B-250).

**Plate 28.** In the French army, military units had attached to them *vivandière* who wore a feminine variant of the unit's uniform. Some American Zouaves copied this practice, including the 114th Pennsylvania. Their *vivandière*, Mary Tippee (also known as Mary Tobee), is shown here in her Zouave uniform with her keg of brandy. Her Zouave jacket is decorated with ball buttons and also exhibits the *tombeaux*. The sash and cuffs are light blue; the rest of the uniform is dark blue trimmed with red. Courtesy United States National Archives, Still Pictures Branch (NWDNS-79-T-2148).

**Plate 29.** A rather racist interpretation of the Zouave dress of the West India Regiment. To be fair, Major Seccombe who produced this image presents equally unflattering portraits of British officers and men in the other plates that illustrate his *Army and Navy Drolleries* (London: Frederick Warne, 1875). The uniform is for the most part correct except that the red jacket laced yellow should be sleeveless revealing the white sleeves and red cuffs laced yellow of the under jacket. The error may lie with the colourist of the plate since the lines of the illustration suggest the sleeveless Zouave jacket. Author's collection.

**Plate 30.** Regimental Sergeant Major, Gold Coast Regiment, c. 1930. Only the red fez and the red laced gold sleeveless Zouave jacket remain from what had been a more complete Zouave uniform at the turn of the century. Khaki shorts and puttees have replaced the baggy Zouave trousers formerly worn. No. 43 in a series of cigarette cards, *Military Uniforms of the British Empire Overseas*, issued by John Player and Sons. Author's collection.

**Plate 31.** Subadar-Major, 8th Punjab Regiment, Indian Army, c. 1930. This illustrates the use of khaki as full dress. The khaki puttees and the blue and white turban arise from the local area, as do the full trousers. The tunic, khaki with blue collar and cuffs, derives from the dress of the Hungarian hussar, with its drab braid, toggles and loops across the chest and decorative braid on the cuff. No. 21 in a series of cigarette cards, *Military Uniforms of the British Empire Overseas*, issued by John Player and Sons. Author's collection.

**Plate 32.** Officer, US Army in khaki uniform, c. 1905. The branch of service was indicated by brass collar badges. His sword, the gold cord on his slouch hat and the rank badges on his shoulder straps distinguish him as an officer; the leggings secured by buckles and straps also differ from the laced canvas leggings worn by enlisted men. Card issued by Recruit Little Cigars. Author's collection.

**Plate 33.** Detail of the *Death of General Wolfe* by Benjamin West. Painted in 1770, eleven years after the event. West was born in Pennsylvania but left to seek his fortune in Europe in 1760. His own testimony indicates he observed and interacted with American Indians; it is possible that he observed American irregulars, 'Rangers', serving in the British army during the Seven Years War. In his composition of officers and men watching their commander die he chose to include an American irregular shown here. He depicts the figure in a green coat and black light infantry cap. The latter is decorated with a band of porcupine quillwork. Indian deer hide leggings are worn over green breeches and deer hide moccasins decorated with quillwork provide footwear. A broad belt of Indian manufacture with a diamond pattern of glass beads and edging of the same is worn over the left shoulder. Robert Rogers, the famous American Ranger who was *not* at the battle of Quebec depicted in the *Death of General Wolfe*, was in London from 1769 to 1775 (Stacey 1979: 681) leaving open the intriguing possibility that he may have posed for, or advised Benjamin West relative to, the dress of the 'Ranger'. However, it is more likely that this image should be taken as a generalized representation from West's memory, since there is no evidence to suggest that West had models or documentary or iconographic information available on the dress of American irregulars at the time he did the painting including this depiction of the 'Ranger'. It is nevertheless an accurate statement of the wearing of items of Indian dress by soldiers on the American frontier in the eighteenth century. Courtesy the National Gallery of Canada, Ottawa, Ontario.

**Plate 34.** Purporting to represent the famous American Ranger, Major Robert Rogers, this print was published in London in 1776. However, similarities between this and the Ranger in Benjamin West's *Death of Wolfe* suggest it is of little value as independent evidence of the dress of soldiers on the American frontier. Courtesy of the John Ross Robertson Collection, Toronto Reference Library, Toronto, Ontario.

Plate 35. The uniform worn by Canadian hero Sir Isaac Brock when he was killed at the Battle of Queenston Heights, 13 October 1812, while leading troops opposing an American invasion of Upper Canada. Noteworthy is the finger-woven sash, which was probably the one that, according to legend, the Shawnee chief Tecumseh presented to Brock in exchange for Brock's British officer's sash of crimson silk. Courtesy the Canadian War Museum, Ottawa, Ontario.

**Plate 36.** This American supporter of the Continental Congress wears a fringed hunting shirt in this print published in 1776 by Johann Martin Will of Augsburg, possibly based on a sketch by a Bavarian officer in the British army (Windrow and Embleton 1973: 27). The hunting shirt probably derives from the smock worn by farmers and labourers ornamented with fringes derived from American Indian styles. A characteristic feature is the fringed cape covering the shoulders. It could be made of leather, but the example here is probably made of white linen. Courtesy Anne S. K. Brown Military Collection, John Hay Library, Brown University, Providence, Rhode Island.

**Plate 37.** The Seneca orator Red Jacket (1750[?]–1830) in a fringed hunting shirt as portrayed late in his life (in 1826) by Robert Walter Weir. A product of the frontier, the hunting shirt was popular among both Indians and non-Indians. Red Jacket, a veteran of both the American Revolution and the War of 1812, has a finger-woven sash tied about his waist. He wears the very large 'peace medal' presented to him by US President George Washington in 1792. Courtesy of the Dana Porter Arts Library, University of Waterloo, Waterloo, Ontario.

**Plate 38.** The Mohawk chief Joseph Brant (Thayendanegea) wears a feather headdress of the 'tiara style' (see Einhorn and Abler 1996: 50–1) popular in the latter portion of the eighteenth century in Northeastern North America. This, one of many portraits of the prominent Mohawk leader, is by Benjamin Gilbert, painted in London in 1786. This elaborate use of feathers seems to provide a model for the extensive use of feathers to decorate the bonnets of Scots Highlanders serving on the frontiers of North America. Brant also wears numerous silver brooches on his headband and shirt and a shell gorget with two silver studs on his chest. Courtesy the New York Historical Association, Cooperstown, New York.

Plate 39. The evolution of the Highland bonnet. On the left is a conservative reconstruction of the appearance of the bonnet of Highlanders on their return to Great Britain after service in North America. Some documentary sources suggest more elaborate and extensive use of feathers. In the centre is the bonnet as worn in the Napoleonic Wars and at Waterloo (see also Plate 18 above). The feathers completely cover the cloth portion of the bonnet above the band. On the left is the final form, still worn today, with the feathers covering all but the bottom row of dicing of the bonnet and with a number of feather 'tails' (the number specific to each regiment) falling to the right of the bonnet. Nos. 6, 10 and 46 of a series of cigarette cards, *Military Head-Dress*, issued by John Player & Sons. Author's collection.

**Plate 40.** Detail of a drawing of the Battle of the Little Big Horn, 25 June 1876, by a Sioux leader in that battle, Kicking Bear. The body of George Armstrong Custer lies surrounded by some of his men. Kicking Bear correctly depicts Custer in the fringed deer hide garments he wore in the battle, but the Sioux name for Custer ('Long Hair') may have influenced his decision to depict Custer with his more usual long tresses rather than with the short haircut he is reported to have had before departing on the 1876 campaign. Courtesy the Southwest Museum, Los Angeles, California, Photo # N.30455 (1026.G.1).

*Khaki*

## Advances in Military Technology

One must put the diffusion of khaki from the north-west frontier of India to armies around the world in the context of changes being made in military technology, which greatly increased the value of camouflage (or at least less visible) clothing. The change in military technology in the nineteenth century was far more revolutionary for the average soldier than any changes or innovations in military technology have been in the twentieth. At the beginning of the nineteenth century the British infantryman was using basically the same weapon (the Brown Bess musket) that his great-grandfather or great-great-grandfather had used a century earlier at Blenheim under Marlborough; by the end of the nineteenth century the British infantryman was using basically the same weapon (the Lee-Enfield) that his grandson or great-grandson would use a half-century later on the beaches of Normandy against the forces of Adolf Hitler.

Four important changes were made to the smoothbore, muzzle-loading, single-shot flintlock that had been the standard weapon of the infantryman in the eighteenth century. Each made the life of the infantryman easier, but also made combat much more dangerous as his enemy had similar arms. First, a percussion cap proved much more reliable than the flint and steel mechanism had been for firing the weapon. Since arms did not misfire as often, the density of a volley aimed at one's position increased. Second, a solution was found to the problems with rifled barrels. It had long been known that rifled barrels, which spin the projectile after the weapon is fired, were more accurate than smoothbores. However, because the bullet must fit tightly in a rifled barrel, rifles were slow to load (in Wellington's day British riflemen were issued with a mallet to hit their ram rods to drive the bullet down the barrel). The invention of the Miné ball showed that the bullet could be made to expand to engage the rifling in the barrel upon firing, so the size of the bullet could be kept small enough for easy loading. In many ways war became more personal in that a soldier had to worry about someone aiming directly at him, whereas in the smoothbore era it had been a matter of chance whether a particular infantryman or the man standing next to him was hit. Both the percussion cap and the Miné ball had been invented and adopted for military use in time for full utilization in the American Civil War, which accounts, in large part, for the appalling loss of life in that conflict. The third change was the development of an effective breech-loading mechanism. This removed the necessity for an infantryman to stand to load his rifle by ramming bullet and charge down the muzzle. However, this had not been adopted at the time of the American Civil War, which also helps account for the appalling loss of life in that conflict. The fourth innovation or development was the magazine, which relieved the infantryman from reloading his rifle after every shot. Over the course of the nineteenth century these innovations made the battlefield a very dangerous place.[3]

The above sequence is somewhat simplified and distorted, for over this period large numbers of inventors were attempting to produce better military technology. Authorities were often reluctant to accept the new technologies, however. As has been stated, the American Civil War was fought with muzzle loaders although a bolt-action breech loader (the needle gun – named after its long firing pin) had been invented by Johann von Dreyse in 1837. This was adopted by the Prussian Army but rejected by both the British and French because the barrel tended to foul and the firing pin to break. It was also a smoothbore weapon, although it served the Prussian army well in its wars with Austria in 1866 and France in 1870. In this last conflict the French had a superior breech-loading rifle (the *chassepot*) which had been approved in 1866 but was not yet in general use in the army of the Second Empire. Captured *chassepots* were enthusiastically used by the Prussians as snipers' weapons. An early model of a magazine rifle was the American Lee box-magazine of 1879 and the French adopted the Lebel, a magazine rifle, in 1886. The invention of smokeless powder in 1887 eliminated the problem of the vision of troops being obscured by battlefield smoke and the range of rifles was extended by the use of the more powerful cordite, giving rifles greater range, invented by the Swede, Alfred Nobel (Young 1973: 73–7).

There were other notable advances in arms besides the musket/rifle of the infantryman. The machine gun was perfected in the latter portion of the nineteenth century. I believe, though, that estimates of its importance on the battlefields of the twentieth century rest on an underestimation of the importance of the magazine rifle. Artillery also became much more effective and developed the capacity to destroy distant enemy positions, out of the actual sight of the gunners.

## Red Coats in the Late Nineteenth Century

The British experience in suppressing the Indian Mutiny did not lead to a quick or wholesale adoption of khaki for general use, or even in combat conditions. An order, dated January 1860, for the Bombay Army noted that khaki was 'more adapted to field service in the hot season but the system of wearing it for all seasons of the year was slovenly and at variance with the proverbial and most correct appearance of officers and soldiers' (quoted in Carman 1969: 184). The 59th Foot did wear drab holland boat coats with red collar and cuffs on campaign in China in 1858, but two years later British troops continuing the fight in China were in red serge frocks (Barthorp 1988a: 24). However, they were accompanied by units from the newly reorganized Bengal Army, such as the 8th Punjab Infantry (later the 20th Brownlow's Punjabis) and the 15th Punjab Infantry (later the 23rd Sikh Pioneers) who fought in loose khaki blouses (Carman 1969: 113–5).

There was some recognition among the British general staff that red or scarlet was not the most practical of colours for waging war. The second and third Maori Wars in New Zealand (1860–1 and 1863–6) were fought by troops in dark blue smocks rather than the red serge usually worn as foreign service dress. The Ashanti War in West Africa, 1873–4, was fought by troops wearing uniforms of Elcho grey, and the Black Watch even abandoned their kilts, substituting trousers, but retained their distinctive red hackle in their tropical helmets (Barthorp 1988a: 33–8). The Sudan campaign of 1884–5 was fought by troops in grey serge, save those dispatched to the region from India who wore the khaki of the Raj (Barthorp 1988b: 44–5). An officer who served on the expedition said the only British troops wearing 'real khaki' was the 1st Battalion of the Royal Irish who had come to Egypt from India. He had journeyed from England to join this regiment on the Nile, but he was dressed in grey serge 'since khaki was unprocurable in England at that time, and it was not to be had in Egypt either' (Shandy 1937).

Elsewhere, red coats continued to be worn on campaign, as when red-coated British regulars and similarly clad Canadian militia beat back the Fenian (Irish nationalist) invasions of Canada from the United States in 1866 and 1870 (Ross and Tyler 1992). In 1863 in India, the 71st Foot wore tartan trews and a scarlet frock and the 101st Foot (an ex-Honourable East India Company regiment) also wore a scarlet serge frock on the Ambela campaign on the North-West frontier (Barthorp 1982: 89–90; 1988a: 45). While troops in the Abyssinian campaign of 1868 who had been serving in India and were mostly in a greyish khaki, both the 33rd Foot and the Royal Engineers wore red serge (Barthorp 1988a: 35, 46). The Afghan War of 1879 was fought in khaki frocks (frequently worn with dark blue home service trousers, kilts or trews) but 59th Foot fought in red serge in the initial stages of the war (Barthorp 1988a: 38). Although the forces in India led the way in the adoption of khaki, some units resisted the trend. Lord Birdwood noted of the 11th Bengal Lancers, 'we were one of the last regiments to adopt khaki – wearing blue through the Hazarq Operations of 1891 and only adopting the more usual khaki about 1895' (quoted in Carman 1961: 84).

Outside of India, the order of dress known as Home Service Dress prevailed. This consisted of a red or scarlet 'frock', somewhat less ornate than the full dress tunic. On 22 January 1879, some 858 British and 470 auxiliaries were killed by the victorious Zulu army at Isandlwana in South Africa (Morris 1982: 155). Most of the former were men of the 24th Foot who died wearing red serge frocks, for the Zulu War was fought in home service dress (scarlet coats and dark blue trousers) but with foreign service helmets dyed khaki (Fosten and Fosten 1989: 112–5). This is the same dress worn by the troops dispatched from England to campaign in Egypt in 1882, where Highlanders wore kilts except for the 2nd Battalion, Highland Light Infantry, and khaki was worn only by those troops who had been serving in India such as the Seaforth Highlanders. It had been decided to replace the Home Service Dress scarlet with grey serge but the 30,000 uniforms manufactured in Britain arrived only after the fighting ceased (Barthorp 1988b: 37–8). The suits of grey were used, however, in the Sudan, including the expedition up the Nile to relieve Gordon at Khartoum, and again troops who had been serving in India fought in khaki. A belief that the old red uniform carried a psychological impact on the battlefield led to its being worn in battle by the Royal Sussex at Khartoum and the Black Watch and the South Staffordshire Regiment at the battle of Kirbekan (Barthorp 1988b: 39–40). The superiority of khaki over grey was eventually recognized, and in February 1885, the Guards Brigade became the first troops to be issued khaki uniforms manufactured in Britain. Although the entire force sent south to counter a Mahdist invasion later that year was clad in khaki, they put on their red serge for the Battle of Ginniss (3 December 1885). A Captain of the 1st Yorkshire Regiment noted, 'it was thought the force would look more formidable to the Dervishes dressed in red than in khakee' (quoted in Barthorp 1988b: 41). This was the last battle fought by the British Army in red uniforms although the Royal Scots wore red serge frocks and government tartan trews in action in Zululand in 1888 (Barthorp 1988b: 45).

## The Puttee

Before outlining the spread of khaki to other armies in the world, mention should be made of one other Indian Army practice that spread to the regular British Army and thence to the rest of the world. This is the wearing of puttees. Inevitably the dust and mud of field conditions are hard on trouser cuffs. One solution is to tuck these into a boot, but this reduces the flexibility of the ankle. Another is to resort to gaiters made of leather or canvas to cover the calf, ankle and top of the shoe. Men on both sides of the American Civil War reached the simple if inelegant solution of tucking the bottoms of their trouser legs into their socks. The puttee is another solution to this problem. 'Puttee' is a word in Urdu meaning 'bandage' and the puttee is simply a long strip of cloth that is wound about the leg from the top of the footwear to mid-calf or slightly higher. Puttees were most often khaki, but were occasionally blue or black. The Scottish United Services Museum in Edinburgh Castle has puttees in the Prince Charles Edward Stuart tartan that were worn with trews of the same tartan by officers of the 72nd Highlanders in the Afghanistan campaign of 1879. Puttees were usually worn by the British Army in the last quarter of the nineteenth century on service in Asia and Africa, and in 1902 they officially became part of the new service dress. Britain and Turkey fielded the only two armies at the start of World War I to wear puttees, but after a year of war their use was nearly universal. The Japanese army continued to wear puttees through World War II.

## Khaki Becomes Universal

Khaki had finally earned its legitimacy with the British military establishment. In 1885 a khaki uniform became official for wear in India and in 1896 it was approved for wear at all foreign stations. Finally, in 1902 khaki became the colour of Service Dress generally in the British Army (Barthorp 1982: 106–9).

Other armies began to follow the example that had been taught to the British in India. The first three to adopt khaki for all their land forces were the United States, Japan and Imperial Russia. The United States had officially adopted khaki when it began the Spanish-American War in 1898, but most of the troops who invaded Cuba were in the old US Army blue. The infantry marched through Cuba in canvas leggings, light-blue kersey trousers, dark-blue flannel shirts and felt campaign hats (Rankin 1967: 52). When khaki reached the American forces in Cuba, it did not arrive as a complete uniform. A frequently seen combination consisted of the dark blue woollen shirt with khaki trousers (Pakula 1960: Plate XLVII). Perhaps the most famous, and certainly the most publicity-conscious, unit in the Spanish-American War was Theodore Roosevelt's 'Rough Riders', the 1st United States Volunteer Cavalry. Personally raised by Roosevelt, who had been an Assistant Secretary of the Navy (a political appointment) with ambitions to be President of the United States, the regiment fought the war on foot (their horses did not reach Cuba) in what was essentially a khaki garb. Roosevelt tried to obtain the new khaki uniform for his men, but for the most part they made do with the drab canvas stable dress of the regular US Cavalry (Todd 1954: Plate 25; Windrow and Embleton 1973: 127).

The initial khaki uniform of the US Army retained flashes of colour. The shoulder straps on the coat were the colour of the officer's or soldier's branch of service – white for infantry, yellow for cavalry, dark blue for staff and red for artillery. Chevrons marking the rank of non-commissioned officers were similarly coloured as were, in some instances, the flaps on the four patch pockets of the coat. This colour was also used for the cords ornamenting the khaki campaign hat of enlisted men; officers wore gold cords (Rankin 1967: 52–3).

The khaki was not greeted with enthusiasm by some in the United States military. One officer found it 'objectionable in every respect' and noted 'the original diversities of colour are multiplied with every washing.' In his opinion the uniform was 'fit neither for campaigning nor garrison purposes' (quoted in Mollo 1972: 222).

In 1902 the colour of service dress in the United States Army became officially 'olive drab' but remained within the wide spectrum of hues that have born the designation khaki (Plate 32). The branch of service colours continued on the cords on campaign hat for other ranks but disappeared elsewhere (Pakula 1960: Plates XVI, XVII). In 1912, the shape of the campaign hat, which had been creased fore-and-aft at the top, was changed to the 'Montana' style, with four indentations giving the hat the appearance of a mountain peak (Windrow and Embleton 1973: 128). This style of headdress had been in use among the North West Mounted Police in Canada since 1897 (Ross and May 1988: 43).

The United State Army wore khaki uniforms as part of the eight-nation force that suppressed the so-called Boxer Rebellion in China in 1900, ensuring continuing foreign domination of that formerly great empire. The United States Marines, however, fought in dark blue shirts, light blue trousers with khaki canvas leggings and a khaki campaign hat (Bodin 1979: 30). Khaki was worn by the only regular British regiment, the Royal Welch Fusiliers, which fought in this war, but there was a large khaki-clad contingent from the Indian Army participating, including infantry, cavalry and support troops. A locally raised unit, Her Majesty's 1st Chinese Regiment, wore khaki clothing with broad brimmed, flat-topped straw hats supplied by the Royal Navy (Bodin 1979: 28, 34). Germany sent marines, the Third Seebataillon, in khaki uniforms with a cork sun helmet, sometimes provided with a khaki cover (Bodin 1979: 31). A British war correspondent observing German troops in khaki with large white straw hats was left unimpressed, remarking that 'their clothing and hats seemed more adapted for suburban summer gardening in Germany than for war purposes' (quoted in Mollo 1972: 230). Italy's contribution was a battalion of *Bersaglieri*, light infantry noted for their rapid drill and the swathe of cock's feathers worn on the right side of their headgear, who arrived with a khaki summer uniform, but its poor quality caused them to revert to their blue uniforms. Both khaki and blue were worn with a white sun helmet ornamented with the black-green feather plume. The khaki cover for this helmet was designed so that the plume could still be worn (Bodin 1979: 34).

Japan furnished the largest number of troops to the allied forces suppressing the Boxer Rebellion, and these troops were clad in blue. By the Russo-Japanese War of 1904–5, however, the Japanese had provided their army with a khaki cotton summer uniform. Both khaki trousers and a khaki tunic, fastened with hooks and eyes rather than buttons, were worn. The blue service cap was provided with a khaki cover usually including a neck curtain. Most wore khaki leggings - although Kannik (1968: 229) says the leggings were white – but some adopted the Indian Army fashion (learned during the Boxer Rebellion?) of wearing puttees. Although most carried a dark blue overcoat rolled like a blanket roll over the left shoulder, a portion of their overcoats were also khaki (Johnson 1969). By the outbreak of the First World War, Japanese army service dress for both summer and winter was khaki and khaki puttees were standard (Funcken and Funcken 1970: 82–4).

In manoeuvres held in the summer of 1906, following the Russo-Japanese War, the Russian Army experimented with khaki uniforms and with Order No. 171 of 1907 instituted a khaki uniform. Officers wore a tunic and other ranks a shirt not unlike the *kurta* but considerably shorter than the item of Indian Army dress. It was pulled over the head and fastened at the front with five buttons. A peaked forage cap was worn with a cockade in the imperial colours of white, orange and black. For a short period of time, there was a version of the khaki tunic for other ranks and, although officially discontinued in 1912, some were still being worn in the initial stages of World War I (Mollo 1978: 164).

The German military establishment was reluctant to accept khaki as appropriate for wear in Europe (Mollo 1972: 228). It was only colonial troops whom Germany chose to dress in khaki. In Africa, khaki drill (in German *Braundrell*) competed with grey cord as the material of choice to be worn in the field. This represents the tendency (already noted in the spread of Zouave uniforms) of a European power to dress its own colonial troops in copies the colonial uniforms of other European powers. Germany in 1889 raised military units termed *Schutztruppen* for its African colonies. In South West Africa all personnel were German; in East Africa, the Cameroons and Togo other ranks and native officers were recruited from the local population. Khaki served as tropical dress for German officers and men. This uniform was piped in cornflower blue for South West Africa, white for East Africa and poppy red for the Cameroons and Togo. Native personnel also dressed in khaki and wore a low red fez with a black tassel and a white metal eagle badge. A 1914 photograph reveals that some German personnel in South West Africa also wore this headdress (Marrion 1970). It was in this khaki uniform with a khaki cover and neck curtain for the fez that these troops battled the British and South Africans for control of East Africa (see Miller 1974).

After considerable experimentation, the German Army adopted a light grey (*feldgrau*) for the regular army in 1910. Although as late as 1913 manoeuvres were still executed in a version of full dress, the entire German Army marched off to fight the Great War in uniforms of *feldgrau* with the spiked helmets (*pickelhaube*) of the infantry, the colbacks of the hussars, and the *czapkas* of the uhlans covered in *feldgrau* cloth (Mollo 1972: 230–1).

In 1914, both France and Belgium still dressed infantry for war primarily in dark blue. France had used khaki overseas, in West Africa, Madagascar and Indo-China, but the metropolitan army[4] resisted changing their uniform, which essentially was the same worn in the Franco-Prussian War of 1870-1 (Mollo 1972: 226). The French did make two concessions to modernity in providing their men with light-blue covers for their red kepis and light-blue overalls to cover their red trousers, although in the initial stages of the war red trousers were often seen in combat. Dragoons wore their dark-blue coats and red trousers into combat, but their gleaming helmets were provided with cloth covers of a variety of colours, including khaki. Similarly, the cuirassiers wore cloth covers on their helmets and cuirasses, the colour varying from regiment to regiment, but some, such as that of the 13th Cuirassiers, being khaki (Kannik 1968: 235; Mollo 1978: 187). Changes to the French uniform – including the adoption of the horizon blue, in April 1915, and the Adrian helmet – in response to conditions on the Western Front in the First World War lay outside the subject of this book. However, it is interesting to note that in November 1915, France decided not to dress her colonial troops (including the French Foreign Legion) in horizon blue, but rather to follow the practice of dressing colonial troops like military in the colonies of other empires and put them in khaki (Funcken and Funcken 1970: 16). Eventually khaki reached metropolitan France, when in 1928 khaki replaced horizon blue as the service dress for the regular army.

Belgian infantry entered World War I in shakos as did the three Belgian regiments of Chasseurs of the cavalry. The five lancer regiments wore the *czapka* but the two regiments of Guides still wore their colbacks. In early 1915 these uniforms were replaced by a khaki dress manufactured in Great Britain. That of the officers reflected British influence but the uniforms imported from Britain for other ranks were still of a decidedly French cut (Mollo 1978: 103–7, 183–6).

The eastern Mediterranean included several countries who had dressed troops in khaki before the outbreak of hostilities in 1914. Turkey had adopted khaki in 1909 (Kannik 1969: 237). A 'greenish khaki field uniform' was worn by the Greek army beginning in 1912 (Mollo 1978: 142). Montenegro obtained khaki cloth for uniforming its army from Russia in 1910 (Mollo 1978: 151). Russian influence was a key in the adoption of khaki by Bulgaria in 1908 (Mollo 1978: 110).

John Mollo identified a chilling result of this diffusion of khaki, but through a circuitous route. In 1908, Robert Baden-Powell, who had commanded in the defence of Mafeking during the Anglo-Boer War, founded the Boy Scouts as an organization designed to inspire healthy living and good citizenship among youth in Britain, and he dressed them 'in a mock South African service dress, which consisted of a slouch hat, khaki shirt and shorts.' Mollo sees this uniform as one of the inspirations for the uniform of the Nazi Party. As Mollo observes: 'Uniform became the weapon of the propagandist. The dress of the Boy Scouts, which was deliberately intended to suggest healthy adventure, with undertones of moral education, was soon added to and adapted to promote a more sinister ideology' (Mollo 1972: 232).

# 8

# North America: Feathers and Leather

'Custer Wore Arrow Shirts'
Bumper sticker on a
*Native American automobile*

## Boundaries to Diffusion

For five centuries the military of expanding Euro-American states have been in contact with native warriors in North America. This contact involved fighting between the two but also included the employment of North Americans as allies and auxiliaries against other native populations and in wars against other imperial powers. As will be seen, there was considerable use of the dress of the Indians by the military, and considerable use of military symbols by the Indians in their own dress.

It is not possible in the space available to detail the varieties of dress worn by North American Indians who fought against or alongside Euro-American armies. There was great diversity across the continent and changes through time within a single area. This chapter will look primarily at the influence of North American Indians on the dress of the French, British and American forces in the woodlands east of the Mississippi from the mid-eighteenth century through the War of 1812, and in the later campaigns undertaken, after the American Civil War, in the trans-Mississippi west. While clashes and wars occurred in other locales (notably the Apache Wars in Arizona and New Mexico), it is in these first two regions that the dress of the American Indians had the most impact on the military.

Male attire for most of the Indian population of North America differed from that of the Europeans who invaded the continent in that only on the Arctic coast (among the Inuit and Eskimo) and in the western portion of the boreal forest (the Yukon and interior Alaska) were trousers worn aboriginally. Elsewhere men usually wore a belt or sash about the waist and passed a breech cloth between their legs and over the belt at both the front and the back. In some areas a simple apron predated the breech cloth, and in others males frequently went completely naked. A pair of leggings, usually fastened to the belt and tied below the knee with garters, protected the legs from mid-thigh to ankle. Footwear consisted of moccasins, the pattern varying from region to region. In the east the sole and top were made of a single piece of soft leather, and on the plains west of the Mississippi a stiff rawhide sole was sewn to a top of softer leather. Robes of fur or leather, and later trade blankets, were worn to protect the upper body; leather shirts and coats of varying patterns were also worn. In the post-contact period Euro-American shirts and coats obtained in trade were frequently worn and trade cloth was often used for the breech cloth and leggings.

Under the French regime, Canada was defended by the Compagnies Franches de la Marine from 1689 until the British conquest of Canada in 1759. A unit in the regular French Army, the Regiment de Carignan-Sallières, had served in Canada from 1665–8, to defend the colony against the Iroquois Confederacy immediately to the south, but with their departure regular army troops were not seen in Canada until 1755, leaving defence of the colony to specially raised colonial forces. Although not formally part of the French Army, the men of the Compagnies Franches de la Marine were full-time soldiers, often referred to as 'colonial regulars'. They provided garrisons for Quebec City and Montreal, but also served at forts and posts far in the interior. Their officers were largely Canadian in origin, but the rank and file was recruited in France. Their uniform – white coat, blue sleeved waistcoat, blue breeches, gaiters and tricorne hat – was like that of the regular French army, but while on service in the interior the men dispensed with the coat in summer and frequently wore Indian leggings (referred to as *mitasses*) and moccasins in place of gaiters and shoes (Summers and Chartrand 1981: 11–2). The leggings were worn with the regulation breeches and replaced the gaiters normally worn.

As breeches reached only to below the knee, in civilian dress they were worn with long stockings, but soldiers on active service required a more substantial leg covering, hence they wore gaiters (or 'spatterdashes', as the gaiters that reached to mid-thigh were often called) over their breeches and stockings. Each gaiter or spatterdash was buttoned all the way from ankle to mid-thigh, with 25 or so buttons. In addition, the white full dress gaiters presented a formidable cleaning task (brown canvas gaiters were often issued for active service and in some European armies black gaiters were worn in winter and white in summer).

It was not just the Compagnies Franches de la Marine who wore Indian leggings. Speaking of French Canada, Windrow and Embleton (1973: 16) assert 'the use of Indian-style cloth leggings, thonged in place, is believed to have dated from the earliest days of colonization' and attribute their use by the régiment Carignan-Sallières, the first regular army unit of a European power to serve in North America, in 1665–8. During the Seven Years War (often called the French and Indian War in the United States) both French and British regulars substituted Indian leggings for gaiters (examples are given below). Indian leggings were probably welcomed as much more convenient by troops commanded by officers sensible enough to authorize their use.

Commencing in 1755, regular French army battalions crossed the Atlantic to Canada to carry on the war with the British in the American colonies.[1] Modern students of the dress of the French military in Canada (based on written rather than pictorial evidence) occasionally illustrate these metropolitan regulars wearing Indian leggings. For example, Robert Marrion depicts an officer of the régiment de Guyenne wearing greyish-white breeches with leather leggings and moccasins (Summers and Chartrand 1981: 28–9) and G. Embleton (1967: 6) states that for the regulars, 'shoes and gaiters were the first to go and moccasins and Indian leggings of leather and cloth were worn'.

The Compagnies Franches de la Marine and their Indian allies achieved their greatest victory on 9 July 1755 near Fort Duquesne at the forks of the Ohio River (now Pittsburgh, Pennsylvania). British General Edward Braddock with some 1,450 men, marching to attack the French fort, was met by 108 of the colonial regulars along with 146 Canadian militia and 637 Indians, led by Daniel-Hyacinthe-Marie Liénard de Beaujeu, a captain of the Compagnies Franches de la Marine. On the trail leading to Fort Duquesne, Braddock's advance guard, under Thomas Gage, encountered a man in full Indian dress but wearing a gorget (a crescent-shaped metal ornament worn just below the throat, which was worn by officers as a badge of rank). This 'Indian' proved to be Liénard de Beaujeu who signalled by waving his hat upon which a volley rang out. By the end of the day the British had lost almost a thousand killed and wounded, including 60 of their 86 officers. Braddock himself was mortally wounded. Beaujeu, who had led his combined force into battle in Indian dress, was among the 23 killed of the French-Indian forces (Fortescue 1910: 280–5; Steele 1994: 188–9; MacLeod 1974: 400–2).

Beaujeu's wearing of native dress was far from unique. G. Embleton (1967: 6) notes 'those who saw service with the Indians came to dress like them and wear paint and feathers partly for convenience, partly diplomacy'. As will be seen, officers in the British Indian Department followed the same practice.

## The North American Ranger

Many British officers became convinced of the need for light troops to campaign in the forests of North America. Britain lacked large numbers of native allies for Britain, although able to convince some groups such as the Mohawks of the Iroquois Confederacy and the Stockbridge Indians (so-called from their home near Stockbridge, Massachusetts, descended from people known as Mahican) to serve as auxiliaries, was not as successful in recruiting Indian warriors as were the French. To supplement these a number of companies of colonials with frontier experience were created, usually styled as 'Rangers'. In 1744 John Gorham led a company of Rangers, the majority of whom were Mohawk Indians, to fight the French and their Micmac allies in what is now the Annapolis Valley of Nova Scotia. In 1747, he recruited New Englanders to defend the region against the Acadian French and the Micmac. When John Gorham died in 1751, his brother, Joseph Gorham,[2] took command of the unit and was the senior officer among the six ranger companies that served under Major General James Wolfe at the 1759 victory before the walls of Quebec City. Captain Henry Knox of the 43rd Foot, also with Wolfe's army, described the Rangers as wearing a blue bonnet, a black sleeved waistcoat with blue cuffs, a black sleeveless jacket with blue lapels, a 'blue skirt or short petticoat', linen or canvas trousers and black leggings (Ray and Elting 1974). These last reflect Indian fashion, for although they buttoned part way up the calf like spatterdashes, Indians were also known to wear similar leggings. The skirt probably reflects Highland Scots influence (as does the bonnet) but it may also be derived from the dress of European seamen. It just might show some American Indian influence, as kilts were recorded a century later as part of native Seneca attire (Morgan 1851: 262–4), but it seems likely the Seneca were also copying the Scots. It is reported that Gorham's Rangers were 'the most highly rated by the British high command' (Chartrand 1995: 49).

By far the most famous corps of Rangers was His Majesty's Independent Companies of American Rangers commanded by Robert Rogers. Colonel Frederick P. Todd of the United States Military Academy expressed the view that 'in the French and Indian War, Robert Rogers and his men established an undying reputation for daring, skill and endurance', and noted that 'when the six modern Ranger battalions were formed [by the US Army] in 1942, the rules laid down by Rogers for his Ranger companies in 1757 were reprinted and used in the training of the new men' (Todd 1954: Plate 28). The extent to which they wore uniform dress is unclear, but for some of their history they wore short green jackets made by the tailors Thomas & Benjamin Forseys from Albany, New York. Their headgear was the Highland bonnet. Deer hide breeches were worn with Indian leggings of green or brown rateen (May 1974: 36).

Our perception of the appearance of Rogers' Rangers has been shaped by two images, not independent of each other, which were produced a decade after the end of the Seven Years War. The first of these is a figure in Benjamin West's painting *The Death of General James Wolfe* completed in 1771. Legend has it that West created a sensation because he dressed his figures in contemporary uniforms rather than in classical togas and armour. However, this ignores the fact that Edward Penny had done the same thing with the same subject in a painting completed in 1765 (Penny's painting is now in the Ashmolean Museum, Oxford), and from which West had blatantly lifted the figure of the running British officer coming to inform the dying commander of his victory. West grouped prominent officers in the command structure of the British force around Wolfe when in fact they were all busy elsewhere on the battlefield. At the extreme left of his painting West placed a figure who is most often identified as an 'American Ranger', although he should not be taken as an exact representation of the dress of rangers. However, I think the image can be considered as evidence of the manner in which the dress and artefacts of the indigenous population of North America were incorporated into the dress of such troops (Plate 33).

West's 'Ranger' illustrates the practice of combining breeches with Indian leggings and moccasins, with the leggings secured below the knee with beaded garters. A band of native quillwork ornaments his black light infantry cap, probably an ordinary tricorne with the brim removed from the back and sides and with the remaining portion of the brim folded up to form a frontlet. He carries a powder horn and a pouch, both supported by beaded straps in Indian style.

Some of the models used by West for the details of indigenous origin in the dress of the 'Ranger' have survived. These were acquired in 1991 by the Museum of Mankind (the Ethnology Division of the British Museum) in London from a descendent of Benjamin West (King 1991). The surviving items included the band of quillwork that decorates the light infantry cap in the painting (King 1991: Figure 7) and the garter constructed of glass beads depicting three males and two females (King 1991: Figure 9). A pair of moccasins decorated with porcupine quills, metal cones and red dyed hair resemble those worn by the Ranger (King 1991: Figure 2). The Ranger's Indian companion in the painting wears a woven pouch, ornamented with beads and cone and dyed hair tassels, which has also survived (King 1991: Figure 6). It is interesting that the broad woven yarn strap decorated with beads attached to the surviving pouch was not included with the pouch in the painting but rather West used it as the model for one of the straps over the left shoulder of the Ranger. The surviving strap does not have the metal cones with red-dyed hair that decorate that of the Ranger, however.

H. Charles McBarron, in reconstructing the uniform of the ranger company of Captain Hezekiah Dunn, organized to protect the New Jersey frontier in 1756, has added Indian leggings and pouches, clearly derived from the 'Ranger' in Benjamin West's 1771 painting, *The Death of Wolfe*. All that is really known of the dress of this unit comes from the description of the dress of a deserter – 'A grey lapell'd Waistcoat and an under green Jacket, a Leather Cap, and Buckskin Breeches' (McBarron and Elting 1974).

In many publications dealing with the exploits of Rogers and his Rangers, one frequently sees a portrait reproduced that purports to depict Robert Rogers (Plate 34). It is seldom mentioned that this mezzotint portrait was published by T. Hart in London in 1776, almost twenty years after Rogers fought the French in the region of Lake Champlain (Lawson 1940–67, Volume 3: 217). Both the hat and the strap worn over the left shoulder by the subject of this print recall strongly the Ranger in West's *Death of Wolfe*. This print, however, has strongly influenced reconstructions of the dress of officers in Rogers' Rangers (as R. Embleton 1967).

### The British Indian Department

The members of the British Indian Department, a quasi-military organization dedicated to maintaining peace and trade with the Indians or, in times of conflict, enlisting the aid of Indians in military expeditions, often wore Indian dress. An American prisoner in Detroit reported that the Indian Department officer Simon Girty wore ordinary clothing while in the fort but donned Indian dress when serving in the field (Calloway 1989: 48). Benjamin West's well known portrait of Guy Johnson (see Einhorn and Abler 1998; King 1991), who became Indian Superintendent for the Northern Department in 1774, again displays the practice of wearing Indian leggings over civilized breeches and the substitution of moccasins for civilized shoes. The moccasins were or became part of the artist's collection and have survived (King 1991: 36–8). In addition, Johnson has wrapped himself in a splendid robe, with geometric decorations suggesting an origin west of the Mississippi, and holds a light infantry cap heavily decorated with quillwork.

Indians in the Ohio country continued to maintain a hostile stance against the United States after the British recognized American independence at the Treaty of Paris of 1783. Complex political issues and a desire to maintain the lucrative fur trade led the British to remain in the western forts and posts in the Upper Great Lakes and the Ohio country. Members of the Indian

Department and the Detroit militia, including the aforementioned Simon Girty, covertly fought alongside native warriors, and are said to have blackened their faces with war paint as they joined Wyandot, Miami, Delaware and Shawnee warriors in their attack of American General Anthony Wayne's Fort Recovery in August 1794 (Calloway 1989: 53). When war broke out between the United States and Britain in 1812, the Indian Department was quick to enlist Indian aid, and Alexander Elliott continued Indian Department tradition as he wore Indian dress in the ambush of an American column attempting to supply Detroit on 5 August 1812 (Stanley 1983: 101).

It seems at least some British Regulars adopted the use of *mitasses* or Indian leggings. For the 1758 campaign Viscount Howe (Brigadier George Augustus Howe), who earlier had attached himself to Rogers' Rangers to learn their tactics and techniques, commanded the 55th Foot making a number of modifications to the uniforms of his officers and men to make them less cumbersome and less conspicuous. Noteworthy, here, is that according to a contemporary female observer 'he set the example of wearing leggins' (Anne MacVickers quoted in Ray and Elting 1974a: 4). Howe may have been wearing these items of native American dress when he was killed near Fort Ticonderoga on 6 July 1758. Some have also suggested that the 60th (Royal American) Regiment of Foot, raised on 25 December 1755, also made use of leggings (Summers and Chartrand 1981: 44; Reid 1995: 35).

## Isaac Brock and Tecumseh

A minor hero in the history of the British Empire is Major General Isaac Brock who in 1812 commanded British forces in Upper Canada (now Ontario). Britain was heavily engaged in the war in Europe against Napoleon when President James Madison of the United States declared war against Britain in June 1812. News of the hostilities reached Brock while he was at dinner in the Officers' Mess in Fort George, the British fort on the Canadian side of the Niagara River, dining with officers from the American garrison at Fort Niagara across the river. The British and their American guests continued their social evening, and the Americans departed, content to begin the war the next morning.

Brock quickly took the offensive and hurried west where Americans under William Hull had crossed the Detroit River into Upper Canada. At Fort Malden (Amherstburg), on 13 August 1812, Brock met the great Shawnee Chief, Tecumseh. The two vigorous warriors made an impression upon each other. Tecumseh is reported to have evaluated Brock with the words: 'this is a man' (Stanley 1983: 106). Brock's opinion of Tecumseh was that 'a more sagacious or a more gallant Warrior does not I believe exist' (Goltz 1983: 798). At one meeting between the two, Brock took off his crimson sash, emblematic of his rank in the British Army and presented it to Tecumseh; Tecumseh removed his finger-woven sash and presented it to Brock (Stacey 1983: 113). Within days the American General William Hull, his men, and Detroit itself were in British hands.

Later that year Brock was fall mortally wounded at the Battle of Queenston Heights, defending Upper Canada from an American invasion. The uniform worn Brock wore on that 13 October 1812 is now in the Canadian War Museum in Ottawa. Tied about the waist is not the crimson sash of a British General Officer, but rather the finger-woven sash of the Shawnee Chief Tecumseh (Plate 35).

## Hunting Shirts

In assessing the impact of North American Indians and North American wars upon military uniforms, one must address questions relating to the origins of the 'hunting shirt', which enjoyed a brief period of use by the American military. It is true that the hunting shirt is a distinctly North American garment, which may have been worn by Rangers and other provincial units during the Seven Years War. It was considered by General George Washington to be an appropriate garment to issue to the entire Continental Army in the American Revolution (Windrow and Embleton 1973: 14–5). Although clearly a frontier garment, the degree to which it owes any ancestry to native North Americans is questionable. The hunting shirt is basically a farmer's or labourer's smock, but embellished with fringes (which may be of American Indian inspiration) on the front, bottom, sleeves and collar and capes which might be added (see Plate 36). That North American Indians wore the garment is not subject to doubt; several images of the great Seneca orator Red Jacket show him wearing a hunting shirt in the 1830s (Plate 37). The garment was very widely used by soldiers during the American Revolution and continued as the summer dress of the US Rifle Regiment through the War of 1812 (McBarron 1941). It was also worn by the Maryland Rifle Volunteers in the defence of Baltimore in 1814 (Windrow and Embleton 1973: 53). Unlike other styles of dress derived from hinterland warriors or the frontier experience described earlier, though, the hunting shirt did not spread beyond its region of origin.

## Light Infantry and Rifle Green

It is sometimes claimed that North American frontier warfare, including the experience of fighting native North Americans, was an important causal variable in the development of light infantry in the British Army and in the adoption of a 'rifle green' uniform by the rifle regiments within the British Army. I do not feel either view is justified. Russell (1978) has demonstrated that by 1750 European military professionals were well aware of the importance of light troops, both infantry and cavalry. In Chapter 3 above, the importance of hussars was emphasized, but many of their compatriots from the Balkans on the Austrian frontier fought on foot rather than on horseback. The most important variable in the recognition of the importance of light infantry on the field of battle lay not in the forests of North America but rather on the frontier of the Austrian empire.

The case for an American cause for the adoption of the 'rifle green' uniforms is equally flawed. It is true that the first battalion to dress in a green uniform in the regular British Army was the 5th Battalion of the 60th Foot (the 'Royal Americans' – which, despite the title, was not particularly American and was largely composed of Germans). It is also true that a large portion of Loyalist regiments during the American Revolution were clad in green, including Simcoe's Huzzars discussed in Chapter 3. However, dark green had long been the colour worn by riflemen in the armies of Prussia and other German states, this being the colour worn by huntsmen on the estates of major and minor German nobility. Long before Britain's wars in America, her continental German allies were fielding bodies of men armed with rifles and dressed in dark green.

## Indians, Feathers and the Highland Bonnet

Thus far I have argued that in Eastern North America in the eighteenth century there had been some impact of the styles of dress of the indigenous population on the military uniforms of units sent from overseas or raised within colonial settlements, but that this impact was limited to local use of such dress and did not introduce any lasting change to the uniforms of world's armies. The one possible exception to this conclusion is the influence of North American Indian feather headdresses on the headgear worn by Scots Highlanders serving on the frontiers of Eastern North America.

I think it significant that the Highland bonnet evolved from a dark blue cloth beret-like cap with a diced band to the tall ostrich feather bonnet of today in the period 1760–90 when several Highland regiments were stationed, and fighting, in North America. Even earlier, as Lawson notes, feathered bonnets were used to describe the dress of the Independent Highland Company in Oglethorpe's North American colony of Georgia. 'The mention of feathered bonnets is curious as none of the pictures of Highlanders at this period show them so ornamented, except some of the portraits of Chiefs of Clans. One can only suppose that one or more feathers had been added in imitation of their Indian friends' (Lawson 1940–67, Volume 4: 108). I would argue that if one compares the arrangement of feathers on the 'stand-up' feather headdress of the native peoples of the Eastern Woodlands of North America with the arrangement of ostrich feathers on contemporary Scots bonnets (the Indians were also fond of ostrich feathers obtained through the fur trade), one must recognize remarkable parallels. It is possible that the two groups influenced each other, but the feathers in the Scots bonnet very much resemble an Indian headdress turned anticlockwise by 90° on the head (see Plates 38 and 39). An official report of 1790 commented on the headdress of the 42nd Foot upon its return to Britain from serving in North America for more than a decade. 'Their bonnets are entirely disfigured. They are so covered with lofty feathers that they appear like grenadier caps of black bearskin' (quoted in Carman 1957: 101).

## US Cavalry and Plains Indians

While there were several wars between native North Americans and the US Army in the years between the War of 1812 and the American Civil War (notably the Black War in Illinois, the second Seminole War in Florida, the slaughter of large numbers of native Californians by gold miners and prospectors and the 'pacification' of the Navajo by Kit Carson) the use of native auxiliaries was limited in these conflicts. As there is not a great deal of evidence to suggest that indigenous dress had a significant impact on the uniforms of the US military in these wars, the discussion will move on to consider the dress of the US Cavalry on the plains of North America.

Colonial experiences elsewhere in the world had an impact on the thinking of some in the US military as it moved to establish control over the nomadic populations of the grasslands of the trans-Mississippi west. When Captain George B. McClellan (later to command the Army of the Potomac in the initial stage of the Civil War) journeyed to the Crimea as an observer in 1855, he saw parallels between the Cossacks and native North Americans and thought Indians could perform a similar role in the American army to that the Cossacks performed for the Russians. Lieutenant William Burnet of the 1st US Infantry saw parallels between the American frontier and the

French experience in North Africa, and when Sir Richard Burton reached America in his worldwide rambles in 1860, he suggested the Americans imitate the British in India as raise battalions of native troops (Dunlay 1982: 24).

The 1866 Act that defined the strength of the United States Army following the Civil War included provision to enlist up to 1000 Indian scouts, who would receive the same pay as regular cavalrymen. In the eyes of the military, there were only two kinds of Indians – hostiles and friendlies – although there were a large number of 'tribes' with differing language and culture. Hostiles and friendlies were fluid categories, and such was the nature of the political structure of the Plains Indians that one group might be 'hostiles' while a second group speaking the same language, practising the same culture and even with kinship ties to the first might be friendlies. It also happened that a single group might move from a hostile stance to a friendly one. That 'friendlies' might become 'hostiles' led some army officers to be reluctant to arm and use Indian scouts.

Space does not allow a prolonged discussion of the contribution of Indian scouts to the success of the US military against 'hostiles' in the trans-Mississippi frontier. However, General George Crook, who utilized the services of Indian scouts on several campaigns, stated that without them 'the white men would be outwitted, exhausted, circumvented, possibly ambushed and destroyed' (quoted in Downey and Jacobsen 1973: 105). Despite the official authorization in the 1866 Act mentioned above, Indian auxiliaries were for the most part raised on an ad-hoc basis to meet a particular crisis or serve on a particular campaign. It is at times confusing as to whether a group of Indians were formally 'Scouts' or simply allies who like the Americans bore a desire to see the 'hostiles' punished militarily. Some of the officers who led these Indians were seconded from a regular army unit; others were non-Indian civilians in the pay of the Quartermaster General. These latter, such as Frank North who commanded a troop of Pawnee Scouts, often wore military uniforms with army badges of rank and received appropriate pay (Dunlay 1983: 101). None of the Indian scouts themselves were allowed to hold a commission – the highest rank available to an Indian who had enlisted for service in the Scouts was First Sergeant (Dunlay 1983: 104). The command structure of these units was such, however, that consultation with the 'other ranks' was required prior to undertaking any action; otherwise, 'orders' would probably be ignored.

The diversity of tribal origins of the Indian scouts plus the differing local circumstances of each campaign make it difficult to summarize issues of dress and appearance. One observer, William F. ('Buffalo Bill') Cody, described a troop of Pawnee Scouts encountered in 1869:

Regular Cavalry suits had been furnished them, but no two of the Pawnees seemed to agree on the correct manner in which the various articles should be worn. As they lined up for dress parade, some of them wore heavy overcoats, others discarded even pantaloons, content with a breech-clout. Some wore large black hats with brass accoutrements; others went bareheaded. Many wore pantaloons but declined shirts, while a few of the more original cut the seats from their pantaloons, leaving only leggings. Half of these were without boots or moccasins, but wore clinking spurs with magnificent pride. (Quoted in Downey and Jacobsen 1973: 160)

These Pawnee Scouts wore uniforms while on the march but stripped to fight, as at Plum Creek in 1867 and at the Dull Knife Fight in 1876 (Dunlay 1983: 82–4, 86–7). North and 400 Pawnees enhanced their reputations by successfully taking on the task of protecting the Union Pacific railroad (Smits 1998: 89).

The ethnic background and history of one unit of these scouts is of interest. The homeland of the Seminole in Florida was a refuge for slaves escaping from southern plantations. Having intermarried with the Seminoles, they were removed with other Seminoles to the Indian Territory (now Oklahoma) where they feared their African ancestry might lead to re-enslavement. They fled to Mexico where they served to protect the state of Coahuila against raids by Apaches and Comanches. In the 1870s they were persuaded to move back to Texas and were enlisted in the US Army as the Seminole Negro Scouts to play an active role in conflicts with the Comanches and others. Four of its men were awarded the Congressional Medal of Honor (Dunlay 1983: 105), and in 1914 the Seminole Negro Scouts were still serving at Fort Clark in Texas (Downey and Jacobsen 1973: 170).

An attempt was also made to recruit Indians within the regular establishment of the US Army as defined in General Order No. 28, March 1891. This proposed a separate troop or company recruited from among Indians for each regiment of cavalry and infantry (Downey and Jacobsen 1973: 13–14). This was opposed by many, including some who were simply prejudiced against Indians. The opposition included George Crook, who had consistently made use of Indian scouts for three decades, but who felt training Indians as regulars would strip them of the very skills that had made them valuable to his troops in the field. These 'regular' units, who wore the same dress and performed the same drills as other members of their regiments, were commanded by officers of high reputation such as Edward Casey who commanded a troop of Cheyennes as L Troop in the 8th Cavalry and Hugh Scott who commanded L Troop, composed of Kiowas, in the 7th Cavalry. The experiment failed, however, and between 1894 and 1897 these all-Indian troops and companies were disbanded. One issue related to the degree of knowledge demanded of the non-Indian officer commanding these units, meaning that successful officers could not easily be replaced. It seems not to have been acceptable to the Americans to recruit native officers from these units to provide a buffer and communication link between the 'imperial' officer and the native troopers as was done in the British Indian army (Dunlay 1983: 195–7).

At about this time the US Army moved to regularize the Scouts themselves. As their duties shifted from an active role in the field to a reserve role in garrison, their dress shifted from being 'modified-native' to being purely imperial, with minor distinctions. A badge was provided with rather anachronistic crossed arrows and the letters 'U.S.S.' (for United States Scouts) and red silk guidons were authorized with four crossed arrows behind a horizontal bow embroidered in white silk. The full dress spiked helmet bore a red and white (were the colours significant?) horsehair plume. When the United States Army moved to khaki, the Scouts followed, but retaining their 'U.S.S.'/crossed-arrows badges. The United States Scouts were not disbanded until 30 November 1943, and the last Indian to have enlisted in the United States Army as a scout retired five years later (Downey and Jacobsen 1973: 163–4, 175–81, 191–2).

## Frontier Dress and the Regular Army

Among the United States Scouts, military dress never evolved beyond the 'modified native' stage, but the dress worn by some officers of the United States Army reached the 'stylized-native' stage. This never had the status of official uniform, but the fringed leather outfit enjoyed widespread use among the officer corps of the US Cavalry who fought the Sioux and others on the Plains. These garments did not precisely follow Indian fashion but rather were tailored to match prevailing Euro-American styles. Their origins lay with those whites who lived among the Indians with Indian wives who produced leather garments cut to European pattern but ornamented with fringes and sometimes beadwork or quillwork.

The most famous of the officers to wear deer hide clothing was George Armstrong Custer. The 'boy general' of the Civil War, Custer was, like other regular US Army officers, reduced in rank because of the drastic reduction in the size of the army following the end of that conflict. As a Lieutenant Colonel he assumed command of the 7th Cavalry. His career came to an end on 25 June 1876 when he and the portion of the 7th Cavalry under his immediate command (Troops C, E, F, I and L) all perished in battle with the

Sioux and Cheyenne defending their village on the Little Bighorn River (Godfrey 1992: 284).

Custer wore a low-crowned light grey hat, deer hide trousers with fringe on the outer seams and a double breasted deer hide blouse with fringe at both the bottom and the outer seams of the sleeves. About his waist, a canvas cartridge belt supported a pair of holsters and a knife in a beaded and fringed sheath. Leather blouses or jackets were also worn by his brothers, Tom Custer who commanded Troop C and Boston Custer, a civilian forage master for the regiment (Hanson 1982: 113–4; Hutchins 1992: 330). Custer's adjutant, Lieutenant William W. Cooke, probably wore fringed leather garments as he had been photographed in such dress (Hutchins 1992: 329). Two other 7th Cavalry officers who were killed in the battle are also known to have worn leather clothing – Lieutenant James E. Porter and Lieutenant Donald McIntosh (Hanson 1982: 114).

Custer's dress is shown in an interesting representation of the battle, drawn by Kicking Bear, one of several Sioux and Cheyenne participants in the battle who drew or painted personal versions of the action. The Sioux leader depicts a dead George Armstrong Custer clad in fringed deer hide clothing (Plate 40).

Custer's defeat was not the worst defeat suffered by the US Army at the hands of American Indians, for the defeats of Brigadier General Josiah Harmar on 20 and 23 October 1790 and Major General Arthur St. Clair on 4 November 1791 in the Ohio country were far more costly in terms of US Army casualties, and both these battles delayed the extension of American control over the Indian country for a greater length of time than did the death of George Custer and the men under his command (Allen 1975: 38–41). The great importance of newspapers in the 1870s, however, gave to Custer publicity denied to earlier participants in epic defeats of the American army on the frontier. Custer, already a hero in the eyes of the public, became one of legendary proportions (see Rosenberg 1974) and the defeat also assumed important symbolic value among native North Americans. Hence bumper stickers now appear on American Indian reservations proclaiming 'Custer died for your sins' and, perhaps more appropriate for this discussion of military uniform, 'Custer wore arrow shirts' (see Deloria 1969).

Evidence indicates that Custer and his officers reflected a common practice in their use of fringed leather clothing. The handsome deer-hide jacket decorated with floral quillwork designs worn by Captain William Ludlow on the 1874 Black Hills expedition is preserved in the museum of the US Military Academy, West Point (Hanson 1982: 114). An elegant double-breasted jacket with brass military buttons, fringed collar, sleeves and pockets from the Smithsonian is illustrated in Mollo (1972: 174).

*North America*

## Chiefs' Coats and Metal Gorgets

European military dress also came to be used by American Indian fighting men and leaders, as the French, British, Spanish and Americans all distributed 'chiefs' coats' or 'captains' coats' during the colonial period and well into the nineteenth century. These coats were cut and laced in the manner of that of a military officer. Andrew Graham, a Hudson's Bay Company trader at York Factory in the 1790s, described such a coat: 'A coarse cloth coat, either red or blue, lined with baize with regimental cuffs and collar . . . ornamented with broad and narrow orris lace of different colours' (quoted in Ray 1996: 85). The Seneca chief Red Jacket (Plate 37) received his English name from a red coat presented to him in his youth by the British during or before the American Revolution. The Spanish presented blue or red coats with facings of the opposite colour to American Indians they hoped to bring or keep under their influence (Hanson 1982: 106). In 1804, the American explorers Meriwether Lewis and William Clark gave what they describe as 'a chief's coat, that is, a richly laced uniform of the United States artillery corps, and a cocked hat and red feather' to a Sioux leader in what is now South Dakota (quoted in Hanson 1982: 106). A Yanktonai Sioux chief is described in 1825 as wearing 'moccasins and leggings of splendid scarlet cloth, blue breech cloth, a fine shirt of printed muslin, over this a frock coat made of fine blue cloth, with scarlet facings, somewhat similar to the underdress uniform coat of a Prussian officer' (quoted in Penny 1992: 46). Calloway has characterized such gifts as 'meddling in the complex world of Indian politics [which] tended to confuse matters further' (Calloway 1987: 43).

Metal gorgets were also distributed. These crescent-shaped metal ornaments, usually silver or brass, were a vestige of the armour protecting the throat of a mediaeval man-at-arms, which, by the seventeenth century, had become a badge of rank of a European military officer. They were worn just beneath the throat on the chest. Military gorgets usually carried a royal cypher, coat of arms or crest. Documents attest to the importance of gorgets as gifts to Indians in securing their services as allies and friends. During a four-month period in 1780, the British Indian Department purchased and placed in store at Fort Niagara some 132 gorgets (Abler 1976: 617). Among the Indian Stores delivered to Michilimackinac in 1814 for distribution to Indians in the Upper Great Lakes were 40 gorgets. One can compare this number to the 248 muskets delivered at the same time (Allen 1975: 98). Gorgets were so popular among the Indians that they were produced, often with engraved motifs designed to appeal to indigenous taste replacing the royal symbols, for the fur trade in eastern North America. For example Fredrickson (1980: 48) describes a gorget, with the mark of silversmith

Narcise Roy, engraved with a leaping bear. Roy is known to have lived and worked in Montreal for 1765 to 1819 (Fredrickson 1980: 39). Fredrickson exhibits a large number of these gorgets (Fredrickson 1980: Figures 11, 31, Catalogue Nos. 44, 48, 56, 63, 71–81, 160, 162–5).

When posing for portraits, North American Indian leaders have frequently chosen to wear gorgets. Table 10 lists the portraits of several such leaders with their tribal affiliation and the date of the portrait. In some cases their are multiple portraits of a particular leader wearing a metal gorget or metal gorgets; in such case the portrait selected is arbitrary. I have also indicated one publication that reproduces the portrait in question, and again, the publication selected is quite arbitrary. It should be emphasized this is in no way a complete list, but it does reflect the widespread geographic area in which the ornament was worn – from Canada to Florida and from the Atlantic Coast to the mid-Missouri Valley. It is also interesting to note that the use of the crescent-shaped military gorget in this list dates from 1762 to 1890. I suspect that an exhaustive study of the pictorial evidence would extend these dates further.

In the early years of the nineteenth century, British colonial officials made similar use of military uniforms and gorgets among the indigenous population of Australia (Troy 1993).

Table 10. *Portraits of American Indians wearing metal gorgets*

| Indian leader | Tribe or nation | Date of portrait | Published source |
|---|---|---|---|
| Joseph Brant | Mohawk | 1776 | Fredrickson 1980: 139 |
| Cornplanter | Seneca | 1792 | Karklins 1992: 79 |
| Ka-be-mub-be | Ojibwa | 1834 | Karklins 1992: 31 |
| Mani-Tow-Wa-Bay | Ojibwa | 1846 | Fredrickson 1980: 133 |
| Brewett | Miami | 1827 | Fredrickson 1980: 59 |
| The Prophet | Shawnee | 1830 | Truettner 1979: 221 |
| Cunne Shote | Cherokee | 1762 | Fundaburk 1958: Figure 120 |
| Hysac | Creek | 1792 | Fundaburk 1958: Figure 136 |
| Hopothle Mico | Creek | 1792 | Fundaburk 1958: Figure 132 |
| Osceola | Seminole | 1838 | Truettner 1979: 101 |
| Billy Bowlegs | Seminole | 1858 | Fundaburk 1958: Figure 310 |
| Billie Stewart | Seminole | 1890 | Hudson 1976: 265 |
| Mouse-colored Feather | Mandan | 1832 | Truettner 1979: 180 |

It also can be argued that the form of clothing produced by American Indians has been influenced by military styles. In most cases, it would be impossible to tell, however, whether it is civilian costume or military uniform (or, for that matter, a 'chief's coat' as described above) which is being copied since these often closely parallel each other. Burnham (1992) has seen changes in the cut of caribou hide coats produced by the Montagnais, Naskapi, and Cree which parallel changes in European male clothing. The influence would appear to be civilian rather than military as there was not a strong military presence in most of the region exploited by these northern hunters.

The case may be different for the Apache in the American Southwest. It has been argued that tailored deer hide coats worn by the Western Apache late in the nineteenth century are a result of cultural borrowing and that they copy the full-dress uniform of the US Army officer. It is noted that the Western Apache for the most part dressed in garments of cotton or wool at the time the tailored deer hide shirt came into use. Gateaume argues that in 'appropriating and redefining the full-dress military coat – the coat they were not allowed to wear [as US Army scouts] – Western Apaches and particularly scouts were expressing themselves . . . in a language that could not but be noticed by white society, especially by members of the U.S. Army' (Gateaume 1998: 54). However, in her interesting discussion Gateaume does not consider the possibility that Western Apache styles might be aping the fringed leather jacket popular among US Army officers rather than their regulation full-dress tunic.

## Native North Americans and Military Uniforms

Despite the widespread use of fringed deer-hide clothing by the American military on the frontier, this style of dress never spread elsewhere nor did it become an accepted part of regulation US military dress. One can hypothesize why this was the case. Part of the answer rests with the prestige of the colonial power. Austria was a major power when the uniforms of the hussar spread from her frontiers to the rest of Europe. The incorporation of Polish lancers into the army of Napoleonic France was a major factor in the spread of that style of dress elsewhere. Again, the continuing military reputation of France led to the diffusion of the Zouave uniform, while the strength of the British empire helped spread the military use of the bagpipe, with its associated costume, and later the Indian army innovation of khaki. In contrast to these examples, America was a backwater when its tiny army with its officers clothed in fringed deer hide was fighting the buffalo-hunting nomads. Although this particular frontier experience did lead to distinctive dress being worn by the imperial army, it did not have an impact beyond the frontier in question. Clearly hinterland warriors have a strong impact on the dress of those who oppose them; other factors determine how widespread the innovations they inspire in military dress will spread.

# 9

# The Frontier Experience and the Military Uniform

> The camp was now a very lively scene, and contained a strange mixture of uniforms and faces, which showed the motley nature of the force which had been scraped together in this desperate crisis of the Empire.
>
> Captain Medley, Bengal Engineers

## Imperial Armies and Hinterland Warriors

Ethnic groups on the frontiers of empires have repeatedly been found to have fighting skills that have proven to have been useful to the military of an expanding state. Although armies of colonial empires had some clear advantages over foes in the hinterland, there were also characteristics of the hinterland warrior lacking in armies recruited in the metropolis. The prevalence and nature of conflict found among hinterland populations and the socialization of hinterland males to bear arms are also pertinent. As Andreski (1968: 12–13) has observed: 'rude rustics made the best soldiers, and refined, comfort-loving city-dwellers – the worst'.

One can contrast the army of the state with the sort of military force typically deployed by their foes and allies in the hinterland. There are several advantages possessed by the armies of the state. As Voltaire noted, 'God is on the side of the big battalions', and the empire is able to typically field larger forces than is possible by polities in the hinterland. The size of an imperial field force is a product of the large population base from which it recruits and the resources the imperial power possesses to logistically support its armies in the field.[1] States also usually possess superior arms to those peoples on the frontier where they are fighting. The technology of war is a double-edged sword, however, for the arms, both offensive and defensive, of the imperial army are advantageous when confronting the enemy in a battle but serve to limit the mobility of the army in the field. The superior logistical organization of the empire serves to slow and inhibit the movement of its forces. While a transport corps and draft animals were able to transport food to keep large numbers of troops in the field, the transport animals themselves have to be fed, as do the personnel who look after them. The actual fighting arm of an imperial army is a small part of the entire force. Sir Robert Napier, campaigning in Abyssinia in 1867–8, needed 36,000 animals and 7,000 teamsters to support his 13,000 fighting men; a Russian expedition to Khiva in 1874 required 8,800 camels to support 5,500 men (Strachan 1983: 81).

It is important to emphasize the 'military revolution' that transformed European armies in the seventeenth century. Drill, drill and more drill was necessary to deliver maximum firepower with the smoothbore muskets of the seventeenth and eighteenth centuries. The pre-eminent military virtue became a willingness to stand in the face of the enemy and calmly deliver precise volleys at the foe while not flinching at the prospect of receiving a volley from those same troops. When shock weapons were used, either in the massed charge of cavalry or in the bayonet charge of foot soldiers, the emphasis again was on acting in close concert with other members of one's unit, and on the unit as a whole exhibiting a willingness to accept casualties.

The European attitude toward battlefield behaviour is perhaps epitomized by the behaviour of Lord Charles Hay, commander of the King's Company[2] of the 1st Foot Guards (now Grenadier Guards), on 11 May 1745, who, before either side had fired, raised his hat in salute to the *Gardes Français* drawn up fifty yards in front of him at Fontenoy and drank a toast to them from the flask he carried (Fortescue 1910: 115).[3] Regimental histories are filled with tales of such behaviour while ignoring or glossing over situations where such ideal behaviour when unrealized. What is significant is that officers of eighteenth and nineteenth century metropolitan armies saw this as the exhibition of prime military virtues.

Typical hinterland warriors did not share this view as to the proper conduct of war. Warfare in the hinterlands most often emphasized mobility and individual action. When possible casualties were avoided, since these societies lack the resources in manpower possessed by the state and empire. However, in these societies the military participation ratio (MPR) was high. Military participation ratio is a concept developed by Andreski (1968: 33): 'the proportion of militarily utilized individuals in the total population'. It is also worthy of note that many of the hinterland warriors alluded to in earlier chapters were recruited from among peoples who raised livestock, whether in the north of Britain or the north of Africa, in the east of Europe or the eastern frontier of Afghanistan. As Gelner (1995: 162) has noted:

> Their [pastoral nomadic] whole lifestyle – their work, after all, consists of the exercise of violence against beasts of prey or other shepherds who would raid their flocks - provides them with a permanent training in the exercise of violence and in resistance to the violence of others. Though pastoral nomadism provides the most obvious example, similar conditions can also sometimes be encountered among peasantries, especially when they are located in difficult terrain. Such societies develop, to use S. Andreski's useful phrase, a high Military Participation Ratio.

Ferguson (1990: 34) recognizes that 'both hunters and gatherers and pastoralists have subsistence techniques and skills which can be carried over into combat'. One can couple this with the fact that the 'blood feud', in which individuals have the responsibility of avenging the death of a kinsman, was institutionalized in many of these hinterland regions, leading to a male population familiar with and willing to bear arms (on the feud, see Otterbein and Otterbein 1963; Boehm 1984). Gelner describes the fighting skills of such men as 'formidable' and notes their value to an expanding state: 'they did not need, like ordinary recruits, to be specially trained and endowed with an artificial *esprit de corps*. They arrived, fully trained and *encadré*, with recognized leaders and a familiarity with the terrain in which they were to be deployed' (Gelner 1995: 185).

Because the sorts of actions involved in livestock raids or in blood revenge emphasize actions by small but highly mobile parties of men, the warriors of the hinterland were trained and experienced in precisely the sorts of warfare in which conventional European armies were deficient. Thus the hinterlands became the depot from which to recruit the light infantryman and the light cavalryman, required to fight as an individual rather than as an unthinking cog in the clockwork manoeuvring of his company and battalion. The hinterlands were not simply the source of more men for the empire (although they were useful in this respect too), they were the source of a particular type of soldier and their dress became associated with the military tasks which were compatible with their socialization as warriors in a frontier society.

One must be careful not to embrace the ideas that all societies in the hinterlands of states are constantly engaged in war.[4] Gelner, though praising Andreski's concept of the military participation ratio, recognizes that 'societies so blessed with a wide military (and hence political) participation would seem to be a minority among agrarian societies' (Gelner 1995: 162). However, as Keeley (1996) has forcefully pointed out, it is also a mistake to subscribe to 'the myth of the peaceful savage'. Another point to be remembered is that the very expansion of empires into the hinterlands can increase conflict among the polities found there (see Ferguson and Whitehead 1992). All in all, it seems a reasonable conclusion that more often than not as imperial forces expanded the empire into the hinterlands, they encountered there veterans of conflict, experienced in handling weapons, who were available to be recruited as auxiliaries in the imperial forces.

## The Evolutionary Path of a Military Uniform

In the initial chapter it was suggested that if the employment of hinterland warriors as auxiliaries led to the native dress of those hinterland warriors being adopted by an imperial army, then the development of that uniform over time might follow an evolutionary path that can be summarized:

Native dress → modified native → stylized native → stylized military

In some of the cases discussed, this evolutionary process stalled before reaching the conclusion of stylized military; in other cases only limited elements of the dress of hinterland warriors reached that stage. The very incorporation of hinterland warriors as auxiliaries in an imperial army leads to the adoption of modified native dress. This is because logistics demand that the hinterland warrior be armed and dressed in a way that proves practical and convenient to the imperial power, so that inevitably standardized equipment supplied by the imperial army will be used by units of the native auxiliaries. The problem of battlefield recognition also encourages native auxiliaries to move to a modified native dress. This is perhaps best illustrated in the discussion of the early hussars (see Plates 1 and 2) and the Highland Scots (Plates 16 and 17). This last illustrates an excellent example of the modified native dress, with the belted plaid and indigenous broadsword being combined with the red coat and the standard Brown Bess musket of the British military.

Regular army personnel serving on the frontier, particularly those whose role involves close interaction with the indigenous population, frequently adopted modified native dress. It has been shown that some of the officers of Highland regiments, not themselves of Highland Scots origin, still wore Highland dress when on duty (Reid 1992: 34). The experiences of the young Frenchman, Marbot, have been described as he effected the Hungarian dress of a hussar. Among the initial Zouave formation, other ranks of French rather than Berber origin still wore North African dress, and the North African dress was retained as the Zouave units in the French army came to be recruited entirely from among Europeans. The North American frontier provided several examples of imperial officers in modified native dress as was seen in the illustrations of rangers and officers in the British Indian Department who wore unaltered items of native costume along with other more conventional military dress (Plates 32 to 36). One can also note that, in India under the Raj, British officers were required to wear a turban, kurta and other elements of indigenous costume in certain orders of dress.

## The Development of Stylized Native Dress

The modified native dress very quickly evolved into a stylized native uniform, as can be seen in the uniform of the French hussar of the Napoleonic era (Plate 3) or his companion in lancer dress (Plate 10). These illustrate how the indigenous costume succumbs to what Laver called the seduction principle, modified to emphasize some elements yet make it 'smarter' and 'more military'. While in both these examples, the native stylized dress is worn by soldiers recruited outside the hinterland in which the dress originated (the hussar recruited in France, not Hungary, and the lancer recruited in the Netherlands, not Poland) the evolution to native stylized dress also could have an impact on the dress of the hinterland itself. For example, regiments recruited in the Highlands of Scotland saw the belted plaid replaced by the *philibeg* or little kilt, as a 'smarter' or 'more military' garment. Comparison of the Highland soldier engaged in the occupation of Paris in 1816 (Plate 18) with the original recruits to the Black Watch some seven decades earlier reflects – beyond general changes in fashion which took place over that time – a considerable stylization and militarization of the dress of the Highland soldier.

The spread of the Zouave uniform also demonstrates this move to stylized native dress, although one could argue that in the French army itself the Zouave uniform never evolved past the modified native stage (Plate 24). French Zouaves were armed and equipped as other French infantry and colour was standardized and regulated so that one could recognize individual Zouave regiments by their dress, but the basic style did not deviate that much from its North African roots. However, when other armies adopted the Zouave uniform, it certainly reached the stylized native stage. In the case of the United States Zouave Cadets (Plate 25) and that of the 1st New York Fire Zouaves (Plate 26) the kepi replaced the fez, although the kepi was red rather than US Army blue[4] and while the trousers were much more full than those of usual military and civilian dress of the time, these American Zouaves utilized stylized rather than 'real' Zouave trousers. As was discussed in Chapter 6, the Americans made other modifications to the Zouave uniform, developing the jacket with a false underjacket. Similarly, when the British put the West India Regiment into Zouave costume, the form of both jacket and trousers were modified (Plate 29).

The *czapka* similarly changed in form through time, being made higher and more extravagant in appearance (in evolution following Laver's seduction principle). The original low and soft square-topped cap (as worn by the *Hulans britanniques* in Plate 11) became the tall, erect and rigid *czapka* of the Lancers of Napoleon's Imperial Guard. Both the hussars colback and the Scots bonnet underwent similar evolution, growing in height over time. These examples reflect a general trend in peacetime dress of the soldier to wear headgear that increases height.

## Transformation to Stylized Military

Uniforms classified as stylized native occur among hinterland units or with troops whose military role is similar to that of the original hinterland warriors. However, some elements of the dress of hinterland warriors, especially when it has reached the stylized native stage, tend to become generalized symbols of the military rather than symbols of a particular kind of soldier. Hence these symbols, now in the realm of stylized military, can be worn by portions of the army performing far different roles from those of the original native auxiliaries who introduced the style.

Hussar braiding is clearly an aspect of military dress that reached this stage. Initially it spread to those troops who fought alongside the hussars, such as horse artillery, and to light infantry and rifles. It was then adopted by others, such as staff officers, who would never be involved in the light cavalry duties of the original hussars. A similar example is that of the shako, which spread from being the specific headgear for Hungarian horsemen to becoming generalized military headwear. The case of the fez is less clear, because of its association with Turkey and Islam which may have independently encouraged its use. However, it would seem that the fez of the Zouave encouraged its use among the military south of the Sahara and even among troops such as the Bersaglieri of Italy who adopted the fez for some orders of dress after fighting alongside French Zouaves in the Crimea. Even the Scottish bagpipe and its associated dress moved well beyond being solely a symbol of Scots heritage, and became a generalized military symbol around the world.

## Diffusion and Evolution

Several forces have encouraged or inhibited the diffusion to general military culture of innovations in military dress that had been made in a frontier setting. For the dress of hinterland warriors to enter the general military culture, three steps must occur. First the hinterland warriors fight in their own dress and establish a reputation for themselves; then the costume must become more widely used within the imperial army; and finally other armies in the world adopt the costume. Military reputation is certainly a major factor in the adoption of a style of military dress in that uniforms are almost universally patterned after those of foreign armies who are perceived as being efficient and successful, although there have been exceptions to this rule, as when those in a position of power reject foreign styles of dress in favour of a 'national' costume as happened from time to time in Imperial Russia (Mollo: 1979). To work backwards, other armies in the world will be more likely to adopt the exotic dress of a hinterland warrior if it has been adopted by what is perceived to be a major world power. It would seem likely, for instance, that if Zouaves had been associated with one of the Italian states rather than France, then the Zouave costume would have been less likely to spread. The fact that hussars were employed by both Austria and Prussia in the mid-eighteenth century almost certainly helped to ensure that other countries would dress their light cavalry as hussars. Although Polish lancers had long been on the fringes of some European armies, it was their prominent incorporation into the army of Napoleonic France that led to the widespread adoption of their style of dress. Similarly, although changes in firearms technology would no doubt have led to use of inconspicuous clothing in time, the importance and prevalence of the khaki of India in armies around the world rests with its initial use by the imperial British army.

On the other hand, there appears to be a tendency to appropriate innovations in dress in one colonial army for use by the colonial armies of other imperial powers. Thus the Zouave uniform was used by the British for its West India Regiment and for troops in West Africa, and the fez spread as the mark of the indigenous colonial soldier in sub-Saharan Africa. For many years, the French and Germans exclusively reserved khaki for their colonial troops. One might also argue, slightly facetiously, that the English tolerated the use of bagpipes by units of hinterland warriors (the Scots) recruited on their northern frontier, and allowed or even encouraged their diffusion to other units of hinterland warriors recruited elsewhere in the empire. This tendency to treat all colonial troops as similar is based, in part, on underlying European ethnocentric assumptions that all peoples on the edges of 'civilization' are alike.

As it seems that the perception of an imperial army's capabilities has been a controlling factor in the adoption of its style of dress by other armies in the industrial world, what, then, leads that imperial power to adopt the dress of native auxiliaries in the first place? One would expect that racist and ethnocentric assumptions held by imperial military officers about abilities of diverse human populations limit the recruiting of hinterland warriors and the adoption of items of their dress. However, although stereotypes of the capabilities of the frontier warriors may have led to them being considered as being in dire need of direction from the imperial officer corps, it was nevertheless granted that some peoples on the edge of 'civilization' were particularly talented in performing specific military tasks. The result is that virtually every population in the world in which men have kept horse herds has found itself being characterized as producing the 'finest light cavalry in the world'. These martial races were perceived as not being capable of fighting like 'civilized' armies, but because they were beyond 'civilization' they were viewed as possessing qualities that made them useful 'if properly led'.

The period covered in this book is a long one, with vast changes in the nature of armies. Certainly a factor in the seventeenth- and eighteenth-century recruitment of frontier warriors was related to the degree to which military units were recruited by individuals who then sold their services to the state. Governments were always anxious to find sources of fighting men, and enterprising leaders – sometimes the élite from among the indigenous hinterland population itself – were happy to profit from the needs of states by seeking willing recruits among frontier peoples. Armies at this time were relatively small, and the proportion of them that was of foreign origin was often quite high. This was changed by the French Revolution and the ensuing creation of the massive armies that took the field after that event. Patriotism began to replace mercenary values as the basis for recruitment of the army, and when patriotism failed to provide the requisite number of men, it was replaced by conscription. Frontier peoples and other foreign elements thus became far less significant to the total picture, although the frontier experience was still of some importance to the metropolitan army.

A major factor relating to the adoption of the dress of the hinterland warrior lay in the relationship between the portion of the imperial officer corps on the frontier and the portion remaining at home in the metropolitan army. The politics surrounding headquarters and the general staff are usually complex, and although, in some cases, service on the frontier seems to have been viewed as a training ground for the officer corps, in other cases it was viewed as a bothersome task, ideally relegated to socially inferior officers. One certainly gets the impression that France, in the mid-nineteenth century, took the former view with respect to North Africa, whereas Britain took the latter view with respect to India. In the United States, despite advances in communication and direct rail links to the edges of the frontier, there seems to have been a considerable gulf between the frontier officers and the staff at headquarters in Washington.

*The Frontier Experience*

## The Periphery Influences the Core

Clearly the expansion of an empire can have tragic consequences for those people who find themselves in its path. At a minimum the frontier population sees the exchange of domination by one state for domination by another (in those regions where two imperial armies compete for control); in the worst cases the frontier population may face enslavement, removal from its homeland or even genocide.

Imperial expansion brings the diverse cultures on the frontier into contact with complex urban civilizations. The latter form the core of the empire while the former forms the periphery. While a good deal of innovation originates in the core, this study demonstrates that the periphery can have an influence on the core. In this book creative innovations in a narrow section of human behaviour – changes in the dress and adornment of the fighting man – have been examined. The examples chosen, I believe, show that fighting against or alongside hinterland warriors has, at least on occasion, led to borrowings, adaptations and improvisational change in the dress of metropolitan armies. Given the conservatism generally associated with the military, and particularly with the military of the 'age of empire', the willingness to accept innovations derived from frontier peoples may be somewhat unexpected. However, I believe the independent nature of some of the officer corps attracted to the frontier, such as Lumsden of the Guides on the Northwest Frontier of India and Frank North with his troop of Pawnee scouts on the American plains, was ultimately a deciding factor. Such officers might not have been as free of ethnocentric or racist attitudes as are those students steeped in the cultural relativism of the twentieth century, but they carried into their frontier duties a total respect for the people they had to deal with on a day-to-day basis. The relatively unusual characteristics and experience required of such leaders is one reason the US Army rejected increased enlistment of Indian personnel. Troops who performed admirably under such an officer might well be completely incompatible with his replacement. Similarly the British in both world wars had difficulties finding men to officer a greatly expanded Indian Army, and also in replacing those officers lost to their units.

The examples in this work have shown how complex military bureaucracies have incorporated frontier peoples, making them integral parts of their institution. They have also shown how similar bureaucracies in other states have been impressed by both the practical and symbolic aspects of the fighting attire of the hinterland warrior – so much so that many intensely patriotic, even chauvinistic, soldiers fighting to preserve their homeland against a feared invader have done so wearing clothing derived from a culture far removed from their own.

# Glossary[1]

Alkhalak – a frock coat worn in the Indian Army cavalry, which reached the knee.

Baldrick – a belt worn over the right shoulder across the body to the left hip; it could support a sword or drum, but in the case of bagpipers it is often simply ornamental.

Balmoral – a flat, broad Highland bonnet, cocked to the right side, with a tourie on the top; see *tam-o'-shanter.*

Barrel sash – a sash consisting of a large number of cords that passed through tubes; worn by hussars.

Battle dress – an order of dress developed for the British Army prior to the World War II, including a khaki waist-length jacket and full trousers with multiple pockets.

Bearskin – a grenadier cap covered completely, or nearly so, with fur. Currently worn in full dress by all five regiments of the British Foot Guards and by the Danish *Livgarde.*

Bicorne – hat that became popular in the late eighteenth century in which the brim is turned up on each side, and which may be worn parallel with the shoulders or 'fore and aft'.

Brandenburg – lace or frogging across the front of a coat or jacket, often with a loop at the end; ornaments the dolman or hussar tunic.

Busby – see colback.

Chasseur – either a light cavalryman (*chasseur à cheval*) or light infantryman.

Coatee – a tailed coat, cut square across the waist at the front; worn in the first half of the nineteenth century.

Cockade – a folded piece of cloth or leather, usually in the form of a rosette, worn on the hat and coloured to indicate national or political affiliation.

Colback – a cylindrical fur cap with a cloth bag emerging from the top and falling to one side. A synonym is *busby.*

Colours – flags carried by a regiment or battalion intended to serve as a rallying point during a battle; in the nineteenth century British battalions carried two, a regimental colour and a Queen's colour, and French battalions carried a single tricolour inscribed with regimental distinctions.

Cossack trousers – very full trousers worn by mounted troops.

## Glossary

Cuirass – armour to protect the upper torso, or sometimes, if a back plate is not worn, simply a plate to protect the chest; although discarded by infantry before the close of the seventeenth century, it was worn by some heavy cavalry in action as late as the first decades of the twentieth and continues in full dress of units such as Britain's Life Guards and the Blues and Royals.

Cuirassier – a designation for heavy cavalry whose upper body is protected by a cuirass.

*Czapka* – a square-topped headdress derived from the *konfederatka* but in its fully evolved form with a rigid rather than a soft-cloth top; worn by uhlans.

Daffadar – a native non-commissioned officer in the British Indian Army; equivalent to a sergeant.

Daffadar-Major – a native non-commissioned officer in the British Indian Army; equivalent to a sergeant major.

Dolman – a jacket with several rows of buttons and horizontal braid across the front. Originally worn by hussars and occasionally worn by other troops.

Doublet – originally the name for a widely worn civilian short jacket in the Middle Ages and Renaissance, doublet is now used for the tunic worn with Highland dress, which may be either single- or double-breasted and terminates with four Inverness skirts or flaps which fall from the waist.

Dragoon – a heavy cavalryman originally intended to dismount for fighting but later serving a role undifferentiated from other battle cavalry.

Eisenhower jacket – a short jacket resembling that of British Battle Dress worn in the US Army during and after the World War II.

Epaulette – a shoulder ornament, usually fringed; sometimes it served as a badge of rank.

Facings – the cloth used for the collar, cuffs, lapels and sometimes lining of a military coat; of a different colour from the coat itself, it served as a regimental distinction.

Feather bonnet – a large ostrich feather headdress worn by Highlanders and others in Highland dress; the feathers cover a cloth bonnet that usually has a diced band or border.

Felie beg – see *philibeg*.

Fez – a cylindrical cap, with a tassel attached to the centre of its flat top, originating from within the Ottoman empire and worn by Zouaves and troops in similar uniforms; the body of the cap is usually red.

Fly plaid – in Highland dress, a tartan scarf which is attached to the left shoulder and falls to the bottom of the kilt.

Foot – infantry.

*Glossary*

Full dress – uniforms designed for wear on gala occasions or ceremonial duties.
Gaiters – coverings for the leg and top of the shoe or boot, with a strap under the instep and closed by buttons up the outside of the leg; see also spatterdashes.
Girdle – a waist belt fastened on the left side, of either silver, gold, white or yellow with two or more horizontal coloured stripes; associated with the dress of uhlans or lancers.
Glengarry – a loaf-shaped cap originally worn by Highlanders ornamented with a tourie; worn fore-and-aft on the head.
Gorget – a metal crescent-shaped badge of rank worn at the throat.
Grenadier cap – originally a cap worn in place of the brimmed hat so that a grenadier could sling his musket freeing his hands to throw grenades; later a tall cap of cloth, metal or fur worn by elite troops.
Grenadiers – in the late seventeenth century soldiers picked for their size and strength to throw hand bombs (grenades); later specially-dressed elite troops picked for their size and courage.
Guards – elite troops, often with more elaborate uniforms, usually associated with the sovereign; distinguished from the line.
Guidon – a flag, usually swallow tailed, carried by cavalry.
Hackle – a plume to decorate a headdress.
Havildar – a native non-commissioned officer of infantry in the British Indian Army; equivalent to a sergeant.
Havildar-Major – a native non-commissioned officer of infantry in the British Indian Army; equivalent to sergeant major.
Horse – in the seventeenth and eighteenth century a designation for some units of heavy cavalry.
Hussar – a light cavalryman with a distinctive dress derived from that of Hungary.
Inverness skirts – the four pointed flaps, decorated with lace and three buttons each, which fall from the waist of the Highland doublet.
Jäger – a German or Austrian light infantryman armed with a rifle.
Jemadar – a native officer in the British Indian Army; second in command of a company of infantry or a troop of cavalry.
Kepi – a peaked cloth cylindrical cap, the top of which is horizontal if the cap is stiffened or slopes from rear to front if the cap is not.
Kilmarnock – either a stiffened bonnet with a broad top, a diced band and ornamented with a tourie and cocks feathers worn by Lowland Scots in full dress or the pill-box cap, also ornamented with a tourie, worn by Ghurkas.
Kilt – the skirt, normally of tartan, pleated at the rear and overlapping at

the front where it is secured with a kilt pin, worn by men in Highland dress; see *plaid* and *philibeg*.

*Konfederatka* – the original form of the square-topped Polish headgear, the top of soft cloth and the brim edged with fur. See *czapka*.

*Kukri* – a broad-bladed knife carried by Gurkhas.

Kurta – a loose blouse worn instead of a tunic or coat in the Indian Army cavalry, put on over the head and buttoning from the neck to the waist, with the skirt sometimes slit (either at the sides or at the front and back).

*Kurtka* – the jacket or tunic associated with lancers or uhlans; fronted with a plastron and piped along the back seams of the sleeves and the back seams of the jacket or tunic.

Lace – braid or tape which ornaments a uniform, often marking regimental affiliation and/or rank.

Lance-Daffadar – a non-commissioned officer in the British Indian Army; equivalent to corporal.

Line – armies organized in European fashion are often divided into guards and the line; the former usually considered the élite of the army while the bulk of the army is the latter.

Mameluk – a slave class employed in a military role by the Turkish empire, some of whom joined the Guard of Napoleon after he led a French invasion of Egypt; these served France until the end of the First Empire.

Mirliton – a cap in the shape of a truncated cone with a long angular flap attached to one side, which can alternatively be allowed to hang over the shoulder or wrapped about the body of the cap. Originally worn by hussars but occasionally worn by others.

Naik – a native non-commissioned officer in the Indian Army; equivalent to a corporal.

Olivet – a large button covered with cloth or thread, often metallic, ornamenting the brandenburg on a hussar tunic.

Overalls – a trouser with a strap under the instep worn by cavalry.

Peak – the extension of a cap or hat from its front to shade the face or occasionally a similar device at the rear of the cap or hat to shade the neck; 'peak' is British usage for what Americans usually call a 'visor'.

Pelisse – a heavily-braided jacket usually lined or edged with fur that, except in cold weather, was slung over the left shoulder or at the back. Associated with hussar dress but sometimes worn by others.

Philibeg – the 'little kilt'; designed to simulate the bottom portion of the belted plaid with pleats permanently sewn into the rear portion of the garment that stretches from the waist nearly to the knee; see *kilt* and *plaid*.

Pickelhaube – the German spiked helmet worn from the latter half of the nineteenth century into World War I.

Pike – a long (four to five metres) spear carried by bodies of infantry prior to the invention of the bayonet.

Pioneer – a soldier with designated tasks involving the construction of defensives and the destruction of obstacles in path of an advancing column.

Plaid – the original Highland garment was belted about the waist, covering the legs almost to the knee, and fastened to the left shoulder; later, after the adoption of the kilt or philibeg, a separate scarf fastened to the left shoulder – see *fly plaid* and *shoulder plaid*.

Plastron – a large coloured cloth buttoned on the sides to the front of a lancer jacket or tunic (*kurtka*) covering the chest and abdomen. The same effect is obtained in a double-breasted coat, cut straight across the waist at the front, by buttoning back the lapels, exposing the facing colour, and fastening the coat by hooks and eyes down the front.

Puggaree – a cloth worn about the head or about a hat or helmet.

Puttees – long strips of cloth wound about the leg from the top of the shoe or boot to somewhere below the knee.

Reversed colours – dress worn by drummers, trumpeters and other musicians in which the coat is in the facing colour of the unit and the collar, cuffs and lapels are the colour of the unit's coat.

Rissalder – a native officer of cavalry in the British Indian Army; commander of a troop.

Rissalder-Major – the senior Indian officer in a cavalry regiment in the British Indian Army.

Sabretache – a flat leather pouch suspended from the sword belt so that it hangs at the knee or lower carried by Hussars and occasionally by others.

*Serouel* – the baggy trousers (really a rectangular bag with a waist band and two openings for the legs) worn by Zouaves.

Sepoy – an ordinary (that is, not an officer but of the other ranks) locally recruited infantryman in India.

Shako – a tall cylindrical cap, although sometimes larger at the top than the bottom, usually with a peak.

Shoulder plaid – a long scarf worn over the left shoulder and under the right arm, fastened with a brooch at the left shoulder and falling down the left side and back to the back of the knee.

Slouch hat – a broad brimmed 'bush' hat with the crown frequently wrapped in a puggaree and indented in various patterns and the brim sometimes turned up on one side.

Spatterdashes – gaiters that reach above the knee, often to mid-thigh.

Sporran – a purse worn with Highland dress at the front of the kilt.

Sowar – an ordinary (that is, not an officer but of the other ranks) locally recruited cavalryman in India.

Subadar – an native officer of infantry in the British Indian Army; commanded a company.

Subadar-Major – a native officer of infantry in the British Indian Army; served on the regimental staff.

Sutleress – see vivandiere.

Tam-o'-shanter – a flat, broad Highland bonnet, cocked to the right with a diced band and a tourie on the top.

Targe – a circular shield, ornamented with brass studs, carried by Highlanders in the early eighteenth century.

Tarleton helmet – named after Sir Banastre Tarleton, commander of the British Legion during the American Revolution, the helmet consists of a leather skull, a peak, a puggaree-like sash about the bottom edge and a fore-and-aft bearskin crest; used by British Light Dragoons and Horse Artillery in the late eighteenth and early nineteenth centuries.

Tartan – the pattern coloured threads woven to form the cloth used to make the plaids, kilts or trews of troops in Highland dress; in military use specific to a regiment or other unit.

Tombeau – a tape or lace that forms a loop and ends in a tri-foil (three additional loops) which decorates the front of jackets of Zouaves and other North African troops.

Tourie – a tuft or small pom-pom that adorns the top of a cap or bonnet.

Trews – tartan trousers.

Tricorne – hat popular for much of the eighteenth century in which the brim was folded up on three sides forming three points, one of which was usually worn pointing forward. Replaced near the end of the century by the bicorne.

Uhlan – a soldier armed with a lance and dressed in the style of Poles who used this arm.

Valise – a pack or satchel carried on the back of an infantryman or behind the saddle of a cavalryman.

Vedette – a cavalry outpost manned to prevent an army being surprised by enemy troops.

Vivandiere – a woman who sells spirits and other refreshments to troops; when associated with a particular regiment, she often wore a modified uniform of the corps.

Voltigeur – a light infantryman in the French army.

Wings – a crescent-shaped ornament of cloth and lace worn on each shoulder where the sleeve joins the body of the coat; associated with élite units and musicians.

Zouave – an infantryman wearing a uniform patterned on colonial troops originally raised by the French in Algeria.

# Notes

## Chapter 1

1. The actual phrase written by W. H. Russell, correspondent from *The Times*, was 'the thin red streak tipped with a line of steel' but it has come down to us as 'the thin red line' (McElwee 1972: 21). It is of course a common phenomenon to alter the text as a saying moves into popular usage. Examples include 'Play it again, Sam' which was never spoken by in the movie 'Casablanca', 'Alas poor Yorick, I knew him well' (Hamlet neglects the 'well' in Shakespear's text) and 'Never-Never Land' of Peter Pan ( J. M.. Barrie's original is 'Never Land').

## Chapter 3

1. However, when Count Hadek's Hussars were among the Austrian troops who briefly occupied Berlin, it was reported 'the Berliners of 1757 found the hussars not the unscrupulous bandits which their reputation hinted at, but disciplined and seasoned troopers' (Heathcote 1976: 120).
2. Any attempt to make sense of uniforms of the Indian Army is compounded by the many orders of dress utilized. The situation was such that when each of the British Officers of the 17th Cavalry donned a different order of dress for a 1922 photograph, both drill order blue (Indian) and khaki service dress were omitted because there were not a sufficient number of officers to provide a model for these orders of dress. Eight orders of dress are illustrated in the photograph (Harris 1979: 33).
3. These fur hats are often misidentified by journalists as 'busbies'. As has been stated above, the busby is the fur headdress with a bag hanging from the top worn by hussars and troops in hussar-style dress.
4. Both the colback and the cylindrical cap worn by hussars were, of course, civilian dress in their original form in their native Hungary, but were distinctive military dress in those countries to which the idea of the hussar

spread. It should be noted that shortly after the initial spread of hussar dress, some units in some European armies adopted helmets of leather or metal with fur, feather or horse hair crests, again distinctly military rather than civilian dress. However, until 1800 the vast majority of soldiers in Europe wore the bicorne.

5. There are of course minor exceptions to this rule. For example, battalion commanders in Napoleonic France enjoyed considerable latitude in dressing musicians and sappers, and frequently these troops (especially drum majors) wore a colback. Voltigeur companies (the second élite company in Napoleonic French Light Infantry battalions) also sometimes wore the colback.

6. Austria also recruited regiments of foot in the same frontier regions that supplied the empire with hussars and these units served as the first light infantry. Like their cousins in the hussars, they wore cylindrical caps. It was in the dress of the hussar, however, that the shako was first introduced to most European armies. Whether one sees the origin of the shako in the dress of the light infantry of the Austrian empire or in the dress of the hussar does not really matter since the dress worn by both reflects the shared ethnicity of these hinterland warriors.

## Chapter 4

1. Among the pejorative ethnic names I recall hearing in two American cities – both with large Polish populations – was a reference to Poles (or persons with Polish ancestry) as 'square-heads'. It is tempting to relate this ethnonym to the *czapka*. The ethnonym was used for Poles by other ethnic minorities; a story circulating in the Native North American community in Milwaukee, Wisconsin, told of a Winnebago Indian who at work was hassled by a foreman of Polish ancestry (a 'Polack' in the story) who insisted on calling him 'Chief', despite requests that he not do this. Fellow workers of the Winnebago asked why he put up with this behaviour. 'Why don't you take his scalp?' they asked the Winnebago. The Indian thought about it, and replied, 'What would I do with a square scalp?'

2. I have seen two functional explanations of the lance pennon. Maurice de Saxe felt the flapping pennons would frighten enemy horses (Heathcote 1976: 118). Others suggested that it prevented the lance from penetrating too deeply and so allowed the uhlan to extract the lance and carry on the fight. That the lance pennon is viewed as attractive is attested to by its use in 'musical rides' by mounted units that never

*Notes*

      considered using a lance in combat, such as the Household Cavalry in the United Kingdom and the Royal Canadian Mounted Police.

3. That Lasalle chose to wear a green dolman and pelisse may also be related to his long association with the cousins of hussars in the French light cavalry, the Chasseurs à Cheval who wore green and whose élite companies were frequently dressed 'à la Hussard'. While often described as the ideal hussar, Lasalle was more frequently in command of chasseurs than of hussars.

## Chapter 5

1. The Royal title was not granted as an honour for the conduct of the regiment at the Battle of Ticonderoga in what is now upstate New York, despite the frequent assertion that it was (see Grant 1971: 10; Lawson 1940–67, Volume 4: 96). The decision to grant the Royal title was made before the regiment suffered appalling casualties (314 killed and 333 wounded, more than half its strength) in the assault on the French positions before Fort Ticonderoga (Reid 1993: 20).
2. I have seen several journalistic references to feather bonnets as 'busbies'. It is likely that the journalists assumed the bonnet was made of fur since journalists also frequently, and equally incorrectly, use the term 'busby' for the bearskins (the fur grenadier caps) worn by the guards on ceremonial duties in London and Windsor. Busby is correct for the fur cap worn by hussars and troops dressed after hussar fashion.
3. The considerable hardships suffered by British forces in the Crimean War have been cited for the change from a coatee to a tunic. However, this was planned before that experience and had occured earlier in other European armies. In the Crimea, the British, still in uniforms essentially of the Napoleonic era, presented a decidedly archaic, unfashionable appearance compared to that of their French and Italian allies and even their Russian foes. The change to the tunic was as much a product of style and fashion as it was a product of concern for the comfort of the common soldier.
4. The regiment wore these scarlet trews with khaki tunics and pith helmets while on campaign in Afghanistan in 1879. Other ranks wrapped their legs from below the knee to their boots with khaki puttees, but officers' puttees were of the regimental tartan.
5. The Scots perhaps gained more respect from their enemies than from some of their comrades in the British Army. Robert Graves was told by the adjutant of the Welch Fusiliers: 'The Jocks are all the same, the

## Notes

trousered variety and the bare-assed variety. They're dirty in the trenches, they shit too much, and they charge like hell – in both directions' (quoted in Farwell 1981: 38).

6. The American Declaration of Independence complained that the King made use of foreign mercenaries against his rebellious colonists. Most Americans now believe that this is a reference to the British employment of Hessians and other German troops in the war. However, when the Declaration of Independence was passed, on 4 July 1776 not a single German 'mercenary' had appeared in North America. The reference in the Declaration of Independence would appear to be to the employment of Highlanders in the British forces.

7. Similar reasoning dictated that cavalry trumpeters wear distinctive dress in reversed colours. In addition the trumpeter in a troop of cavalry was the only one to ride a grey horse, a practice still followed by the Life Guards and the Blues and Royals on mounted ceremonial duties in London. The reverse of this rule was the practice of the Royal Scots Greys who rode grey horses, hence their name. Their trumpeters rode blacks.

8. Pioneers performed tasks such as building fortifications. Their work was much the same as that of the Engineers and most of the Canadian Pioneer battalions were absorbed into the Canadian Engineers in 1917 (Stewart 1970: 152).

9. The barrel of the screw gun could be unscrewed into two sections, each of which could be carried on the back of a mule. A third mule carried the wheels of the gun while a fourth carried the trail. Kipling expressed his admiration for this gun in a poem, part of which reads:

> For you all love the screw-guns – the screw-guns they all love you!
> So when we take tea with a few guns, o' course you know what to do – hoo! hoo!
> Jest send in your Chief an' surrender – it's worse if you fights or runs:
> You may hide in the caves, they'll be only your graves, but you can't get away from the guns!
>
> Rudyard Kipling, *Screw-Guns*

10. In 1949 the 10th became the 10th Princess Mary's Own Gurkha Rifles while in 1959 the 6th became the 6th Queen Elizabeth's Own Gurkha Rifles and the 7th became the 7th Duke of Edinburgh's Own Gurkha Rifles (on the lineage of Gurkha regiments, see Chappell 1993; Marrion and Fosten 1970).

Notes

11. The *kukri* is the famous broad-bladed knife carried on the right hip of each Gurkha. The *kukri* used in the buffalo sacrifice is a two-handed version, much larger and heavier than the one-handed *kukri* used in combat by the Gurkhas. It is expected that the head of the buffalo will be severed with a single blow.
12. The purpose of the cut-away, rounded skirt fronts on the tunic, which goes back to the late nineteenth century, is to allow the sporran to be worn and displayed with the kilt. However, the pattern came to be associated with Scottish, rather than just Highland, dress and it came to be worn by Lowland regiments whether with trews or with ordinary service dress netherwear.

## Chapter 6

1. It was not uncommon to dress kettle drummers in the mounted bands of cavalry regiments in a Mameluk-like costume. However, in military bands from the late-eighteenth century, well before the appearance of Mameluks in the imperial French forces, it was common to dress musicians who played bass drums, cymbals and similar percussion instruments in 'oriental' or 'Turkish' dress because of the popular association of this type of instrument with eastern peoples.

## Chapter 7

1. The Indian Army utilized the ordinary titles of rank for British officers, but had special titles for native officers and non-commissioned officers. This was because all British officers outranked all Indian officers. Indeed, the largest unit the most able of native officers could command was a company. The senior Indian infantry officer was the subadar major, who served on the regimental staff. A subadar commanded a company (as did a captain in the British Army), a jemadar was second in command of a company (as was lieutenant in the British Army), a havildar major was the equivalent of a British sergeant major, a havildar was the Indian equivalent of a British sergeant, a naik that of a British corporal, a lance naik the equivalent of a British lance corporal (American private first class) and the sepoy the ordinary infantryman. In the cavalry the senior Indian officer was the rissaldar major, a rissalder commanded a troop, a jemadar was the junior Indian officer in the cavalry, the daffadar major was the equivalent of a sergeant-major,

the daffadar the equivalent of a sergeant, the lance daffadar equivalent of a corporal, the unpaid Lance daffadar equivalent to a lance corporal and the sowar equivalent to a trooper (Farwell 1989: 367). The kot daffadar ranks between the daffadar major and the daffadar (Harris 1979: 5). The ressaidar ranked below a rissalder but higher than a jemadar (Wilson 1970: 19).
2. 'Puggaree' (in its variety of spellings) is used to designate a cloth wrapped about the head (it can be used meaning 'turban') or about a helmet, hat or cap worn on the head.
3. It has been pointed out that, for most of the history of warfare, a soldier was far more likely to die of disease on campaign than from a wound inflicted by an enemy. The development of better sanitation and health-care reversed this probability, but the increased firepower found on recent battlefields certainly meant that life there was much more precarious than it was in the time of Marlborough or Wellington.
4. French military organization formally distinguished between the metropolitan army (based in Europe) and the colonial army (based overseas, but available for service in Europe).

## Chapter 8

1. Earlier Louisbourg had been garrisoned by the Compagnies Franches de la Marine and the Swiss Regiment Karrer. The latter was not one of the foreign regiments in the French Army but rather was raised specifically for colonial service. Both regiments served as part of the garrison of Louisbourg when it was captured by British colonial troops from Massachusetts in 1745 (Windrow and Embleton 1973: 17). Administratively, Louisbourg, on Cape Breton Island, was not part of Canada but rather the separate colony of Île Royale. A small detachment of Karrer's Swiss Regiment served at Quebec City from 1747 to 1749 (Chartrand 1993: 113).
2. The surname is often spelled Goreham (Chartrand 1993: 173; 1995: 49).

## Chapter 9

1. While the anthropological literature on warfare in small-scale societies is of fair size (Ferguson and Farragher 1988), logistics is one area largely ignored in these discussions. A significant part of war is the provisioning of troops in the field.

## Notes

2. The King's Company of the 1st Foot Guards (now the Grenadier Guards) has the duty to attend the sovereign at Westminster Abbey at the time of the Coronation and to guard the body of the Sovereign at his or her funeral. It is currently known as the Queen's Company as the reigning sovereign is female (Fraser 1978: 40).
3. There are several versions of what was said and why it was said. Jacques Boudet presents one in which the English guards fire first. Lord Charles Hay, Lord Albemarle and Robert Churchill stepped out in front of their men and raised their hats in salute to the French guards. The officers of the French guards replied in kind. Boudet reports that Lord Charles Hay addressed the Comte d'Auteroche, 'Tell your men to fire' and received the reply, 'No, gentlemen, we never shoot first. The honour is yours.' Boudet argues that the reply was not 'dictated by the spirit of chivalry' but rather that the French guards had been under orders not to fire first since the battle of Lens in 1648 when they had fired too soon and experienced difficulty reloading under enemy attack (Boudet 1969: 52–4). Fortescue, however, dismisses as a legend (which 'every one knows') the exchange – 'Messieurs les Gardes Français, tirez les premiers.' 'Non, messieurs, nous ne tirons jamias les premiers' – because English accounts state the French did fire first (Fortescue 1910: 115n). Fortescue states that Hay alluded to an earlier rout of the French guards. ' "I hope, gentlemen", he shouted, "that you are going to wait for us to-day and not swim the Scheldt as you swam the Main at Dettingen. Men of the King's Company," he continued, turning round to his own people, "these are the French Guards, and I hope you are going to beat them to-day"'. As the French prepared to fire first one of Hay's British guards muttered 'For what we are about to receive may the Lord make us truly thankful' (Fortescue 1910: 115). General Sir David Fraser combines both stories in dealing with the incident having Hay initially asking the French to fire first, and then following with the reference to the rout of the French at the Battle of Dettingen which took place two years before Fontenoy (Fraser 1978: 8–9).
4. Some seem to have done so. Chagnon (1968) has suggested his ethnographic data on warfare among the Yanomamö is representative of non-state societies and has argued the violent men among the Yanomamö enjoy an enhanced Darwinian fitness (Chagnon 1988; see Ferguson 1989). Hallpike argues that violence and war are simply part of human nature (Hallpike 1973).
5. The officers of the French Zouaves wore a red kepi (as did the French army generally), a frock coat and conventional trousers rather than Zouave dress. Some American Zouave units were clothed in dress more

closely resembling that of the officers rather than the rank and file of the French Zouaves.

## Glossary

1. For an excellent, well-illustrated dictionary of terms relating to military uniform, see Carman 1977.

# Bibliography

Abler, Thomas S. (1975), 'Presents, Merchants, and the Indian Department: Economic Aspects of the American Revolutionary Frontier', *Canadian Ethnology Society Proceedings*, National Museum of Man Canadian Ethnology Service Mercury Series, paper no. 28, vol. 2, pp. 603–21.

Ahliny, Anders B. (1972), 'The First Swedish Hussars', *Tradition*, no. 63, pp. 30–1.

Allen, Robert S. (1975), 'The British Indian Department and the Frontier in North America, 1755–1830', *Canadian Historic Sites: Occasional Papers in Archaeology and History*, no. 14, pp. 5–125, Ottawa: Parks Canada.

Anderson, Donald (1939), 'Cape Corps, Officer's Jacket, 1820', *Journal of the Society for Army Historical Research*, vol. 18, p. 115.

Anderson, Douglas N. (1989), *The Brigade of Gurkhas*, British Army Series nos 54–60, Blackwell: Geoff White Ltd.

Andreski, Stanislav (1968), *Military Organization and Society*, Berkeley: University of California Press.

Asquith, Stuart (ed.) (1997a), 'The Royal Logistic Corps', *Regiment: The Military Heritage Collection*, no. 23.

——, (1997b), 'The Royal Tank Regiment 1916–1997', *Regiment: The Military Heritage Collection*, no. 26.

——, (1998), 'The Royal Gloucestershire, Berkshire and Wiltshire Regiment 1694–1881: History, Standards, Uniforms & Equipment', *Regiment: The Military Heritage Collection*, no. 27.

Bailey, Thomas Andrew, ed. (1968), *The American Spirit*, 2nd Edition, Lexington: Heath.

Baines, Anthony (1960), *Bagpipes*, Pitt Rivers Museum, University of Oxford, Occasional Papers on Technology 9, Oxford: Oxford University Press.

Balaguer, José and Fernández, Cristián (1974a), 'Argentine Army 1814–1819: Husares y Guias de la Guardia del Director Supremo', *Tradition*, no. 74, pp. 32–3.

——, (1974b), 'Some Argentine Uniforms', *Tradition*, no. 76, pp. 2–3.

Balaguer, José and Girado, Ernesto Denvi (1972), 'National Guard Hussars Brazilian Empire – 1840,' *Tradition*, no. 64, pp. 12–3.

——, (1973), 'The Argentinean Army 1813,' *Tradition*, no. 67, pp. 2–4.

Bard, Bob and Craver, Charles H. (1960), 'The Soldiers on the Cover', *Military Miniature Collector*, vol. 2, p. 87.

Barnes, R. Money (1954), *A History of the Regiments & Uniforms of the British Army*, London: Seeley Service.

# Bibliography

——, (1956), *The Uniforms & History of the Scottish Regiments: Britain – Canada – Australia – New Zealand – South Africa: 1625 to the Present Day*, London: Seeley Service.

——, (1960) *Military Uniforms of Britain and The Empire*, London: Sphere Books [reprint 1972].

Barroso, Gustavo (1922), *Uniformes do Exercito Brasileiro*, Rio de Janeiro: Ministerio da Guerra.

Barthorp, Michael (1979), *Indian Infantry Regiments 1860–1914*, London: Osprey.

——, (1982), *British Infantry Uniforms Since 1660*, Poole, Dorset: Blandford.

——, (1984), *British Cavalry Uniforms Since 1660*, Poole, Dorset: Blandford.

——, (1988a), *The British Army on Campaign 1816–1902 (3): 1856–1881*, London: Osprey.

——, (1988b), *The British Army on Campaign 1816–1902 (4): 1882–1902*, London: Osprey.

Berenger, Jean (1980), 'L'influence des peuples de la steppe (Huns, Mongols, Tartares) sur the conception européenne de la guerre de mouvement et l'emploi de la cavalerie ($V^e$ – $XVII^e$ siècle)', *Revue internationale d'histoire militaire*, vol. 49, pp. 33–50.

Bodin, Lynn E. (1979), *The Boxer Rebellion*, London: Osprey.

Bodley, John H. (1996), *Anthropology and Contemporary Human Problems*, Third Edition, Mountain View, California: Mayfield.

Boehm, Christopher (1984), *Blood Revenge: The Enactment and Management of Conflict in Montenegro and Other Tribal Societies*, Philadelphia: University of Pennsylvania Press.

Bordewich, Fergus M. (1996), *Killing the White Man's Indian: Reinventing Native Americans at the End of the Twentieth Century*, New York: Doubleday.

Botkin, B. A. (ed.), (1960), *A Civil War Treasury of Tales, Legends and Folklore*, New York: Random House.

Boudet, Jacques (1969), '1745 Fontenoy', in Cyril Falls (ed.), *Great Military Battles*, London: Spring Books, pp. 51–7.

Bowling, A. H. (1971), *Indian Cavalry Regiments 1880–1914*, London: Almark.

——, (1972), *British Hussar Regiments 1805–1914*, New Malden, Surrey: Almark.

Bradbury, Jim (1985), *The Medieval Archer*, Woodbridge: Boydell.

Brussell, Eugene E. (ed.), (1970), *Dictionary of Quotable Definitions*, Englewood Cliffs: Prentice-Hall.

Burnham, Dorothy K. (1992), *To Please the Caribou: Painted Caribou Skin Coats Worn by the Naskapi, Montagnais, and Cree Hunters of the Quebec-Labrador Peninsula*, Seattle: University of Washington Press.

Calloway, Colin G. (1987), *Crown and Calumet: British-Indian Relations, 1783–1815*, Norman: University of Oklahoma Press.

——, (1989), 'Simon Girty: Interpreter and Intermediary', in James A. Clifton (ed.), *Being and Becoming Indian: Biographical Studies of North American Frontiers*, Chicago: Dorsey, pp. 38–58.

Calthrope, Lt. Col. Somerset J. Gough (1979), *Cadogan's Crimea. Illustrated by General the Hon. Sir George Cadogan K.C.B. Written by Lt. Col. Somerset J. Gough Calthrope*, London: Hamish Hamilton.

Campbell, Horace (1975), *Four Essays on Neo-Colonialism in Uganda: The Military Dictatorship of Idi Amin*, Toronto: Better Read Graphics.

Canada. Department of National Defence (1995), *Special Commission on the Restructuring of the Reserves Report*, Brian Dickson, Chairman; Charles H. Belzile and Jack L. Granastein, Commissioners, Ottawa: Canada Communication Group – Publishing, Public Works and Government Services Canada.

Carman, W. Y. (1957), *British Military Uniforms from Contemporary Pictures: Henry VII to the Present Day*, London: Hill.

——, (1961), *Indian Army Uniforms under the British from the 18th Century to 1947: Cavalry*, London: Leonard Hill.

——, (1969), *Indian Army Uniforms under the British from the 18th Century to 1947: Artillery, Engineers and Infantry*, London: Morgan-Grampian.

——, (1977), *A Dictionary of Military Uniform*, London: Batsford.

——, (1982), *Richard Simkin's Uniforms of the British Army: The Cavalry Regiments*, Execter: Webb & Bower.

——, (1985), *Uniforms of the British Army: Infantry, Royal Artillery, Royal Engineers and Other Corps*, Exeter: Webb & Bower.

Carneiro, Robert L. (1992), 'The Role of Warfare in Political Evolution: Past Results and Future Projections', in G. Ausenda (ed.), *Effects of War on Society*, San Marino: Center for Interdisciplinary Research on Social Stress, pp. 87–102.

Cassin-Scott, Jack and Fabb, John (1973), *Ceremonial Uniforms of the World*, London: Stephen Hope.

Caton, A. S. (1969), 'German Uhlans, c. 1910,' *Tradition*, no. 34, pp.8–13.

Chaduc, Gérard (1986), 'Les Hussards au XVIII$^e$ Siècle, des marginaux au Service du Roi de France', *Révue historique des Armes 1986*, no.1, pp. 60–7.

Chagnon, Napoleon (1968), *Yąnomamö: The Fierce People*, New York: Holt, Rinehart & Winston.

——, (1988), 'Life Histories, Blood Revenge, and Warfare in a Tribal Population', *Science*, vol. 230, pp. 985–92.

Chandler, David (1976), 'The Age of the Sun King', in James Lawford (ed.), *The Cavalry*, Indianapolis: Bobbs-Merrill, pp. 93–105.

Chant, Christopher (1985), *Gurkha: The Illustrated History of an Elite Fighting Force*, Poole, Dorset: Blandford.

Chappell, Gordon (1972), *The Search for the Well-dressed Soldier 1865–1890: Developments and Innovations in United States Army Uniforms on the Western Frontier*, Arizona Historical Society Museum Monograph no. 5. Tucson: Arizona Historical Society.

Chappell, Mike (1993), *The Gurkhas*, London: Osprey.

——, (1994), *Scottish Units in the World Wars*, London: Osprey.

Chartrand, René (1991), *The French Army in the American War of Independence*, London: Osprey.

——, (1993), *Canadian Military Heritage. Volume I. 1000–1754*, Montreal: Art Global.

——, (1995), *Canadian Military Heritage. Volume II. 1755–1871*, Montreal: Art Global.

―, (1996), *British Forces in the West Indies 1793–1815*, London: Osprey.
Chaucer, Geoffrey (1979), *The Canterbury Tales*, Paul G. Ruggiers (ed.), Norman: University of Oklahoma Press.
Cochrane, Peter (1987), *Scottish Military Dress*, London: Blandford.
Cohen, Ronald (1984), 'Warfare and State Formation: Wars Make States and States Make War', in R. Brian Ferguson (ed.), *Warfare, Culture, and Environment*, Orlando: Academic Press, pp. 329–58.
Collinson, Francis (1975), *The Bagpipe: The History of a Musical Instrument*, London: Routledge & Kegan Paul.
Crescent Books (1973), *Military Uniforms: The Splendour of the Past*, New York: Crown.
Cunliffe, Marcus (1980), 'Elmer Ellsworth', in Peter Karsten (ed.), *The Military in America: From the Colonial Era to the Present*, New York: The Free Press, pp 117–21.
D'Ami, Rinaldo D. (1969), *World Uniforms in Colour, Volume 2, Nations of America, Africa, Asia and Oceania*, F. Dubrez Fawcett (trans), London: Patrick Stephens.
Das, Chand N. (1984), *Traditions and Customs of the Indian Armed Forces*, New Delhi: Vision Books.
Deloria, Vine (1969), *Custer Died for your Sins: An Indian Manifesto*, New York: Macmillan.
Downey, Fairfax, and Jacobsen, Jacques Noel, Jr. (1973), *The Red/Bluecoats: The Indian Scouts*, Fort Collins, Colorado: Old Army Press.
Duffy, Christopher (1974), *The Army of Frederick the Great*, Newton Abbot: David & Charles.
―, (1977), *The Army of Maria Theresa: The Armed Forces of Imperial Austria, 1740–1780*, North Pomfret, VT: David & Charles.
―, (1981), *Russia's Military Way to the West: Origins and Nature of Russian Military Power 1700–1800*, London: Routledge & Kegan Paul.
―, (1988), *The Military Experience in the Age of Reason*, New York: Antheneum.
Dunlay, Thomas W. (1982), *Wolves for the Blue Soldiers: Indian Scouts and Auxiliaries with the United States Army, 1860–90*, Lincoln: University of Nebraska Press.
Dutailly, Henry (1978), 'Les premiers Zouaves (1830–1841)', *Revue Historique des Armes*, vol. 5, no. 4, pp 42–52.
Einhorn, Arthur, and Abler, Thomas S. (1996), 'Bonnets, Plumes, and Headbands in West's Painting of Penn's Treaty', *American Indian Art Magazine*, vol. 21, no. 3, pp. 44–53.
―, (1998), 'Tattooed Bodies & Severed Auricles: Images of Native American Body Modification in the Art of Benjamin West', *American Indian Art Magazine*, vol. 23, no. 4, pp. 42–53, 116–7.
Elting, John R. (1988), *Swords Around a Throne: Napoleon's Grande Armée*, New York: The Free Press.
Embleton, Gerry (1967), 'The French Army in Canada', *Tradition*, no. 24, pp. 4–7.
Embleton, R. S. (1967), 'Rogers' Rangers', *Tradition*, no. 23, pp. 22–5.

Farwell, Byron (1981), *Mr Kipling's Army*, New York: W. W. Norton.
——, (1984), *The Gurkhas*, New York: W. W. Norton.
——, (1989a), 'A Reputation for Intimidation', *MHQ: The Quarterly Journal of Military History*, vol. 1, no. 3, pp 82–9.
——, (1989b), *Armies of the Raj: From the Mutiny to Independence, 1858–1947*, New York: W. W. Norton.
Feest, Christian (1980), *The Art of War*, London: Thames & Hudson.
Ferguson, R. Brian (1989), 'Do Yanomamo Killers Have More Kids?', *American Ethnologist*, vol. 16, pp. 564–5.
——, (1990), 'Explaining War', in Jonathan Haas (ed.), *The Anthropology of War*, Cambridge: Cambridge University Press, pp. 26–55.
——, and Farragher, Leslie (1988), 'The Anthropology of War: A Bibliography', *Occasional Papers of the Harry Frank Guggenheim Foundation*, no. 1, New York: Harry Frank Guggenheim Foundation.
Ferguson, R. Brian, and Whitehead, Neil L. (1992), 'The Violent Edge of Empire', in R. Brian Ferguson and Neil L. Whitehead (eds), *War in the Tribal Zone: Expanding States and Indigenous Warfare*, Santa Fe: School of American Research Press, pp. 1–30.
Fortescue, J. W. (1910), *A History of the British Army*, Vol. II, London: Macmillan.
Fosten, D. S. V. (1969), 'Some Notes on Military Costume Worn During the Indian Mutiny 1857–1858', *Tradition*, no. 29, pp. 10–7; no. 30, pp. 13–20.
——, and Fosten, B. K. (1989), *The Thin Red Line: Uniforms of the British Army between 1751 and 1914*, London: Windrow & Greene.
Fraser, David (1978), *The Grenadier Guards*, London: Osprey.
Fredrickson, N. Jaye (1980), *The Covenant Chain: Indian Ceremonial and Trade Silver*, Ottawa: National Museums of Canada.
Funcken, Liliane, and Funcken, Fred (1970), *L'uniforme et les Armes des Soldats de la Guerre 1914–1918: 1. Infanterie – Blindés – Aviation*, Tournai: Casterman.
Fundaburk, Emma Lila (1958), *Southeastern Indians Life Portraits: A Catalogue of Pictures 1564–1860*, Luverne, Alabama: Fundaburk.
Ganteaume, Cécile R. (1998), 'Western Apache Tailored Deer Hide Shirts: Their Resemblance to Full-dress Coats Worn by Officers in the U.S. Army and Possible Meaning', *American Indian Art Magazine*, vol.23, no. 2, pp. 44–55, 104.
Gelner, Ernest (1995), *Anthropology and Politics: Revolutions in the Sacred Grove*, Oxford: Blackwell.
Gernsheim, Helmut and Gernsheim, Alison (1954), *Roger Fenton: Photographer of the Crimean War*, London: Secker & Warburg.
Gibbs, Gary (1998), 'The Royal Artillery Sunset Ceremony', *Military Modelling*, vol. 28, no. 15, pp. 46–8.
Glubb, John Bagot (1948), *The Story of the Arab Legion*, London: Hodder & Stoughton.
——, (1957), *A Soldier with the Arabs*, London: Hodder & Stoughton.
Godfrey, Edward S. (1992), 'Custer's Last Battle', in Paul Andrew Hutton (ed.), *The Custer Reader*, Lincoln: University of Nebraska Press, pp. 257–318.

## Bibliography

Goltz, Herbert C. W. (1983), 'Tecumseh', *Dictionary of Canadian Biography*, vol. 5, pp. 795–801, Toronto: University of Toronto Press.
Grant, Charles (1971), *The Black Watch*, Reading: Osprey.
Grant, Roderick (1977), *The 51st Highland Division at War*. London: Ian Allan.
Hagger, D. H., Fosten, D. S. V. and Marrion, R. J. (1974), *Hussars and Mounted Rifles: Uniforms of the Imperial German Cavalry 1900–1914*, New Malden, Surrey: Almark.
Hallpike, Christopher (1973), 'Functionalist Interpretations of Primitive Warfare', *Man, ns*, vol. 8, pp. 451–73.
Hanson, James A. (1982), 'Laced Coats and Leather Jackets: The Great Plains Intercultural Clothing Exchange', in Douglas H. Ubelaker and Herman J. Viola (eds.), *Plains Indian Studies: A Collection of Essays in Honor of John C. Ewers and Waldo R. Wedel*, Smithsonian Contributions to Anthropology No. 30, Washington: Smithsonian Institution Press, pp. 105–17.
Harris, R. G. (1979), *Bengal Cavalry Regiments 1857–1914*, London: Osprey.
Haswell Miller, A. E. and N. P. Dawnay (1966–70), *Military Drawings and Paintings in the Collection of Her Majesty the Queen*, London: Phaidon.
Haythornthwaite, Philip J. (1975), *Uniforms of the Civil War 1861–1865 in Color*, New York: Macmillian.
——, (1977), *World Uniforms and Battles in Colour 1815–50*, Poole, Dorset: Blandford.
——, (1981), *Uniforms of the French Revolutionary Wars 1789–1802*, Poole, Dorset: Blandford.
——, (1986), *Austrian Army of the Napoleonic Wars (2): Cavalry*, London: Osprey.
——, (1987), *The Russian Army of the Napoleonic Wars (2): Cavalry 1799–1814*, London: Osprey.
——, (1988), *Victorian Colonial Wars*, London: Arms and Armour Press.
——, (1991), *Frederick the Great's Army (1): Cavalry*, London: Osprey.
——, (1994), *The Austrian Army 1740–80 (1): Cavalry*, London: Osprey.
Heathcote, T. A. (1976), 'The Age of Frederick the Great', in James Lawford (ed.), *The Cavalry*, Indianapolis: Bobbs-Merrill, pp. 107–21.
Hefter, J. (1958), *El Soldado Mexicano 1837–1847*, Mexico City: Nieto, Brown, Hefter.
——, (1982), 'Hungarian Hussars, Mexico, 1864–1867', in John R. Elting and Michael J. McAfee (eds.), *Military Uniforms in America: Volume III: Long Endure: The Civil War Period 1852–1867*, Novato, California: Presidio Press, pp. 122–3.
Heggoy, Alf Andrew and John M. Haar (1984), *The Military in Imperial History: The French Connection*, New York: Garland.
Henderson, Diana M. (1993), *The Scottish Regiments*, Glasgow: HarperCollins.
Hesketh, Christian (1961), *Tartans*, London: Weidenfeld & Nicolson.
Hills, R. J. T. (1936), 'Khaki and Service Dress', *Journal of the Society for Army Historical Research*, vol. 15, pp. 150–1.
Holding, T. H. (1894), *Uniforms of the British Army, Navy, and Court,* London: T. H. Holding [reprinted, 1969, London: Frederick Muller].

Hooker, Terry (1972), 'Uniforms of the Mexican Army 1839–1847, Part II, Cavalry', *Tradition*, no. 66, pp. 22–5.
——, and Poulter, Ron (1991), *The Armies of Bolivar and San Martin*, London: Osprey.
Hourtoulle, F. G. (1979), *Le Général Comte Charles Lasalle 1775–1809*, Paris: Copernic.
Howarth, David (1968), *A Near Run Thing: The Day of Waterloo*, London: Collins.
Hudson, Charles (1976), *The Southeastern Indians*, Knoxville: University of Tennessee Press.
Hutchins, James S. (1992), 'The Cavalry Campaign Outfit at the Little Big Horn', in Paul Andrew Hutton (ed.), *The Custer Reader*, Lincoln: University of Nebraska Press, pp. 319–35.
Jansson, Per-Eric (1973), 'The Swedish Army: Organization, Potential and Uniforms during the Latter Part of the 19th Century'. *Tradition*, no. 70, pp. 9–12.
Johnson, David (1978), *Napoleon's Cavalry and its Leaders*, New York: Holmes & Meier.
Johnson, Ray (1969), 'The Japanese Infantry Uniform, 1904–05', *Tradition*, no. 32, pp. 14–6.
Johnson, Rossiter, Lee, Fitzhugh, Ridpath, John Clark, Morgan, John T., and Kilmer, George L. (1895), *The American Soldier in the Civil War: A Pictorial History of the Campaigns and Conflicts of the War between the States, Frank Leslie's Illustrations*, New York: Bryan, Taylor.
Johnson, Samuel (1755), *A Dictionary of the English Language*, London: W. Strahan [reprinted New York: AMS Press, 1967].
Jones, Tom, and Milligan, Ed (1991), 'Pipes and Drums, United States Corps of Cadets, 1972–1990', *Military Collector and Historian*, vol. 43, no. 2, p. 82.
Joseph, Nathan (1986), *Uniforms and Nonuniforms: Communication through Clothing*, New York: Greenwood.
Kannik, Preben (1968), *Military Uniforms in Color*, New York: Macmillan.
Karklins, Karlis (1992), *Trade Ornament Usage among the Native Peoples of Canada: A Source Book*, Ottawa: National Historic Sites, Parks Serve, Environment Canada.
Katcher, Philip (1973a), *The American Provincial Corps 1775–1784*, Reading: Osprey.
——, (1973b), *King George's Army 1775–1783: A Handbook of British, American and German Regiments*, Reading: Osprey.
——, (1975), *Armies of the American Wars, 1753–1815*, New York: Hastings House.
——, (1989), *American Civil War Armies (5): Volunteer Militia*, London: Osprey.
——, (1992), 'A Legion of Strangers: European Military Images in the Era of the American Civil War', *Military Images*, vol. 14, no. 3, pp. 20–4.
Keegan, John (1976), *The Face of Battle*, New York: Viking.
——, and Darracott, Joseph (1981), *The Nature of War*, New York: Holt, Rinehart & Winston.
Keegan, John, and Holmes, Richard (1986), *Soldiers: A History of Men in Battle*, New York: Viking.

## Bibliography

Keeley, Lawrence H. (1996), *War Before Civilization: The Myth of the Peaceful Savage*, New York: Oxford University Press.

Ketchum, Richard M. (ed.), (1960), *The American Heritage Picture History of the Civil War*, New York: American Heritage.

Kieran, Brian L. (1992), *The Lawless Caymanas: A Story of Slavery and Freedom*, Bournemouth: Bourne Press.

King, J. C. H. (1991), 'Woodlands Artifacts from the Studio of Benjamin West, 1738–1820', *American Indian Art Magazine*, vol. 17, no. 1, pp. 34–47.

Knötel, Richard, Knötel, Herbert and Seig, Herbert (1937), *Handbuch der Uniformkunde*, Hamburg: H. G. Schulz.

Lachouque, Henry (1961), *The Anatomy of Glory: Napoleon and his Guard*, adapted from the French by Anne S. K. Brown, Providence: Brown University Press.

Laffin, John (1982), *Arab Armies of the Middle East Wars 1948–73*, London: Osprey.

Large, Hector (1965), *Le costume militaire Français de 1789 à 1848*, Paris: Librairie Clavreuil.

Larter, Harry C., and Todd, Frederick P. (1982), '6th Pennsylvania Volunteer Cavalry Regiment (Rush's Lancers), 1862', in John R. Elting and Michael J. McAfee (eds), *Military Uniforms in America: Volume III: Long Endure: The Civil War Period 1852–1867*, Novato, California: Presidio Press, pp. 78–9.

Laver, James (1945), 'Fashion and Class Distinction', *Pilot Papers*, vol. 1, pp. 63–74.

——, (1948), *British Military Uniforms*, London: Penguin.

——, (1969), *Modesty in Dress: An Inquiry into the Fundamentals of Fashion*, Boston: Houghton Mifflin.

Lawford, James (1976), 'Origins', in James Lawford (ed.), *The Cavalry*, Indianapolis: Bobbs-Merrill, pp. 33–43.

Lawson, Cecil C. P. (1940–67), *A History of the Uniforms of the British Army*, 5 vols.., London: Kaye & Ward.

Lefferts, Charles M. (1926), *Uniforms of the American, British, French, and German Armies of the War of the American Revolution*, New York: New York Historical Society.

Leliepvre, Eugene, Hefter, Joseph and Elting, John R. (1982), 'French Contra-Guerrillas, Mexico, 1865–1867', in John R. Elting and Michael J. McAfee (eds.), *Military Uniforms in America: Volume III: Long Endure: The Civil War Period 1852–1867*, Novato, California: Presidio Press, pp. 126–7.

Lodolini, Elio (1976),'Les Volontaires du Canada dans l'armee Pontificale (1868–1870)', *National Museum of Man Mercury Series. History Division Paper*, no. 19, pp. 68–156, Ottawa: National Museum of Man.

Luard, John (1852), *A History of the Dress of the British Soldier, from the Earliest Period to the Present Time*, London: William Clowes & Sons (facsimile edition, 1971, London: Muller).

Lucas, James (1987), *Fighting Troops of the Austro-Hungarian Army 1868–1914*, Tunbridge Wells, Kent: Spellmount.

Lumsden, General Sir Peter S. and Elsmie, George R. (1899), *Lumsden of the Guides: A Sketch of the Life of Lieut.-Gen. Sir Harry Burnett Lumsden with Selections from his Correspondence and Occasional Papers*, London: John Murray.

McAfee, Michael J. (1991), *Zouaves: The First and the Bravest*, Gettysburg, PA: Thomas Publications.

——, (1993), 'What Is a Zouave – Not?', *Military Images*, vol. 14, no. 5, pp. 6–10.

——, and Grube, Harry T. (1982), '146th New York Volunteer Infantry Regiment, 1863–1865', in John R. Elting and Michael J. McAfee (eds.), *Military Uniforms in America: Volume III: Long Endure: The Civil War Period 1852–1867*, Novato, California: Presidio Press, pp. 68–9.

McBarron, H. Charles, Jr. (1941), 'American Military Dress in the War of 1812. IV. Regular Riflemen', *Military Affairs*, vol. 5, pp. 138–44.

——, (1977), 'Boston Hussars, Massachusetts Volunteer Militia, 1810–1817', in John R. Elting, (ed.), *Military Uniforms in America: Volume II: Years of Growth 1796–1851*, San Rafael, California: Presidio Press, pp. 54–5.

——, and Elting, John R. (1974), 'Captain Hexekiah Dunn's Company of Rangers, New Jersey Frontier Guard, 1756–1760', in John R. Elting (ed.), *Military Uniforms in America: The Era of the American Revolution 1755–1795*, San Rafael, California: Presidio Press, pp. 16–7.

McBarron, H. Charles, Jr., and Smith, Rutledge F. (1974), 'The Queen's Rangers (1st American Regiment), 1778–1783', in John R. Elting (ed.), *Military Uniforms in America: The Era of the American Revolution 1755–1795*, San Rafael, California: Presidio Press, pp. 44–5.

McBarron, H. Charles, Jr., and Todd, Frederick P. (1982a), '3rd Regiment (Hussars), New York State Militia, 1850–1860', in John R. Elting and Michael J. McAfee (eds.), *Military Uniforms in America: Volume III: Long Endure: The Civil War Period 1852–1867*, Novato, California: Presidio Press, pp. 24–5.

——, (1982b), '155th Pennsylvania Volunteer Infantry Regiment, 1864–1865', in John R. Elting and Michael J. McAfee (eds), *Military Uniforms in America: Volume III: Long Endure: The Civil War Period 1852–1867*, Novato, California: Presidio Press, pp. 76–7.

——, and Elting, John R. (1977), 'Chatham Light Dragoons, Georgia Volunteer Militia, 1811–1816', in John R. Elting (ed.), *Military Uniforms in America: Volume II: Years of Growth 1796–1851*, San Rafael, California: Presidio Press, pp. 8–9.

McBarron, H. Charles, Jr., Todd, Frederick P. and the Editors (1982), 'United States Zouave Cadets, 1859–1860', in John R. Elting and Michael J. McAfee (eds), *Military Uniforms in America: Volume III: Long Endure: The Civil War Period 1852–1857*, Novato, California: Presidio Press, pp. 14–5.

McChristian, Douglas C. (1995), *The U.S. Army in the West, 1870–1880: Uniforms, Weapons, and Equipment*, Norman: University of Oklahoma Press.

McClellan, George B. (1861), *The Armies of Europe*, Philadelphia: Lippincott.

McElwee, William (1972), *Argyll and Sutherland Highlanders*, Reading: Osprey.

McKay, James B. (ed.), (1993), 'The National Character of the Scottish Regiments 1808–1861' [reprinting a pamphlet published in 1862], *Dispatch: The Journal of the Scottish Military Historical Society*, no.132, pp. 9–12, no.133, pp. 16–18, no. 134, pp. 14–16.

## Bibliography

McKenzie, John (1998), 'The Royal Army Ordnance Corps T.A. Presence in Scotland & their Pipe Bands 1850–1967', *Dispatch: The Journal of the Scottish Military Historical Society*, no. 147, pp. 6–7.

MacKinnon, C. R. (1970), *Tartans and Highland Dress*, Glasgow: Collins.

MacLeod, Malcolm (1974), 'Liénard de Beaujeu, Daniel-Hyacinthe-Marie', *Dictionary of Canadian Biography*, vol. III, pp. 400–2, Toronto: University of Toronto Press.

MacLeod, Ronald (1959), 'Pipers are International', *Military Miniature Collector* vol. 1, pp. 100–4.

Mains, Tony (1997), '9th Gurkha Rifles: Uniform Particulars from the 1930s'. *Journal of the society for Army Historical Research*, vol. 75, pp. 138–42.

Marchal, Gustave (1888), *La Guerre de Crimee*, Paris: Firmin-Didot.

Margerand, J. (1945), *L'armée Française en 1845*, Paris: Les Éditions militaires illustrées.

Marrion, Robert W. (1965), 'Prussia 1756–63 Frei Corps v Kleist', *Tradition* no. 11, pp. 2–8.

——, (1970), 'German Kaiserliche Schutztruppen 1889–1914', *Tradition,* no. 43, pp. 2–7, no. 44, pp. 24–7, no. 46, pp. 9–12, no. 47, pp. 34–5.

——, (1987), 'The West India Regiment', *Military Modelling*, vol.17, pp. 614–7.

——, and Fosten, D. S. V. (1970), 'Special Gurkha Issue', *Tradition: Journal of the International Society of Military Collectors*, No. 45.

——, and Jones, Ken (1992), 'Gurkha Rifles', *Military Modelling*. vol. 22, no. 11, pp. 33–6.

Martin, Paul (1963), *European Military Uniforms: A Short History*, London: Spring Books.

Mason, Philip (1976), *A Matter of Honour: An Account of the Indian Army, Its Officers and Men*, Harmondsworth: Penguin.

Masters, John (1956), *Bugles and a Tiger*, New York: Viking.

Mathews, Hazel C. (1963), *The Mark of Honour*, Toronto: University of Toronto Press.

Mauldin, William H. (1945), *Up Front*, New York: Henry Holt.

May, Robin (1974), *Wolfe's Army*, London: Osprey.

Melegari, Vezio (1969), *The World's Great Regiments*, New York: G. P. Putnam's Sons.

Miller, Charles (1974), *Battle for the Bundu: The First World War in East Africa*, New York: Macmillan.

Mollo, Andrew (1978), *Army Uniforms of World War I: European and United States Armies and Aviation Services*, New York: Arco.

Mollo, Boris (1979), *Uniforms of the Imperial Russian Army*, Poole, Dorset: Blandford.

Mollo, John (1972), *Military Fashion: A Comparative History of the Uniforms of the Great Armies from the 17th Century to the First World War*, New York: G. P. Putnam's Sons.

——, (1977), *Uniforms of the Seven Years War, 1756–1763*, Poole, Dorset: Blandford.

——, and Mollo, Boris (1991), *Into the Valley of Death: The British Cavalry Division at Balaclava 1854*, London: Windrow & Greene.

Morgan, Lewis H. (1851), *League of the Ho-dé-no-sau-nee or Iroquois*, Rochester: Sage.

Morris, Jan (1982), *The Spectacle of Empire: Style, Effect and the Pax Britannica*, Garden City, NY: Doubleday.

Moyse-Bartlett, Hubert (1956), *The King's African Rifles: A Study in the Military History of East and Central Africa, 1890–1945*, Aldershot: Gale & Polden.

Nash, David (1972), *The Prussian Army 1808–1815*, London: Almark.

Nevill, Ralph (1909), *British Military Prints*, London: Connoisseur Publishing.

Nevins, Edward M. (1992), *Forces of the British Empire 1914*, Arlington, Virginia: Vandamere Press.

Nicholson, J. B. R. (1970a), 'British Staff Uniforms 1897', *Tradition*, no. 39, pp. 7–10, no. 40, pp. 14–19.

——, (1970b) 'Introduction [to Special Indian Cavalry Issue]', *Tradition*, no. 50, pp. 2–13.

——, (1974), *The Gurkha Rifles*, Reading: Osprey.

Niemeyer, Joachim and Ortenburg, Georg (eds), (1977), *The Hanoverian Army During the Seven Years War*, Kopenhagen: Bent Carlsens.

Norman, C. A. (1972a), 'Further Notes on the Uniforms Worn During the Indian Mutiny 1857–58', *Tradition*, no. 62, pp. 5–7, 11; no. 63, pp. 2–6, 9.

——, (1972b), 'The French Army in the Franco-Prussian War, 1870–71', *Tradition*, no. 64, pp. 6–14.

Otterbein, Keith, and Otterbein, Charlotte (1963), 'An Eye for an Eye, a Tooth for a Tooth: A Cross Cultural Study of Feuding', *American Anthropologist*, vol. 67, pp. 1470–82.

Pakula, Marvin (1960), *Uniforms of the United States Army: Second Series*, Plates by Harry Alexander Ogden, New York: Yoseloff.

Parker, Geoffrey (1988), *The Military Revolution: Military Innovation and the Rise of the West, 1500–1800*, Cambridge: Cambridge University Press.

Penny, David W. (1992), *Art of the American Indian Frontier: The Chandler-Pohrt Collection*, Seattle: University of Washington Press.

Pimlott, John (1977), *British Light Cavalry*, London: Almark.

Potheir, Bernard, and Grant, Roddick (1975), 'The Leslie Collection', *National Museum of Man Mercury Series, Canadian War Museum Paper*, no. 5, Ottawa.

Prebble, John (1975), *Mutiny: Highland Regiments in Revolt 1743–1804*, Harmondsworth: Penguin.

Rankin, Robert H. (1967), *Uniforms of the Army*, New York: G. P. Putnam's Sons.

Ray, Frederick E., Jr., and Elting, John R. (1974a), '55th Regiment of Foot, 1758', in John R. Elting (ed.), *Military Uniforms in America: The Era of the American Revolution 1755–1795*, San Rafael, California: Presidio Press, pp. 4–5.

——, (1974b), 'Gorham's Rangers, 1759–1761', in John R. Elting (ed.), *Military Uniforms in America: The Era of the American Revolution 1755–1795*, San Rafael, California: Presidio Press, pp. 10–1.

*Bibliography*

Ray, Frederic E., Jr., Strurcke, Roger D., and McAfee, Michael J. (1982), '33rd New Jersey Volunteer Infantry Regiment ("2nd Zouaves"), 1863–1865', in John R. Elting and Michael J. McAfee (eds.), *Military Uniforms in America: Volume III: Long Endure: The Civil War Period 1852–1867*, Novato, California: Presidio Press, pp. 52–3.

Read, D. B. (1890), *The Life and Times of Gen. John Graves Simcoe*, Toronto: George Virtue.

Reid, Stuart (1992), *Wellington's Highlanders*, London: Osprey.

——, (1993), *18th Century Highlanders*, London: Osprey.

——, (1995), *King George's Army 1740–93: (1) Infantry*, London: Osprey.

Richard, Jules (1992), *L'Armée Française: An Illustrated History of the French Army 1790–1885*, New York: Waxtel & Hasenauer.

Riehn, Richard K. (1959), 'The French Imperial Army: The Campaigns of 1813–1814 and Waterloo,' *Helenic Uniform Color Guides*, Series No. 1, Booklet No. 1.

——, (1960), 'The French Infantry and Artillery, 1795–1812,' *Helenic Uniform Color Guides*, Series No. 1, Booklet No. 2.

Risley, Cylde A., Elting, John R. and Sturcke, Roger D. (1982), '3rd New Jersey Volunteer Cavalry Regiment (1st U.S. Hussars) 1864–1865', in John R. Elting and Michael J. McAfee (eds), *Military Uniforms in America: Volume III: Long Endure: The Civil War Period 1852–1867*, Novato, California: Presidio Press, pp. 54–5.

Roberts, Michael (1967), *Essays in Swedish History*, London: Weidenfeld & Nicolson.

Rogers, H. C. B. (1960), *Weapons of the British Soldier*, London: Sphere Books.

Rosenberg, Bruce A. (1974), *Custer and the Epic of Defeat*, University Park: Pennsylvania State University Press.

Ross, David, and Chartrand, René (eds) (1977), *Canadian Militia Dress Regulations 1907: Illustrated, with Amendments to 1914*, Saint John: The New Brunswick Museum.

Ross, David, and May, Robin (1988), *The Royal Canadian Mounted Police 1873–1987*, London: Osprey.

Ross, David, and Tyler, Grant (1992), *Canadian Campaigns 1860–70*, London: Osprey.

Roubicek, Marcel (1978), *Modern Ottoman Troops 1797–1915: Al Nizam El-Gedid Ottoman Army Uniforms, 1797–1915 in Contemporary Pictures*, Jerusalem: Franciscan Printing Press.

Russell, Peter E. (1978), 'Redcoats in the Wilderness: British Officers and Irregular Warfare in Europe and America, 1740 to 1760', *William and Mary Quarterly*, vol. 35, pp. 629–52.

Seaton, Albert (1985), *The Horsemen of the Steppes: The Story of the Cossacks*, London: The Bodley Head.

Seccombe, Major Thomas S. (1875), *Army and Navy Drolleries*, London: Frederick Warne.

Severin, John P., and Todd, Frederick P. (1982), '79th Regiment, New York State Militia, 1860–1861', in John R. Elting and Michael J. McAfee (eds), *Military*

*Uniforms in America: Volume III: Long Endure: The Civil War Period 1852–1867*, Novato, California: Presidio Press, pp. 66–7.

Shandy, Tristam (1937), 'Khaki and Service Dress', *Journal of the Society for Army Historical Research*, vol. 16, pp. 58–9.

Shann, Stephen and Delperier, Louis (1991), *French Army 1870–1871: Franco-Prussian War: 1 Imperial Troops*, London: Osprey.

Sigel, Gustav A. (1989), *Germany's Army and Navy by Pen and Picture*, New York: Military Press [originally published 1900].

Simcoe, John Graves (1962), *Simcoe's Military Journal*, Toronto: Baxter [original edition London, 1784].

Smith, Robin (1996), *American Civil War Zouaves*, London: Osprey.

Smits, David D. (1998), '"Fighting Fire with Fire": The Frontier Army's Use of Indian Scouts and Allies in the Trans-Mississippi Campaigns, 1860–1890', *American Indian Culture and Research Journal*, vol. 22, pp. 73–116.

Spicer, Ron and Elting, John R. (1967), 'United States Air Force Pipe Band, 1965–1966', *Military Uniforms in America*, plate no. 303, Washington, DC: Company of Military Historians.

Stacey, C. P. (1979), 'Rogers, Robert', *Dictionary of Canadian Biography*, vol. 4, pp. 679–83, Toronto: University of Toronto Press.

——, (1983), 'Brock, Sir Isaac', *Dictionary of Canadian Biography*, vol. 5, pp. 109–15, Toronto: University of Toronto Press.

Stacke, Major H. FitzM. (1970), 'The First Hussars', *Tradition*, no. 39, pp.2–6, 28 [originally published, *Cavalry Journal*, 1934].

Stanley, George F. G. (1983), *The War of 1812: Land Operations*, Canadian War Museum Historical Publication No. 18, Toronto: Macmillan of Canada in collaboration with National Museum of Man, National Museums of Canada.

Steel, William D. (1998), 'Editorial', *Dispatch: The Journal of the Scottish Military Historical Society*, no. 146, p. 3.

Steele, Ian K. (1994), *Warpaths: Invasions of North America*, New York: Oxford University Press.

Steele, Russel V. (1958), '"Khakee" at the Siege of Delhi, 1857'. *Journal of the Society for Army Historical Research*, vol. 36, p. 42.

Stewart, Charles H. (1970), *"Overseas": The Lineages and Insignia of the Canadian Expeditionary Force 1914–1919*, Toronto: Little & Stewart.

Strachan, Hew (1983), *European Armies and the Conduct of War*, London: George Allen & Unwin.

Summers, Jack L. and Chartrand, René (1981), *Military Uniforms in Canada 1665–1970*, Canadian War Museum Historical Publication No. 16, Ottawa: National Museums of Canada.

Sumner, Percy (1941), 'Indian Mutiny Recollections of Bugler Johnson, 52nd Light Infantry', *Journal of the Society for Army Historical Research*, vol. 20, pp. 172–3.

Thompson, Leroy (1985), *Uniforms of the Soldiers of Fortune*, Poole: Blandford.

Thorburn, W. A. (1969), *French Army Regiments and Uniforms from the Revolution to 1870*, London: Arms and Armour Press.

## Bibliography

——, (1973), 'Tartans: Origins and Military Significance', *Regiments of the Scottish Division: Histories, Tartans and Music*, Bassingstoke, Hampshire: Macmillan, pp. 3–4.

Todd, Frederick P. (1954), *Soldiers of the American Army 1775–1954*, Drawings by Fritz Kredel, Chicago: Henry Regnery.

——, and the Editors (1982), '114th Pennsylvania Volunteer Infantry Regiment (Collis Zouaves), 1852–1865', in John R. Elting and Michael J. McAfee (eds), *Military Uniforms in America: Volume III: Long Endure: The Civil War Period 1852–1867*, Novato, California: Presidio Press, pp. 74–5.

Trevor-Roper, H. (1983), 'The Invention of Tradition: The Highland Tradition of Scotland', in Eric Hobsbawm and Terrance Ranger (eds), *The Invention of Tradition*, Cambridge: Cambridge University Press, pp. 15–41.

Troy, Jakelin (1993), *King Plates: A History of Aboriginal Gorgets*, Canberra: Aboriginal Studies Press.

Trubowitz, Neal L. (1985), 'Cracked Flints and Singed Fingers: Lessons from Living History of Firearms Archaeology', *Proceedings of the 1984 Trade Gun Conference, Rochester Museum and Science Center Research Records*, vol. 18 (Part II), pp. 89–99.

Truettner, William H. (1979), *The Natural Man Observed: A Study of Catlin's Indian Gallery*, Washington, DC: Smithsonian Institution Press.

Tylden, G. (1938), 'The Cape Mounted Riflemen, 1827–1870', *Journal of the Society for Army Historical Research*, vol. 17, pp. 227–31.

Tyrrell, F. H. (1922), 'Busby', *Journal of the Society for Army Historical Research*, vol. 1, p. 137.

von Pivka, Otto (1979), *Armies of the Napoleonic Era*. Newton Abbot: David & Charles.

Walton, Colonel P. S. (1986), *Simkin's Soldiers: The British Army in 1890. Volume II. The Infantry*, Chippenham: Picton.

Warner, Philip (1975), *Army Life in the '90s*, London: Country Life.

Warry, John (1995), *Warfare in the Classical World*, Norman: University of Oklahoma Press.

Webster, Graham (1985), *The Roman Imperial Army of the First and Second Centuries A.D.*, Third Edition, London: A. & C. Black.

Whitehorne, A. C. (1936), 'Khaki and Service Dress', *Journal of the Society for Army Historical Research*, vol. 15, pp. 180–3.

Wilkinson-Latham, Christopher (1977), *The Indian Mutiny*, London: Osprey.

Wilkinson-Latham, Robert (1977), *North-West Frontier 1837–1947*, London: Osprey.

Wilkinson-Latham, Robert and Wilkinson-Latham, Christopher (1970), *Infantry Uniforms Including Artillery and Other Supporting Corps of Britain and the Commonwealth 1855–1939*, London: Blandford.

Wilson, Frank (1970), 'Special Indian Cavalry Issue, Part I', *Tradition*, no. 50.

——, (1974), 'Special Indian Cavalry Issue, No. 2', *Tradition*, no. 73.

Windrow, Martin, and Embleton, Gerry (1973), *Military Dress of North America 1665–1970*, London: Ian Allan.

## Bibliography

——, (1974), *Military Dress of the Peninsular War 1808–1814*, London: Ian Allan.
Wise, Terence (1981), *Ancient Armies of the Middle East*, London: Osprey.
Wiseman, Edric (1974), 'The New South Wales Lancers', *Tradition*, no. 76, pp. 34–7.
Wolf, Eric R. (1969), *Peasant Wars of the Twentieth Century*, London: Faber.
Wood, Stephen (1987), *The Scottish Soldier*, Urmstrom: Archive Publications.
Woodbridge, George, and Grube, Harry T. (1982), '14th Regiment, New York State Militia, 1861–1864', in John R. Elting and Michael J. McAfee (eds.), *Military Uniforms in America: Volume III: Long Endure: The Civil War Period 1852–1867*, Novato, California: Presidio Press, pp. 60–1.
Woodham-Smith, Cecil Blanche FitzGerald (1953), *The Reason Why*, London: Constable.
Young, Peter (1971), *Chasseurs of the Guard*, Reading: Osprey.
——, (1972), *The Arab Legion*, Reading: Osprey.
——, (1976), 'The Napoleonic Wars', in James Lawford (ed.), *The Cavalry*, Indianapolis: Bobbs-Merrill, pp. 129–40.
——, (1977), *The Machinery of War*, New York: Crescent Books.

# Index

Alexander III, Tsar of Russia, 59
Alsace, 28, 32
Amin, Idi, 81
Angus, Felix, 105
Apache Indians, 131, 147
Argentina, 28, 76
  army,
    Cazadores a Caballo, 38
    Guias de Caballeria, 38
    Húsares de la Patria, 38
    Húsares de Pueyrredón, 38
    Húsares del Rey, 37
    Union Hussars, 38
Army & Navy Gazette, The, 19, Plate 19
Atkinson, John Augustus, Plate 14
Australia,
  Aboriginal population, 146
  army,
    Byron Regiment, 80
    Cameron Highlanders of Western Australia, 80
    New South Wales Lancers, 55–6
    New South Wales Scottish Regiment, 80
    South Australian Scottish Regiment, 80
    Sydney Light Horse Troop, 55
    Victoria Scottish Regiment, 80
Austria, 28, 29, 64, 147, 155
  army,
    Archduke Carl Regiment, Plate 9
    Baranyay Hussars, 30
    Beleznay Hussars, Plate 2
    Bethlen Hussars, 30, Plate 2
    Carlstädter Hussars, 30
    Count Schwarzenberg Regiment, Plate 9
    cuirassiers, 25
    Dessöffy Hussars, 30
    dragoons, 25
    Esclavonier Hussars, 30
    Esterhazy Hussars, 30
    1$^{st}$ Lancers of the Polish Legion, 60
    1$^{st}$ Uhlans, 49
    4$^{th}$ Uhlans, 49
    Galician Noble Guard, 49
    generals, 44
    Ghilany Hussars, Plate 2
    Hadik Hussars, 30, 167n1, Plate 2
    hussars, 25, 29, 41
    Kaiser Hussars, 30
    Kalnoky Hussars, 30
    Karoly Hussars, Plate 1
    Kukez Hussars, 30
    light infantry, 139
    Nadasdy Hussars, 30
    Palatinal Hussars, 30
    Palffy Hussars, 30, Plate 1
    2$^{nd}$ Uhlans, 49
    Spleny Hussars, 30
    Szeczeny Hussars, 30
    3$^{rd}$ Uhlans, 49

Baden-Powell, Robert, 129
bagpipes, 81–97, 154–5, Plate 19, Plate 20, Plate 22
Baker, John B., 54
barrel sash, 27, 29, 41, 159
Barthélémy, Colonel, 99
battles,
  Alma, 101
  Antietam, 105
  Austerlitz, 46
  Balaclava, 1–2, 27, 40
  Blenheim, 121
  Brandywine, 33
  Bull Run, 105

# Index

Canne, 4
Constantine, 101
Culloden, 72
Delhi, siege of, 93, 113, 116–18
Germantown, 33
Gettysburg, 105–6
Falkirk, 4
Fontenoy, 72, 150, 173n3
Fort Ticonderoga, 73, 169n1
Ginniss, 124
Gorindghar, 113–14
Isandlwana, 123–4
Jena, 46
Khartoum, 124
Kirbekan, 124
Kojuck Pass, 109
Little Big Horn, 5, 143–4, Plate 40
Lucknow, 112, 118–19
Madrid, 100
Mafeking, 129
Mardan, 117
Meerut, 115
Minden, 32
Multan, 113
New Orleans, 75
Normandy, 121
Pyramids, battle of the, 63
Quebec (Plains of Abraham), 134, Plate 33
Queenston Heights, 138, Plate 35
Rivoli, 63
Sangao, 114
Somosierra, Spain, 51
Stettin, 64, Plate 15
Wagram, 64
Waterloo, 39, 40, 47
*see also* campaigns, wars
Bavaria, 28
bearskins, 45, 159, 167n3
Belgium, 60, 128
Berbers, 101, 152
Berchény, Count Ladislaw de, 32
Berthier, Louis, Marshal of France, 64
blood feud, 151
Bolivar, Simon, 38
  forces of,
    1st Venezuelan Hussars, British Legion, 38
    Hussar Guards, Irish Legion, 38
    2nd Venezuelan Hussars, British Legion, 38
    Peruvian Legion, 38
Bonaparte, Joseph, King of Spain, 100
Bonaparte, Josephine, 100
bonnet, Highland, 71, 74, 139–40, 154, 169n2, Plate 16, Plate 17, Plate 18, Plate 19, Plate 39
Bonney, William (Billy the Kid), 104
Booth, John, Plate 3, Plate 7, Plate 9
Bosquet, General, 1
Bouillé, Marquis Louis de, 52
Bowlegs, Billy, 146
Boy Scouts, 129
Braddock, General Edward, 133
brandenbergs, 40, 42, 159
Brant, Joseph, 146, Plate 38
Brazil,
  army,
    National Guard Hussars, 38, 57
    Zuavos da Bahia, 109
Brewett, 146
Brock, Major General Isaac, 137–8, Plate 35
'Brown Bess' musket, 12, 71–2, 121, 152, Plate 17
Bulgaria, 129
Burnet, Lieutenant William, 140–1
Burton, Sir Richard, 141
busby, 26, 32, 159
Byron, Lord, 67

cadenettes, 27, 40
Cameron of Erracht, Allan, 75
campaigns,
  Abyssinian, 123, 150
  Ambela, 123
  Georgia, 105
  Egypt, 63, Plate 7
  Hazarq Operations, 123
  Italy, 63
  Medeah expedition, 101
  Yorktown, 36
  *see also* battles, wars
Campbell, George, 116
Canada,
  army,

## Index

Black Watch (Royal Highland Regiment) of Canada, 79
Corps of Guides, 55
8th Princess Louise's New Brunswick Hussars, 37
Essex Scottish, 80
48th Highlanders of Canada, 79–80, 85
Lake Superior Scottish, 80
Lorne Scots, 79–80
New Brunswick Scottish, 80
Nova Scotia Highlanders, 80
Perth Regiment, 80
Princess Patricia's Canadian Light Infantry, 84–5
6th Hussars, 37
Toronto Scottish, 79
Canadian Expeditionary Force, 80, 84–5
Canadian Forestry Corps, 85
15th Battalion, 80, 85
1st Canadian Mounted Rifles, 84
1st Pioneer Battalion, 85
16th Battalion, 80, 85, Plate 21
French regime, 132–3
Compagnies Franches de la Marine, 132–3, 172n1
Regiment de Carignan-Sallières, 132–3
Regiment de Guyenne, 133
North West Mounted Police, 16, 42, 126
Pontifical Zouaves, 107
Royal Canadian Mounted Police, 55, 169n2
Cardigan, Lord, 2
Cardwell reforms, 76–7
Casey, Edward, 142
Catherine the Great, 61
Charles II, King of England and Scotland, 68
chassepot rifle, 122
Cherokee Indians, 146
Cheyenne Indians, 5, 142, 144, Plate 40
Childer, H. E., 92
Chisholm, James, 72
Chisholm, John, 72
Chisholm, Roderick, 72
Clark, William, 145
Cody, William F. ('Buffalo Bill'), 141–2
colback, 26, 32, 40, 41, 44, 159, 167n4, 168n5, Plate 1

Confederate States of America, army,
Army of Northern Virginia, 105
8th South Carolina Infantry, 37
Highland Company, Charleston, South Carolina, 81
Louisiana Zouaves, 103
Wheat's Tigers, 106
Cooke, William W., 144
Cornplanter, 146
'Cossack' trousers, 52, 63–4, 160, Plate 14, Plate 15
Creek Indians, 146
Crook, General George, 141–2
Crow Indians, 5
Cumberland, William, Duke of, 72, 83
Cunne Shote, 146
Custer, Boston, 144
Custer, George Armstrong, 5, 131, 143–4, Plate 40
Custer, Tom, 144
czapka, 1–2, 48–9, 53–4, 57, 58, 60, 153, 160, Plate 9, Plate 10, Plate 11, Plate 12, Plate 13

Daly, Sir Henry, 113
De Haviland, Olivia, 1
Detaille, Edouard, 64
Dieudonné, Lieutenant, 41
Dighton, Robert (the younger), 31
dolman, 27, 29, 32, 36, 37, 39, 40, 41, 64, 160, Plate 1, Plate 2, Plate 3, Plate 5, Plate 7
Don Cossacks, 61–2
Dos Mayo, 100
doublet, 74, 77, 81, 88, 92–3, 95, 160, Plate 19, Plate 20, Plate 22
Duff, Colonel Sir Beauchamp, 95
Dunn, Captain Hezekiah, 136
Duvier, Captain, 99
dyes, 18–19

Edward I, King of England, 4
Egyptian empire, 4
Elliott, Alexander, 137
Ellsworth, Elmer Ephriam, 103–5, Plate 25, Plate 26
Enfield Rifle, 115–16

## Index

Erskine, Sir William, 34

Fenton, Roger, 20
Flameng, François, 64
Flynn, Errol, 1
France, 28, 29, 64, 147
  army, 128
    Chasseurs à Cheval, 16
    Chasseurs á Cheval of the Guard, 41, 99
    Chasseurs d'Afrique, 58
    Consular Guard, 99
    dragoons, 128
    8th Chevau-lèger lanciers, 52
    8th Hussars, 31
    11th Hussars, 31
    5th Hussars, 31, 153, Plate 3
    1st Hussars, 31
    1st Lancers of the Imperial Guard, 51
    Foreign Legion, 128
    4th Hussars, 31
    Gardes Français, 150, 173n3
    horse artillery, 42
    Hussar Regiment Berchény, 32
    Hussar Regiment Royal-Nassau, 32
    hussars, 27, 40–1
    Lancers of Berg, 51
    Lauzun's Legion, 36
    Légion du Nord, 51
    Legion of the Vistula, 51
    Lithuanian Tartars of the Imperial Guard, 63
    Mamluks of the Imperial Guard, 99–100, Plate 23
    9th Chevau-lèger lanciers, 52
    9th Hussars, 31
    Régiment de dromadaire, 41–2, Plate 7
    Royal Guard, 58
    2nd (Dutch) Lancers of the Imperial Guard, 51, 57, 153, Plate 10
    2nd Hussars, 31
    7th Chevau-lèger lanciers, 51
    7th Hussars, 31, 64
    6th Hussars, 31
    6th Orléans Lancers, 58
    Spahis, 102
    10th Hussars, 31, 64
    3rd Éclaireurs de la Garde, 63
    3rd Lancers of the Imperial Guard, 51
    3rd Hussars, 31
    13th Cuirassiers, 128
    Tirailleurs algériens (Turcos), 101–2, 104, 106
    24th Cavalry, 63
    22nd Chasseurs á Cheval, 63
    23rd Chasseurs á Cheval
    Voluntaires de l'Ouest, 107
    Voluntaires de Saxe, 48
    Zouaves, 20, 101–5, 109–10, 154, 173n5, Plate 24
    Pontifical Zouaves, 107
  see also Canada, French regime
Frank Leslie's Illustrated Newspaper, Plate 25
Frederick the Great, King of Prussia, 25, 29, 49, Plate 6
Frederick William, King of Prussia, 28

Gage, Thomas, 133
Gault, Andrew Hamilton, 84
George II, King of England and Scotland, 71
Géricault, Théodore, 41
Germany, 28, 59–60
  army, 128
  hussars, 40
  Life-Guard Hussars, 40, Plate 6
  uhlans, Plate 13
  colonial troops, 127–8
  marines (3rd Seebataillon), 126
Gielgud, John, 1
Gilbert, Benjamin, Plate 38
Girty, Simon, 136–7
Glubb, John B., 14, 97
Goebel, Carl, Plate 24
Gordon, Charles, 124
gorget, 95, 133, 145–6, 161
Gorham, John, 134
Gorham, Joseph, 134
Goya, Francisco, 100
Great Britain, 28, 29, 64, 147
  army, 125
    Argyle and Sutherland Highlanders, 77, Plate 19
    Black Watch (Royal Highland Regiment, originally 43rd Foot, later

# Index

42nd Foot), 6, 70–7, 97, 123–4, 169n1, Plate 17
Blues and Royals, 23
Cameronians (Scottish Rifles), 77, Plate 20
18th (Queen Mary's Own) Hussars, 54
8th Foot, 117
8th (King's Royal Irish) Hussars, 2, 54
11th (Prince Albert's Own) Hussars, 2, 54
15th (The King's) Hussars, 32, 54
5th (Royal Irish) Lancers, 54, 55
55th Foot, 137
59th Foot, 122–3
52nd Foot (Oxfordshire Light Infantry), 116
1st Yorkshire Regiment, 124
40th Foot, 34
14th (King's) Hussars, 54
4th Light Dragoons (later 4th Hussars), 1, 54
General Staff, 44
Gordon Highlanders, 77–8
Grenadier Guards, 150, 173n2, 173n3
Highland Light Infantry, 77–8, 124
Irish Guards, 97
King's Own Scottish Borderers (formerly 25th Foot), 68, 77, 83
King's Royal Rifle Corps, 20
Light Dragoons, 16
Life Guards, 23
19th Light Dragoons (Lancers), 52
19th (Queen Alexandra's Own) Hussars, 54
9th Light Dragoons (Lancers), 52, 54, 118
91st Foot, 76, 118
92nd Foot, 76
97th (Inverness-shire) Regiment of Foot, 75
93rd (Highland) Regiment of Foot, 2, 74–6, 118
Northamptonshire Regiment, 20
Oglethorpe's Regiment (42nd Foot), 70
101st Foot, 123
Prince of Wales's Leinster Regiment, 117
Princess of Wales's Own (Yorkshire Regiment), 19–20
Queen's Own Cameron Highlanders, 77–8
rifle regiments, 42
Royal Artillery, 116
Royal Engineers, 123
Royal Horse Artillery, 40, 42
Royal Horse Guards, 23
Royal Irish Regiment, 123
Royal Logistic Corps, 84
Royal Scots Fusiliers (formerly 21st Foot), 68, 77
Royal Scots (The Royal Regiment), 67, 72, 77, 83, 96, 124
Royal Sussex Regiment, 124
Royal Tank Regiment, 83
Royal Welch Fusiliers, 126
Scots Guards, 7, 68, 72, 85, 95
Seaforth Highlanders, 77, 124
2nd Dragoon Guards (the Queen's Bays), 118
17th (Duke of Cambridge's Own) Lancers, 1, 54, 118
7th Light Dragoons (Hussars), 32, 54, 118
70th Foot, 117
78th Foot, 76
75th Foot, 118
71st Foot (Highland Light Infantry), 76, 118, 123
74th Foot, 76, 117
79th Foot, 75, 76, 81
72nd Foot, 76, 125
73rd Foot, 76
16th Light Dragoons (Lancers), 52, 54
6th Dragoon Guards, 116, 118
60th (Royal American) Regiment of Foot (later 60th Rifles), 114, 116, 137, 139
61st Foot (South Gloucestershire), 116
South Staffordshire Regiment, 124
10th Light Dragoons (Hussars), 32, 39, 54
3rd (King's Own) Hussars, 54, 118
13th Foot (Somerset Light Infantry), 117
13th Light Dragoons (later 13th Hussars), 1, 54

193

# Index

35th Foot (Royal Sussex), 118
39th Foot, 111
32nd Foot (Duke of Cornwall's Light Infantry), 117–18
33rd Foot, 123
12th Light Dragoons (Lancers), 52–3, 54, Plate 12
20th Hussars, 54
21st (Empress of India's) Lancers, 54
24th Foot, 123–4
23rd Light Dragoons (Lancers), 52
see also Gurkhas
colonial units,
 Gold Coast Regiment, 108, Plate 30
 Her Majesty's 1st Chinese Regiment, 126
 Hongkong Volunteer Defence Force, 80–1
 King's African Rifles, 81
 Rangoon Volunteer Rifles, 80
 Sarawak Rangers, 43
 2nd Selangor Battalion Federated Malay States Volunteer Force, 81
 Shanghai Volunteer Corps, 80
 Singapore Volunteer Corps, 81
 West India Regiment, 107–8, 153, Plate 29
Indian Department (North America), 133, 136–7, 145, 152
irregular units,
 British Legion, 30
 Choiseul's Hussars, 34
 Damas Hussars, 34
 Diemar's Huzzars, 35
 1st Rohan Hussars, 34
 Hompesch Hussars, 34
 Hulans britanniques, 52, Plate 11
 Hussars de Béon, 26, 34
 Irwin's British Hussars, 33
 Queen's Rangers, 33–6, 139, Plate 4
 Rogers' Rangers (His Majesty's Independent Companies of American Rangers), 33, 134–5
 2nd Rohan Hussars, 34
 Slam Hussars, 34
 Warren's Hussars, 34
 York Hussars, 33, 34
Royal Air Force,
 No. 602 (City of Glasgow) Squadron Auxiliary Air Force, 84
Royal Navy, 126
Territorial Army, volunteers and fencibles,
 51st Highland Division Signal Regiment, 95
 1st or Strathespay Fencibles, 75
 40th Regiment Royal Artillery (The Lowland Gunners), 84
 Liverpool Scottish, 77
 London Scottish, 77–8
 19th Regiment Royal Artillery (The Highland Gunners), 84
 105th Regiment Royal Artillery (Volunteers), 84
 104th Regiment Royal Artillery (Volunteers), 84
 103rd Regiment Royal Artillery (The Lancashire Artillery Volunteers), 84
 Royal Army Ordnance Corps (Territorial Army), 84
 204th (Tyneside Scottish) Battery, 84
 Scottish Transport Regiment (Volunteers), 84
Greece, 53, 129
grenadier cap, 45, 161
Guemes, General Martin Miguel de, 38
Gurkhas, 89–97, 120
 8th Gurkha Rifles, 90, 95, Plate 22
 11 Gorkha Rifles, 90–1
 Gurkha Transport Regiment, 96
 5th Royal Gurkha Rifles (Frontier Force), 90, 93–4
 1st King George V's Own Gurkha Rifles (The Malaun Regiment), 90–2
 4th Prince of Wales's Own Gurkha Rifles, 90–3
 9th Gurkha Rifles, 90, 95
 Queen's Gurkha Signals, 96
 2nd King Edward VII's Own Goorkhas (the Simoor Rifles), 90, 93, 117
 7th Duke of Edinburgh's Own Gurkha Rifles, 7, 94–5
 6th Queen Elizabeth's Own Gurkha Rifles, 90
 10th Gurkha Rifles, 90–1
 3rd Queen Alexandra's Own Gurkha Rifles, 90, 93

# Index

Gustavus Adolphus, King of Sweden, 12, 67–8, Plate 16

Hanger, Colonel, 12
Hannibal, 4
Hanover,
  army,
    Luckner's Hussars, 32–3
Harmar, Brigadier General Josiah, 144
Hart, T., 136
Havelock, Henry, 118–19
Hay, Lord Charles, 150, 173n3
Hemmings, David, 1
Hepburn, John, 67
hierarchical principle, 13
Hitler, Adolf, 121
Homer, Winslow, 55
Honourable East India Company, 54, 108, 111–12, 117, 119, 123
Hoffmann, Nicholaus, Plate 23
Hopothle Mico
Howard, Trevor, 1
Howarth, David, 47
Howe, Brigadier George Augustus Viscount, 73, 137
Howe, William, 34
Hugo, Victor, 26
Hull, General William, 138
Hungary, 28, 32
  irregular cavalry, 24–5
  national dress and hussar uniform, 26
hunting shirt, 138, Plate 36, Plate 37
Hysac, 146

India,
  army,
    Assam Regiment, 90
    Bengal Cavalry, 39, 43, Plate 5
    Bengal Engineers, 117, 149
    Bengal Horse Artillery, 111, 119
    Bombay Lancers, 56
    Bombay Volunteer Rifles, 80
    Brigade of Guards, 90
    Calcutta Scottish, 80
    Central Indian Horse, 43
    Dogra Regiment, 90
    18th Lancers, 57
    18th Royal Garhwal Rifles, 88–9
    8th Lancers, 57
    8th Punjab Infantry, 123, Plate 31
    11th Prince of Wales's Own Lancers (Probyn's Horse), 57, 123
    Erinpura Irregular Horse, 43
    15th Lancers (Cureton's Multanis), 57
    15th Punjab Regiment, 88, 123
    5th Punjab Infantry, 114
    55th Bengal Native Infantry, 117
    59th Bengal Native Infantry, 111
    1st Bengal Native Infantry, 120
    1st Duke of York's Own Lancers (Skinner's Horse), 57, 120
    1st Punjab Cavalry, 119
    1st Punjab Rifles, 19, 86, 88, 114, 117
    1st Sikh Regiment (Punjab Frontier Force), 89, 115
    40th Pathans, 88
    42nd Deolis, 87
    47th Sikhs, 89
    14th Ferozepore Sikhs, 88
    14th Murray's Jat Lancers, 57
    4th Bombay Grenadiers, 88
    4th Bombay Native Infantry, 89
    4th Lancers, 57
    4th Punjab Infantry, 114
    4th Sikhs, 115
    Frontier Force Cavalry, 43
    Garhwal Rifles, 90
    Governor General's Body Guard, 39, 43, 56, Plate 5
    Governor's Bodyguard, Bengal, 43
    Governor's Bodyguard, Madras, 43
    Grenadiers, 90
    Guides, Corps of, 19, 43, 88, 111–14, 120, 157
    Hodson's Horse, 119
    Hyderabad Contingent, 43, 120
    Jammu and Kashmir Light Infantry, 90
    Jammu Kashmir Rifles, 90
    Jat Regiment, 90
    Java Hussars, 39, Plate 5
    Ladakh Scouts, 90
    Madras Pioneers, 88
    Madras Regiment, 90
    Mahar Regiment, 90
    Maratha Light Infantry, 90
    Mountain Artillery, 87

# Index

19th Lancers (Fane's Horse), 57
9th Hodson's Horse, 57
9th Jat Regiment, 88
106th Hazara Pioneers, 89
130th King George's Own Buluchis (Jacob's Rifles), 87
125th Napier Rifles, 87
Parachute Regiment, 90
President's Bodyguard, 56
Punjab Irregular Force (Punjab Frontier Force), 114–15, 120
Rajput Regiment, 90
Rajputana Rifles, 90
2nd Bengal Native Infantry, 109, 120
2nd Bombay Native Infantry, 88
2nd Lancers (Gardner's Horse), 57
2nd Punjab Cavalry (Probyn's Horse), 119
2nd Punjab Regiment, 89, 114
2nd Sikhs, 115
17th Cavalry, 57, 89, 167n2
17th Dogra Regiment, 88
7th Lancers, 57
Sikh Light Infantry, 90
16th Bengal Native Infantry, 109
16th Cavalry, 57
6th Rajputana Rifles, 87
10th Baluchs, 88
10th Duke of Cambridge's Own Lancers (Hodson's Horse), 57
3rd Bengal Light Cavalry, 115–16
3rd Bombay Europeans, 117
3rd Punjab Cavalry, Plate 8
3rd Punjab Regiment, 114
3rd Sikhs, 115
13th Duke of Connaught's Lancers, 57
13th Frontier Force Rifles, 88
30th Lancers (Gordon's Horse), 57
38th Dogras, 87
31st Duke of Connaught's Own Lancers, 57
32nd Lancers, 57
37th Lancers (Baluch Horse), 57
37th (The Prince of Wales' Own) Dogras, 89
12th Frontier Force Regiment, 88
20th Deccan Horse, 57
28th Bengal Native Infantry, 109
28th Light Cavalry, 57
29th Lancers (Deccan Horse), 57
22nd Bengal Native Infantry, 89
27th Bengal Native Infantry, 89
27th Bombay Native Infantry, 119
27th Light Cavalry, 57
26th Bombay Native Infantry, 89, 119
26th Light Cavalry, 57
see also Gurkhas
Dutch Bengal Lancers, 56
Iroquois Confederacy, 132, 134
see also Mohawk Indians, Seneca Indians
Italy,
 Bersaglieri, 126–7, 154

Jackson, James W., 104
Japan,
 army, 125, 127
 cavalry, 43–4
Johnson, Dr. Samuel, 23, 72
Johnson, Guy, 136
Jordan,
 Arab Legion, 14, 96–7

Ka-be-mub-be, 146
Kahn, Dilawar, 113
Kahn, Risaldar Fateh, 113
Kahn, Subadar Rasul, 113–14
Karganoff, Major-general, 2
Kennington, Eric Henry, Plate 21
kepi, 37, 161
khaki, origins, 114, 116–17
Kicking Bear, 144, Plate 40
Kiowa Indians, 142
Kipling, Rudyard, 19, 111, 170n9
kilt, 19, 69–70, 73, 77–8, 134, 153, 162, Plate 18, Plate 19, Plate 21
Knox, Captain Henry, 134
konfederatka, 48–9, 162
kurtka, 48, 52, 55–6, 58, 162

Lasalle, Antoine-Charles Louis Comte de, 23, 63–4, 169n3, Plate 15
Laver, James, 13, 21, 36, 154
Lawrence, Sir Henry, 112
Lee, Robert E., 105
Lee-Enfield rifle, 121
Leeke, Major R. H., 81

## Index

Lejeune, General Baron Louis-François, Plate 10
Lewis, Meriwether, 145
Liénard de Beaujeu, Daniel-Hyacinthe-Marie, 133
Light Brigade, charge of, 1–2, 27, 40
Louis-Philippe, King of France, 58
Luckner, Nicolaus von, 32–3
Ludlow, Captain William, 144
Lumsden, Harry B., 111–14, 157
Lumsden, Thomas, 111–12

McClellan, Major-General George B., 99, 102–3, 140
McIntosh, Lieutenant Donald, 144
magazine rifle, 122
Mahican Indians, 134
Mandan Indians, 146
Mani-Tow-Wa-Bay, 146
Marbot, Baron, 27, 152
Marlborough, Duke of, 121
martial races, stereotypes, 156
Masters, John, 91–3
Mauldin, William, 15
Maumet, Captain, 101
Maurice of Nassau, Count, 12
Maximilian, Archduke (Emperor of Mexico), 38
Medley, Captain, 147
Mexico, 28
  army,
    Contra-Guerrillas, 39
    Empress' Own Hussars of the Guard (Red Hussars), 38
    Hussars of the Guard of the Supreme Powers, 38
    Jalisco Lancers, 58
Miami Indians, 146
Micmac Indians, 134
military participation ratio, 150–1
'military revolution', 11–13, 24, 150
Miné ball, 121
mirliton, 26, 36, 162, Plate 2
Mohawk Indians, 134, 146, Plate 38
Montenegro, 129
Morgan, Lieutenant Colonel David, 7
Morier, David, Plate 1, Plate 2
Mouse-colored Feather, 146

Munro, Lieut.-Col. Sir Robert, 72
Murat, Joachim, Marshal of France, 51
Murray, Captain James, 35, Plate 4
museum collections, 18, 54, 125, 135–6, 138, 144

Napier, Sir Robert, 150
Napoleon, Emperor of France, 45–6, 50–2, 60, 63, 99–100
Napoleon III, Emperor of France, 58–9, 102, 107, 109–10
Nassau, Prince of, 32
Nazi Party, 129
needle gun, 121
Netherlands, 28
New Zealand Scottish, 80
Nicholas II, Tsar of Russia, 59
Nigeria,
  Presidential Mounted Guard, 58
Nobel, Alfred, 122
North, Frank, 141–2, 157

Ojibwa Indians, 146
Osceola, 146
Ottoman empire,
  army,
    Albanian Guards, 110
    1st Cossack Regiment, 63
    Gendarmes, 110
    2nd Ottoman Dragoons, 63
    Zouaves of the Guard, 110

Pakistan, artillery, 87
Palestine Liberation Army, 97
Pawnee Indians, 141–2, 157
Peake, Captain Frederick G., 97
Penny, Edward, 135
Persian empire, 4
pelisse, 28, 29, 32, 36, 40, 41, 44, 162
Peter the Great, Tsar of Russia, 61
plaid, belted, 19, 69, 73, 153, 163, Plate 16, Plate 17
Pitt, William, 71
Poniatowski, Marshal, 60
Poniatowski, Stanislas, King of Poland, 49
Pontifical Zouaves, 106–7
Porter, Lieutenant James E., 144
Prophet, The, 146

## Index

Prussia, 28, 29, 155
  army,
    Bosniaks, 49–50
    cuirassiers, 29
    5th (Black) Hussars, 26, 29, 49
    1st (Green) Hussars, 29
    4th (White) Hussars, 29
    Frei Korps von Kleist, 50
    Garde-Kosaken-Eskadron, 63
    hussars, 25
    Landwehr, 50
    Leib-Uhlanen, 50
    9th Hussars, 49–50
    riflemen, 139
    2nd (Red) Hussars, 29
    7th Silesian regiment, 50
    3rd (Blue) Hussars, 29
    3rd Silesian regiment, 50
puttees, 124–5, 127, 163

Queen Elizabeth II (ship), 7

rangers, 33, 134–6, 138, 152, Plate 33, Plate 34
Rapp, Jean, 99
Rawlinson, Thomas, 70
Red Jacket, 138, 145, Plate 37
Redgrave, Vanessa, 1
Reid, James, 83
Richardson, Tony, 1
Rogers, Robert, 33, 134–6, Plate 33, Plate 34
Roosevelt, Theodore, 125
Rose, Sir Hugh, 117
Roy, Narcise, 146
Russia, 28, 29, 61–3, 155
  army, 127, 150
    Akhtyrsk Hussars, 31
    Alexandria Hussars, 31
    Caucasian Corps, 59
    Cossacks, 60–2, Plate 14
    Elizabethgrad Hussars, 31
    Grodno Hussars, 31
    Isum Hussars, 31
    Loubny Hussars, 31
    Mariupol Hussars, 31
    Olviopol Hussars, 31
    Pavlograd Hussars, 31
    Soum Hussars, 31
    White Russia Hussars, 31

sabretache, 28, 163
St. Clair, Major General Arthur, 144
Sali, Marquisse de, 63
San Martin, José de, 38
Saxe, Maurice de, Marshal of France, 48, 168n2
Saxony, 28
Scots mercenaries, Plate 16
Scott, Hugh, 142
Seccombe, Major Thomas S., 107–8, Plate 12, Plate 29
seduction principle, 13–15, 21, 36, 154
Seminole Indians, 140, 142, 146
Seneca Indians, 134, 138, 145–6, Plate 37
shako, 26, 36, 39, 44–6, 168n6
Shawnee Indians, 137–8, 146, Plate 35
Sherman, William T., 105
Simcoe, John Graves, 34–5, Plate 4
Simkin, Richard, 19–20, Plate 19, Plate 20, Plate 22
Sioux Indians, 5, 144–5, Plate 40
Smith, C. Hamilton, Plate 5
South Africa,
  Cape Mounted Rifles, 42
  First City, 80
  Presidential Guard, 42–3
  Pretoria Highlanders, 80
  Queen's Own Cape Town Highlanders, 80
  Transvaal Scottish, 80
sporran, 73–4, 78, 81, 86, 164, Plate 19
Stewart, Billie, 146
Stockbridge Indians, 134
Stride, Michael, 78
Stuart, Charles Edward, 72
Sweden, 28
  army,
    Kungliga Husarregementet, 29
    Royal Horse Guards, 53
    Wrangel's Hussars, 29

Tarleton helmet, 30, 164
Tarleton, Lieutenant-Colonel Banastre, 30
tartan, 69, 164
  Cameron of Erracht, 80–1

## Index

Campbell, 86
Campbell of Argyle, 80
Charles Edward Stuart, 125
'Childers', 92–3
Davidson, 80
Douglas, 80, 95
Duff, 95
Ferguson, 88
Forbes, 77
Gordon, 80
government (Black Watch or Sutherland), 77, 80, 88–9, 92–3, 95, Plate 19, Plate 20
Graham, 87
Graham of Montrose, 80
Grant, 96
Hay, 88
Hunting Stewart, 80, 85, 96
Lennox, 80, 85
Leslie, 80
MacDonald, 86
MacDuff, 95
McGillivary, 80
MacGregor, 80
Mackenzie, 80, 88–9, 92–3, Plate 21
McQueen, 86
Mitchell, 86
Murray of Athol, 80
Old Stewart, 88
Robertson, 88
Rose, 88–9
Royal Stewart, 84, 86, 88, 96
Stewart of Fingask, 85
Urquhart, 87
US Air Force, 86
US Military Academy, 86
Tecumseh, 137–8, Plate 35
Tennyson, Alfred, Lord, 1
Tobee, Mary (Mary Tippee), 106, Plate 28
trews, 74–7, 81, 164, Plate 20
Turkey, 125, 128–9
 see also Ottoman Empire

Uganda, 81
United States of America,
 Air Force Pipe Band, 86
 army, 125–6, Plate 32, Plate 36
  Army of the Potomac, 102, 105–6, 140

 8th Cavalry, 142
 Light Dragoons, 36
 Pawnee Scouts, 141–2, 157
 Rangers, 134
 Rifle Regiment, 138
 Second Army pipe band, 85
 Seminole Negro Scouts, 142
 7th Cavalry, 142–4
 Sixth Army pipe band, 85
 62nd United States Army Band, 86
 United States Military Academy (West Point), 86, 103
 United States Scouts, 143
Marines, 102, 126
volunteers (militia), 36
 Boston Hussars, 36
 Boston Light Infantry Company, 55
 Chatham Hussars, 36
 Chatham Light Dragoons, 36
 Duryée's Zouaves (5th New York Volunteer Infantry), 103, 105
 11th Indiana Regiment, 104
 11th New York Volunteer Infantry (New York Fire Zouaves), 103–4, 153, Plate 26
 1st United States Volunteer Cavalry ('Rough Riders'), 125
 44th New York (Ellsworth's Avengers), 104
 14th New York State Militia (14th Brooklyn), 104–5
 Georgia Hussars, 36
 Governor's Guard Battalion, 53
 Governor's Horse Guards of New Hampshire, 37
 Maryland Rifle Volunteers, 138
 National Lancers, 53–4
 19th Illinois Volunteers (Ellsworth's Zouave Cadets), 104
 155th Pennsylvania, 106
 140th New York, 106
 146th New York, 106
 114th Pennsylvania (Collis Zouaves), 105–6, Plate 28
 2nd Ohio Cavalry, 37
 79th New York Volunteers, 81
 6th Pennsylvania Volunteer Cavalry (Rush's Lancers), 55

*Index*

3rd New Jersey Volunteer Cavalry (1st US Hussars), 37
3rd Regiment (Hussars) of New York, 37
33rd New Jersey Volunteer Infantry, 105
United States Zouave Cadets, 103, 105, 153, Plate 25
utility principle, 13–14

Vernet, Horace, 64, Plate 15
Victoria, Queen-Empress, 107
vivandiere, 106, 164, Plate 28

Wade, General George, 68–70
Wallace, Lewis, 104
Wallace, William, 4
wars,
  Afgan War, 123
  American Civil War, 9, 15, 55, 81, 103–6, 121–2, 124, 140, 143, 153, Plate 26, Plate 27, Plate 28
  American Revolution, 6, 21, 33–6, 136, 138, Plate 4, Plate 36
  Anglo-Boer War, 7, 78–9, 129
  Ashanti War, 123
  Boxer Rebellion, 126–7
  Crimea, 1–2, 20, 27, 32, 40, 101–2, 140, 154
  8th Kaffir War, 117
  Falkland Islands, 7, 95
  Fenian raids (Canada), 79, 123
  First World War, 60–1, 78, 79, 84–5, 93, 125, 128–9, Plate 13, Plate 21
  Franco-Prussian War, 15–16, 59, 107, 122, 128
  Indian Mutiny, 6, 93, 111–12, 115–19
  Indian Wars (American west), 140–4, 157, Plate 40

  Italian unification, 106–7
  Jacobite Rebellion (1715), 68
  Jacobite Rebellion (1745), 72, 83
  Napoleonic wars, 24, 39–40, 41–2, 45–6, 50–2, 62–4, 75–6, 99–100, 153, Plate 3, Plate 7, Plate 9, Plate 10, Plate 14, Plate 23
  Northwest Rebellion (Canada), 79
  Peninsular War, 24, 42, 51, 64, 75, 100
  Second Maori War, 123
  Second World War, 15, 78, 79, 121, 125, 129, 134
  Seven Years War, 32, 33, 73, 133–5, Plate 33
  Spanish-American War, 125
  Third Maori War, 123
  Thirty Years War, 67, Plate 16
  War of Austrian Succession, 72, Plate 1, Plate 2
  War of 1812, 36, 75, 79, 137–8, Plate 35
  Zulu War, 123–4
  *see also* battles, campaigns
Washington, George, 138
Wayne, General Anthony, 137
Weir, Robert Walter, Plate 37
Wellington, Arthur Wellesley, Duke of, 75–6, 121
West, Benjamin, 135–6, Plate 33
White House (Washington), 103
Will, Johann Martin, Plate 36
William Louis of Nassau, Count, 12
Wilson, Major-General Sir Robert, 62
Wolfe, Major General James, 134–6, Plate 33
Württemberg, 28

Xerxes, 4